CYCLE OF LEARNING

Anne Fitzpatrick

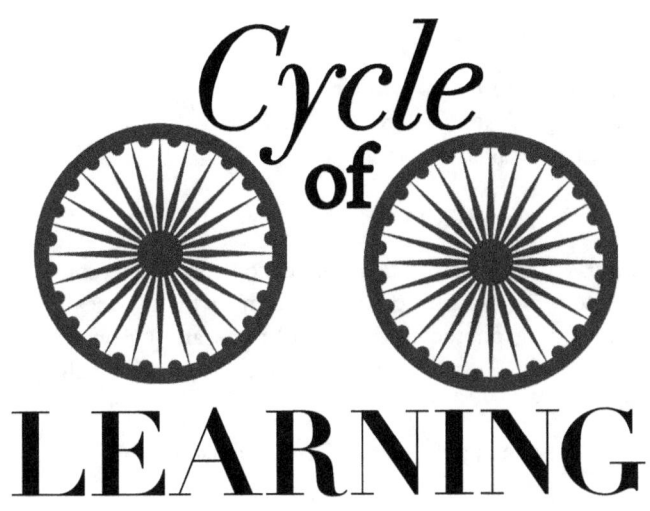

Cycle of Learning

Anne Fitzpatrick

[Lacuna]
2015

Published in 2015 by Lacuna

http://www.lacunapublishing.com

Lacuna is an imprint of Golden Orb Creative
PO Box 185, Westgate NSW 2048, Australia
http://www.goldenorbcreative.com

© Copyright Anne Fitzpatrick 2015

All rights reserved. No part of this publication may be reproduced, stored in a retrievals system, or transmitted in any form or by any means, electronic or mechanical, including photocopying, recording, scanning or otherwise, except under the terms of the Australian *Copyright Act 1969*, without the permission of the publisher.

All enquiries to the publisher: general@lacunapublishing.com

Cover credits:

Photographs: Anne Fitzpatrick, Mark Brenmuhl and "Dan".
Map of Australia: Topography of Australia. PIA06665: Australia, Shaded Relief and Colored Height. Courtesy NASA/JPL-Caltech.
Cover design by Golden Orb Creative.

Internal credits:

Photographs: Anne Fitzpatrick, unless otherwise credited.
Route maps created by Golden Orb Creative.
Design and typesetting by Golden Orb Creative.
Typeset in 11.5pt Adobe Caslon Pro (text) and Didot (titles).

National Library of Australia Cataloguing-in-Publication entry:

Fitzpatrick, Anne E., author

Cycle of learning / Anne Fitzpatrick.

ISBN 9781922198181 (paperback)

ISBN 9781922198198 (ebook)

Fitzpatrick, Anne--Travel.
Travelers--Asia--Anecdotes.
Volunteer workers in education--India--Kodaikanal--Anecdotes.
Fund-raising--Australia.
Bicycle touring--Australia--Anecdotes.

Dewey Number 796.640994

Contents

Author's Notes and Acknowledgements	ix
Prologue	1
Introduction	3

1. **See You If You Get Back** — 9
   - Wednesday 2 February 2005: Adelaide to Murray Bridge, SA — 9
   - Saturday 5 February: Meningie to Kingston, SA — 11
     - *Valli* — 11
     - *Eswaran* — 12
   - Monday 7 February: Southend to Mount Gambier, SA — 14
   - Wednesday 16 February: Geelong to outer Melbourne, Vic — 16

2. **Dirty and Altitudinally Challenged** — 19
   - Sunday 20 February: Bonnie Doon to Benalla, Vic — 19
   - Thursday 24 February: Albury to Walla Walla, NSW — 22
     - *Return to Kodaikanal* — 23
   - Saturday 12 March: Bundeena to Sydney, NSW — 26

3. **Nipple Confusion and Corporate Uniforms** — 31
   - Friday 18 March: Sydney, NSW — 31
     - *Pandimeena and the Grihini program* — 32
   - Sunday 20 March: Ku-Rin-Gai Chase National Park to Berowa Heights, NSW — 36
   - Monday 21 March: Berowra Heights to Wyong, NSW — 37
   - Monday 28 March: Taree to Kempsey, NSW — 39
   - Tuesday 29 March: Kempsey to Nambucca Heads, NSW — 40
   - Friday 1 April: Coffs Harbour to Woolgoolga to Pacific Highway, NSW — 42

4. **Thighs of Mass Destruction** — 45
   - Saturday 9 April: Coolangatta to Brisbane, Qld — 45
   - Wednesday 13 April: Brisbane to Plainland, Qld — 47
   - Tuesday 19 April: Chinchilla to Jandowae, Qld — 49
     - *The Road to Kodaikanal* — 50

5. Lost and Found — 55

Thursday 21 April: Kingaroy to near Nanango, Qld — 55
Tuesday 26 April: Yandina to near Gympie, Qld — 56
Friday 29 April: Childers to Bruce Highway, Qld — 59
   Kodaikanal Welcome — 60
Wednesday 4 May: Byfield State Forest to The Caves, Qld — 65

6. Gender, Bottoms and Nudists — 69

Monday 9 May: Mackay to Kolinjo, Qld — 69
Sunday 15 May: Ingham to Bluewater, Qld — 71
Friday 20 May: Pentland to Hughenden, Qld — 73

7. Desert Craziness on a Bike with No Name — 79

Sunday 22 May: Richmond to Julia Creek, Qld — 79
Wednesday 25 May: Fountain Springs to Mount Isa, Qld — 80
   Kalaivani — 82
Sunday 29 May: Frewena Rest Area to Tennant Creek, NT — 83
Thursday 2 June: Aileron to Alice Springs, NT — 87

8. The Wondrous Glory of the Everlasting Stars and the Vomit that Missed Banjo Paterson — 93

Friday 10 June: Stuart Highway Rest Area to Attack Creek Rest Area, NT — 93
   Rajkumar — 94
Saturday 11 June: Attack Creek Rest Area to Renner Springs Road House, NT — 96
Thursday 16 June: Mataranka to Katherine, NT — 98

9. No Fire-Twirling Inside — 105

Wednesday 22 June: Stuart Highway to Darwin, NT — 105
Tuesday 12 July: Darwin to Hayes Creek, NT — 107

10. Liberating the Sock — 113

Sunday 17 July: Vic Highway to Kununurra, WA — 113
Sunday 24 July: Great Northern Highway to Fitzroy Crossing, WA — 115
Wednesday 27 July: Broome to Roebuck Plains, WA — 120
Monday 1 August: South Hedland, WA — 122

11. The Fifth-Best Cycle Fundraiser in Town	127
Friday 5 August: Karratha to North Western Coastal Highway, WA	127
Karuppusamy	128
Life at the PEAK hostels	128
Friday 12 August: Carnarvon to North West Coastal Highway, WA	131
Murugalakshmi	134
12. Escaping the Outback	137
Saturday 13 August: North West Coastal Highway to Overlander Roadhouse, WA	137
Thursday 18 August: Geraldton to Allanooka Springs Road, WA	139
Sunday 21 August: Watheroo to Bindoon, WA	141
13. Getting Muftied	145
Tuesday 30 August: Perth to Mandurah, WA	145
Meals at the Siruvar Ilum	145
My education in Kodaikanal	147
Sunday 4 September: Margaret River, WA	149
14. The Demise of Poncho and the Rise of TYPHOON JACKET	153
Thursday 8 September: Pemberton to Albany, WA	153
Monday 12 September: Denmark to Chester's Pass Road, WA	157
Sunday 18 September: Great Eastern Highway to Kalgoorlie, WA	158
Karnan	158
Packialakshmi	159
Tuesday 27 September: Kalgoorlie to Coolgardie–Esperance Highway, WA	162
15. The March Flies Made Me Do It	167
Friday 30 September: Eyre Highway, WA	167
Saturday 8 October: Yalata Roadhouse to Eyre Highway, SA	169
16. Kindness Allergies	179
Monday 17 October: Ceduna, SA	179
Friday 21 October: Tod Highway to Tumby Bay, SA	183
Tuesday 25 October: Port Lincoln to Lincoln Highway, SA	185
Monday 31 October: Cowell to Lincoln Highway, SA	186

17. Headwinds, Hayfever, Huge Heads and Hankies	191
Thursday 3 November: Woomera to Roxby Downs, SA	191
Monday 7 November: Port Augusta to Quorn Road, SA	193
Saturday 12 November: Bute to Blyth, SA	196
Monday 21 November: Balaklava to Port Wakefield, SA	198
18. Home	203
Sunday 27 November: Adelaide to Auburn, SA	203
Thursday 1 December: Burra to Greenock, SA	206
Tuesday 6 December: Langhorne Creek to Kangarilla, SA	209
Friday 9 December: Adelaide, SA	212
19. Zip-Lock Bags Can't Solve Everything	215
Wednesday 15 March 2006: Adelaide, SA, to Launceston, Tas	215
Tuesday 21 March: Burnie, Tas	217
Thursday 23 March: Lake Barrington to Launceston, Tas	221
20. Cycles	227
Tuesday 28 March: St Peter's Pass Rest Area to Oatlands to Hobart, Tas	227
Monday 3 April: Hobart, Tas	229
Wednesday 5 April: Oatlands to Kempton to Hobart, Tas	230
Malar	232
Conclusion	235
June 2006: Adelaide, SA	235
Epilogue	236
December 2007: Kodaikanal, India	236
2013: Kodaikanal, India	238

Author's Notes and Acknowledgements

Stories and interviews

This book features the stories of people I met on my visits to Kodaikanal in 2001, 2004, 2007, 2008, and most recently in 2013. On the second visit, I interviewed some of the children and young people there through an interpreter. I have tried to leave these stories as close to what was relayed through the person interpreting as possible. Permission has been given by those profiled to use the stories and photos that are included in this book.

Permission to be included by name was also given by the people I've written about who I met during my bike ride. I met so many other wonderful people that I was not able to include or track down everyone who was part of my journey. I have changed the names of people who I wanted to include when I wasn't able to locate them to ask permission.

Geography and chronology

The book follows the format of diary entries from my cycling journey. They are snapshots, days or weeks apart, along the route, based on the daily blog I posted online throughout the year of my ride.

Acknowledgements

I would like to thank the Fathers, Brothers, Scholastics and staff of Sacred Heart College who have hosted me during my trips to Kodaikanal and also the students, supporters and friends of PEAK and Grihini who have welcomed me into their worlds and shared their work and knowledge with me.

I also would like to express my gratitude to the people who supported me on my bike ride of 2005 and 2006. New and old friends hosted me, people I met along the way encouraged and took care of me, and friends and family supported me in so many ways via phone calls, email, text messages, thoughts and prayers. Thanks also to all of those people who generously donated to the Cycle of Learning trust fund. I have not mentioned by name all the wonderful people and communities I visited, but I am grateful to each and every one of you.

Without the assistance and support of Colleen Fitzpatrick, Christine Knight, Bonnie Fraser and Steph Davis this book would not be possible. My late aunt, Jenny Wagner, provided invaluable work in editing the manuscript for this story. Warm thanks go to Linda Nix from Lacuna Publishing who has been wonderful to work with. I really appreciate how you have taken up and contributed to this cycle of learning.

Lastly, I would like to acknowledge Father Prem Kumar – the person who made my initial three months in Kodaikanal the world-shaking, eye-opening, perspective-spinning time it was. He guided my reading, discussed ideologies and spirituality with me, and took me with him on his work, to his masses and to visit his family. This is where I learnt the most important things from him through his actions – his respect of others, compassion for any person experiencing oppression, courage to speak out, a willingness to debate with an open mind, and a warm sense of humour. Over the years, Prem has remained a good friend, and continued his work with the poor and oppressed, most recently as country director of the Jesuit Refugee Service in Afghanistan.

In June 2014, Prem was abducted by an armed group at a school he worked with in Herat, western Afghanistan. At the time of publication of this book, no group has yet claimed responsibility, and Prem's family and friends continue to wait in uncertainty for news of his whereabouts and well being.

The author and the publisher will be donating a proportion of the proceeds of the sale of this book to support the Grihini Program in Kodaikanal and the work of the Jesuit Refugee Service.

For
Maureen Thomas
and
Jenny Wagner

Prologue

The rush of wind and the roar of traffic drove me to pedal harder and harder along the path to work. My new bike, with a wonderfully light frame and pedals that my shoes clicked into, took me to speeds I'd never experienced before.

I felt unstoppable. This new bike made me feel like I was flying. The clunky blue bike which I'd retired with the purchase of this smooth and speedy silver one had served me well for years, carting me across town, between university, casual jobs and social events. It was slow but steady, towing me and my changes of clothes, books and day's food supplies wherever we needed to go.

Six months ago, I had been pushing my way up South Road on Clunky Blue while mulling over my plans for the coming year. My brain has a particular gear that it slips into when in steady motion: I get my best thinking done when I'm coasting along by train, bus, foot or bicycle.

As I slowly pushed up the hill, dodging the broken glass near the curb, I realised I didn't want to go straight into a teaching job after my study. I was almost finished a Bachelor of Education, and happy with the plan of being a teacher at some stage of my life, just not yet. I wasn't ready to be tied down to a job, a place and a routine.

I slipped past the line of cars waiting for the lights to change and considered saving up some money to do something else for a while after graduating. Maybe a bike ride. I could carry a tent. How far would I go? I could go part way around Australia. No, that would be just stupid. Why go part way around anything? I'd have to go the whole way! And, if I did that, I could raise money for PEAK, a program in India where I had spent time volunteering a few years ago. I could visit schools along my ride and tell the students about the young people I met in India, and how education was helping them.

I made the decision within a few kilometres of congested South Road. The next year I would ride my bike around Australia and raise money for PEAK.

The wheels started turning. I travelled back to south India in the mid-semester break to meet with PEAK once again. I started contacting schools, community groups and the media. I tracked down equipment and a new, less clunky bike. This sleek, silver Shogun made cycling so easy that, as I raced towards work that afternoon, I felt like Around Australia was going to be a piece of cake.

The grin on my face lasted just a few seconds before a flash of movement in my peripheral vision warned me to slam on my brakes. I wobbled on the spot with the hybrid terror of being centimetres away from riding into the path of the car and not being able to get my feet off the new clip-in pedals.

I finally crashed to the ground, landing sandwiched between the bitumen and my bike. As I untangled bike and body parts, avoiding eye contact with the driver of the car, the enormity of what I was planning to do settled back on my shoulders, a load heavier than that piece of cake I was just contemplating. I had three unfinished assignments to complete in the next week, only $3000 in the bank to cover food and accommodation costs for the coming year, scores of letters, emails and press releases to write to get my fundraising organised, a chronic lack of sleep – and somehow I was expecting to ride this bike solo and unsupported around Australia. I couldn't even ride it to work without embedding bitumen into my knees and grating strips of skin from my forearms. What was I thinking?

Introduction

In 2001, after almost a year of backpacking through Asia, I found myself in the Kodaikanal hills of Tamil Nadu, India. Most of the people who unload from the buses that start in the plains and then zigzag through the hills to chilly Kodaikanal town are tourists from around India. Honeymooners in particular come for the very un-Indian cool climate, views of green, unlittered hills, pony-rides and home-made chocolate, and for the chance to take a row boat out onto man-made Kodai Lake (something that probably seems more romantic in theory than the splashy, hard-to-steer, ill-fitting life-jacket reality).

This town of Kodaikanal, or "Kodai" as it is often referred to, is named after the region with the same name in which it lies – a chain of hills

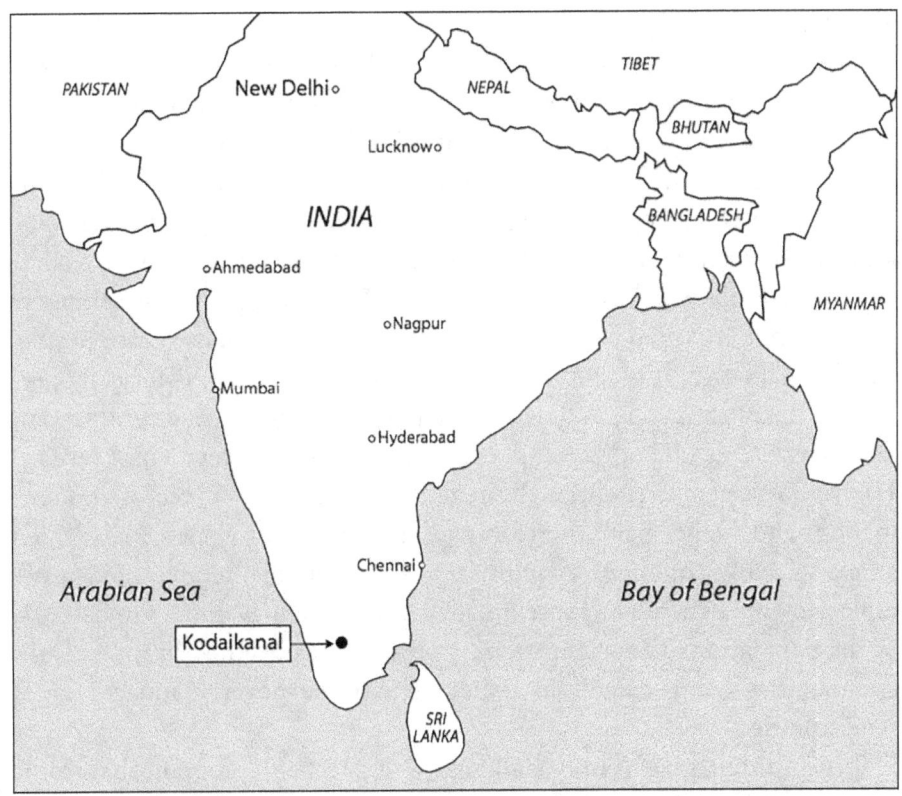

Marker showing location of Kodaikanal region in Tamil Nadu, India.

with over one hundred villages tucked into its pockets, some close to the zigzagging roads, some in places so remote that they are almost impossible to reach.

The Kodaikanal area has been settled for thousands of years and, in recent centuries, been subject to waves of immigration. Pulaiyairs and Paliyars, known as Tribals or Adhivasis, are considered the indigenous people of the area. Adhivasis make up about 8% of the population of India. As other groups moved into Kodaikanal, the Adhivasis were forced from their traditional lands to poorer quality lands. Without the land or capital they needed to be self sufficient, many Adhivasi families were forced into virtual slavery as bonded workers on plantations. Generally, they have been paid very low wages, sometimes being paid in kind, such as with poor quality rice. A large proportion of adult Adhivasis are illiterate, live below the poverty line and have had little or no access to government assistance. They are outside the caste system that still operates in India, particularly in the rural areas, and therefore have limited access to economic, political and social resources.

Dalits (a name that means "the oppressed" – a term chosen by the community themselves, instead of the names given to them by others, such as "untouchable" or "outcaste") are also outside of the caste system and another group of highly vulnerable people in Kodaikanal. Within the Dalit communities, there are those of higher and lower status. Low-status Dalits, known as Maadharis, constitute about 25% of the population in Kodaikanal hills villages. A high proportion of Maadhari people are illiterate and children are often sent out to graze the cattle of higher-caste people, which means they miss out on an education. Dalits have historically performed the most menial and degrading jobs, including agricultural labour, disposing of dead bodies, and cleaning toilets and removing sewage. Higher-caste people traditionally regarded Dalits as a source of contamination, and Dalits have therefore at times been segregated and denied access to many community facilities, such as schools, temples and water tanks. In India there are approximately 240 million Dalits – almost 20% of the population. Their long-term oppression has resulted in many Dalit communities being caught in cycles of extreme poverty and a lack of opportunities.

I spent three months in Kodaikanal, as a guest of a program that works with the Dalit and Adhivasi communities of the area: People's Education and Action in Kodaikanal (which comes to the latitudinally-relevant

Sacred Heart College, Kodaikanal, where PEAK has its headquarters.

acronym of PEAK). PEAK is a program that aims to provide opportunities in education, vocational training, health, finance and activism that will empower Dalit and Adhivasi communities to be able to step out of the cycles of poverty and oppression that have marginalised them for generations.

I spent most of my time in Kodai with the staff and students of two projects that PEAK has involvement with: Grihini, a residential training centre for young women, and Liberative Education for Adhivasis and Dalits (LEAD), which provides hostels and support for primary and secondary students.

The Grihini program, at that time, was a six-month residential course designed to equip illiterate and disadvantaged young women, who are often the most vulnerable members of their communities, with leadership and life skills in order to improve their own and their communities' health, social, economic and political standing. Participants in the course were girls who had only attended a few years of primary school, if any school at all.

Participants came from the Dalit, Adhivasi and Sri Lankan repatriate communities in the Kodai area. Graduates of the Grihini program moved into roles running the program and staffing the LEAD hostels.

The LEAD program concerns itself with the formal education of Adhivasi and Dalit children, mainly through three hostels run exclusively for underprivileged children who are attending school. Two hostels are co-educational and cater to primary students (up to Year 5) and one is for high school-level boys (from Year 6 to Year 10). Girls continuing through high school stay in a hostel run by a local convent, with on-going pastoral support from the PEAK program. The first primary hostel, which started in 1991, began with 30 children; by the time of my first visit 10 years later, the numbers had expanded to 140 young people.

The hostels focus on literacy and numeracy, communication skills, development of leadership qualities, organisational and problem-solving skills, critical social and political analysis skills, banking and saving knowledge, physical education, agricultural skills, and exploring the role of young people in justice campaigns and organisations. The children are also given the opportunity to participate in games, singing and dancing, cultural events, sport, and their traditional religious observances.

As more students have continued through primary and lower secondary school, a need for higher education has arisen. Senior high schools, colleges and universities are geographically and financially difficult to access for the young people of the Kodai hills. In 2001 when I visited, PEAK supported a few students to continue their studies, but the funds for regular and ongoing financial support to a significant number of students was not available in PEAK's budget.

This issue was on the mind of Father Kulandai, PEAK's director, when I visited for a second time in 2004. I had come to sound out my cycling fundraising idea with the PEAK team.

One afternoon I was sitting with Father Kulandai, overlooking the sports field that the students from one of the primary hostels were playing on. Never enjoying conversations about money, I broached it rather awkwardly: "Hypothetically, if I could raise some money for PEAK's work here, what would you use it for?"

Father Kulandai digested the hypothetical offer as quietly and serenely as he does most things. It didn't take long though for him to come to a decision. "A trust fund. We need a trust fund for our senior students."

Father Kulandai had it already thought out: with capital of the equivalent of $200,000, this amount could be invested in a long-term, secure bank account as a trust fund and the interest be used to help fund the secondary and tertiary students' education. It would be an ongoing, sustainable and reliable way to fund an incredibly important investment in the communities of the Kodaikanal hills.

I had already done my calculations too, and informed him that I thought I could maybe raise a quarter of that – $50,000 – by riding around Australia and speaking to schools and community groups along the way. I admitted that I had an inherent aversion to fundraising, and knew my skills in marketing and publicising myself were wanting. However, I was so excited by the way that PEAK worked through education and activism, and felt such affection and admiration for the young people I met in their programs, that I felt, in a year, if I could talk to enough people, and share enough stories about PEAK and the people they worked with, $50,000 might show up.

The rest of my time in Kodaikanal was spent collecting the stories of young people in PEAK's programs and gathering information from Father Kulandai and other members of the PEAK team. I returned to Australia with notebooks full of the interviews and facts and figures – and a small knot of responsibility in my stomach, now I'd made a promise to people and a cause that I had overwhelming amounts of respect for.

With a small group of friends who knew enough about the worlds of fundraising, development and communication, and enough about me and what I was and wasn't capable of, some goals for the endeavour emerged. First, to raise money to help establish a trust fund for higher education for disadvantaged young people in the Kodaikanal hills. Second, to raise awareness with Australian students about the social issues faced by young people in India and the role that education can play in overcoming disadvantage. And lastly, to promote bike riding as a healthy and ecological means of transport.

Christine, the most dexterous with words of the group, christened the project "Cycle of Learning". And with a name, the hard work began.

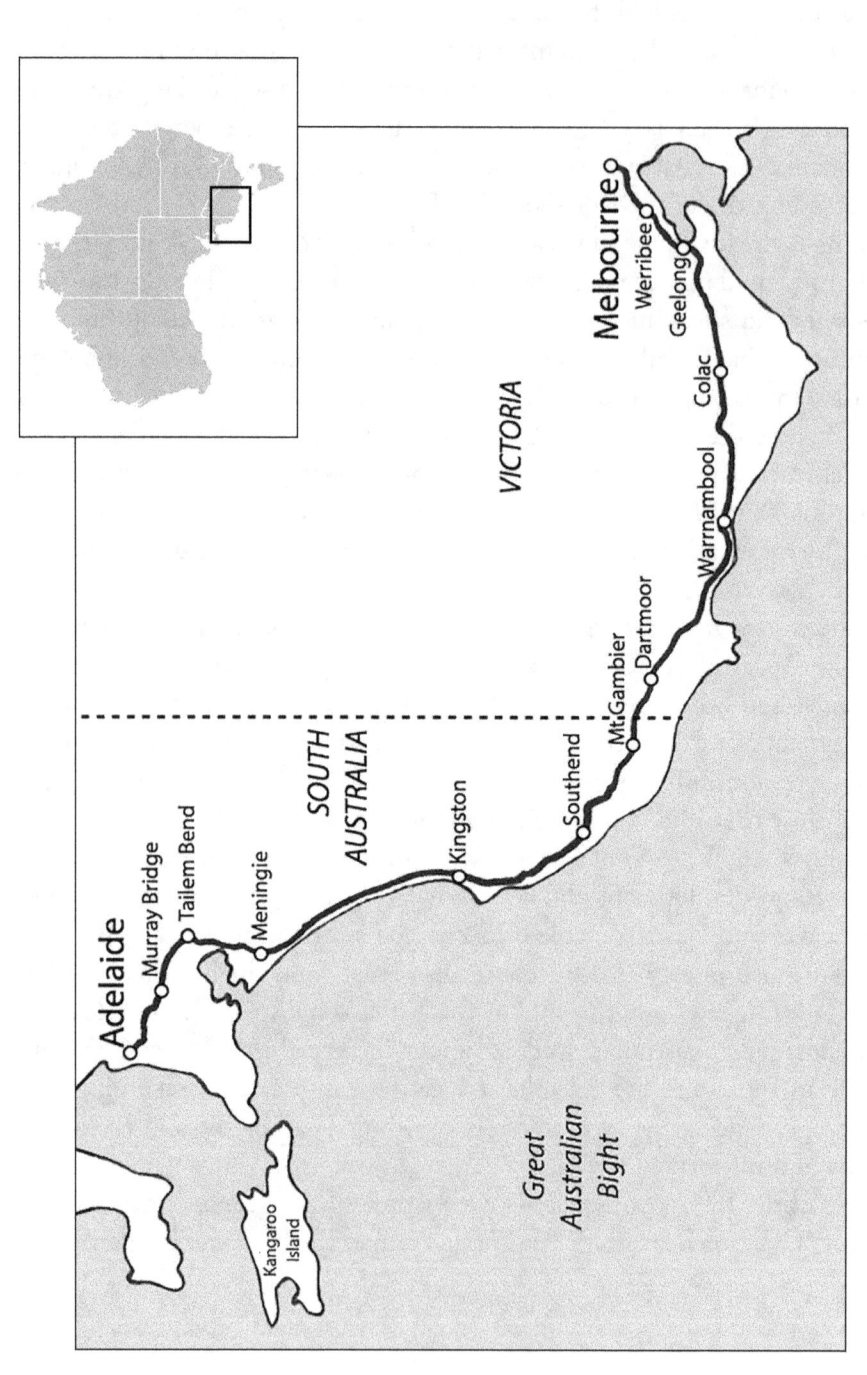

Chapter 1
See You If You Get Back

Adelaide – Murray Bridge – Tailem Bend – Meningie – Kingston – Southend – Mount Gambier – Dartmoor – Warrnambool – Colac – Geelong – Werribee – Melbourne

Totals: 1,148 kilometres – 63 hours 3 minutes – $1,139 raised

Wednesday 2 February 2005
Adelaide to Murray Bridge, South Australia
96 kilometres – 6 hours

As the digital display on my odometer clicked over to 45 km/h, I felt my bicycle trailer begin wobbling from left to right. The wobbles spread through the trailer, into the frame of the bike and then the handlebars. I tried to keep my centre of balance low as I battled to get control back. 48 km/h. Through the drizzle and the wet hair in my eyes, I took note of the sharp turn racing to meet me. 51 km/h. I flicked my eyes to the left to check how many inches I had between me and the embankment. 53 km/h. I willed my bike, still shaking and shuddering from side to side, closer to the edge to leave room for the car I heard approaching from behind.

Just as I was ducking under a rogue branch encroaching onto my limited part of the road, I had a vivid flash of recollection from a few weeks ago. I could clearly see the bright yellow sticker I'd peeled off the trailer, printed in an important-looking font: *WARNING. DO NOT EXCEED 42 KM/H.* I glanced down and saw my odometer click over to 56.

I gritted my teeth and tried to ease on the brakes, but let go as the wheels started skidding.

In the midst of my panic, one more useless memory resurrected itself: Susannah handing me a good-luck card as she left my send-off party. "See you next year. If you get back," was her earnest farewell.

Dying on the first day of my bike ride would be so humiliating.

"So, she was riding her bike around Australia? How far had she travelled?" the investigating police would ask my parents.

"About 20 kilometres, Sergeant."

"And was she adequately prepared, Mrs Fitzpatrick?"

"Well, she did do one practice ride last week. I had to pick her up though, after half an hour, when she got a puncture."

The officer would add something to his notebook about possible genetic megalomania and incompetence, while the representative from the trailer company would pull my odometer from the wreckage. Through the cracked screen, the number 56 would still be visible. "It's a bright yellow sticker. We use capitals AND italics. What more can we do?" the rep would mutter.

We survived though. All three of us – Bike, Trailer and I – made it to the bottom of the hill, shaken but intact. The rest of the day we stayed below the sacrosanct 42 km/h but I continued to have some leadership issues. Before starting my ride today, I had assumed that *I* would be the one in charge of this small, but – thanks to three metres of marine-quality tape – highly reflective crew. This was not proving to be the case. The entire ride to Murray Bridge was a series of wrestling bouts between the three of us. Generally, it was one on one, but at times, it turned into an all-in brawl with everyone wanting to go in conflicting directions and some of us sliding down embankments or lying down on the side of the road stubbornly refusing to get up.

Bike and Trailer do have the upper hand on me in that I'm not well informed when it comes to mechanical objects. Bike is a silver Shogun Metro-LX and people say he has good components. I generally respond with a nod and respectful look on my face to hide the fact I don't know what "components" are. I have managed to attach bar-ends, a bell, rack and side mirror to him along with the reflective tape. The last thing I added was a kickstand. I was warned by bike-expert friends that this is not a hard-core accessory and will add unnecessary weight, but I love a bike that can stand up for itself. After commenting on Bike's components, people turn to Trailer and ask if he is made of aluminium, which leads me to suspect that he is. He has a single wheel at the rear and a tall yellow flag, which I am hoping will prevent us from getting squashed by a truck.

Trundling into Murray Bridge at 7 pm tonight, I couldn't be happier. A damp and wobbly 96 kilometres through the Adelaide hills was a welcome change from wading through administrative preparations for this solo, fundraising bike-ride around Australia. I've still got some logistical issues to deal with, namely, a lack of outdoor expertise, a daunting fundraising target, and a deep-set aversion to asking people for anything, but I've started. 96 kilometres down. 20,000 to go.

Saturday 5 February
Meningie to Kingston, South Australia
150 kilometres – 9 hours 3 minutes

Having an emu trot past me while gliding along a sunny, empty highway felt like a suitable birthday present today. While I'm feeling rather sore as I get used to the physical demands of my new lifestyle, the freedom of the open roads is wonderful compensation. Cycling provides just the right speed, lack of engine noise and wealth of sensory input to enjoy the landscape in a way that is unique to this mode of transport. Some of the sensory input, such as the smell of roadkill, requires extra commitment to appreciate but, overall, having the space and time to fully take in where I am has been enjoyable.

I'm not usually one to anthropomorphise, but today's birthday emu seemed much friendlier than the two lycra-clad Danes who passed me yesterday. When I saw them in the distance behind me, just out of Tailem Bend, I stopped and waited, assuming that when cyclists meet each other on the road they share camaraderie and cycling tales with each other. And maybe there was some camaraderie in the indifferent glance the duo gave me as they sped past. I dejectedly watched the Danish flags on the backs of their shirts fade into the distance. It seems I have a bit to learn about social conventions among long-distance cyclists. Or maybe I just need to learn Danish.

While my confidence is still a little low in the bike-riding department, the school-visiting side of my project has had a solid start. I met with about 150 students at a high school in Murray Bridge yesterday. After looking at a map to find India and, more specifically, the region of Kodaikanal in Tamil Nadu, I told the stories of some children from that area.

Valli

When I first went to Kodaikanal in 2001, I met an 11 year-old girl called Valli who was staying in the primary school hostel run by PEAK. Like the other 100 or so children there, she stayed in the hostel during term time so she could go to school. The village that she was from had a school, which she could not attend because Valli is from the Dalit community. Valli's family, for generations, has done jobs that other people in the village consider unclean, such as cleaning sewage, slaughtering animals or making things from leather. In the urban centres of India, discrimination against Dalits has subsided and is less of an issue, but in many rural areas, it persists. In Valli's village, Dalits either can't go to the village school, or if they do, may be ignored or treated badly.

Staying at the hostel during term time meant that Valli went to school regularly, had help with her homework, ate three healthy meals a day and learnt about social issues as well. A small group of Jesuit Fathers and Brothers oversee the hostel organisation, while local women, referred to as "Akkaa" (older sister), look after the day-to-day needs of the children. When parents bring and pick up their children at the beginning and end of term, they stay for programs discussing hygiene, nutrition, education and agricultural techniques, and hear from local Dalit and Adhivasi activists.

Being one of the oldest in her hostel, Valli often looked after the younger children and helped prepare meals. She was a clever girl, was doing well at school, and had a cheeky sense of humour.

When I returned to Kodaikanal in 2004, Valli wasn't in the hostel anymore. I hoped she had moved on to the hostel in town for girls in high school, but it turned out that she had returned to her village soon after my last visit. She was working with her parents as a coolie (agricultural labourer), picking beans for a nearby landowner. Given she would have been 14 by then, there was a good chance that her parents had already arranged her marriage.

Eswaran

Another student I met on my first visit was a nine-year-old Adhivasi boy called Eswaran. He was the first person in his village to be studying at Year 5 level. When I returned in 2004, I met Eswaran again, this time at the senior boys hostel, and he greeted me with a handshake and a "Hello, sister". Eswaran smiled proudly as the hostel warden informed me he was ranked first in his class at the local high school.

This is Eswaran's story.

Eswaran, aged 12 years, 2004.

To reach the village I am from you must catch one bus down to the plains, catch another bus for a half-hour trip, and then climb on foot for three hours. It is very isolated and has no facilities. The government refuses to help the people of my village build houses, so we live in huts.

The government also refused to supply water to the village, so the villagers saved and put their money together to get a pipe that brings in water from a nearby stream. Otherwise, we would have to carry water a very long way. There is no hospital. If someone becomes sick, they have to walk for three hours to get help. There is also no school, although there is a village television.

I go back to my village four times a year, where I play cricket, go swimming and work as a coolie to help earn money for my family. There are eight people in my family; I have two older sisters, one older brother, one younger brother and one younger sister. My older siblings did not go to school, but my younger brother and sister do. My family do not live in the village proper, but on the property of the landlord of a nearby plantation, which we look after for him.

My family and the other people who work for this landlord get paid 50 rupees a day for men and 40 rupees for women. [At this time one Australian dollar was equivalent to 30 Indian rupees.] They have to travel a long way to a different village where the landlord lives, though, to collect their wages.

I enjoy studying, particularly English and Tamil. When I'm older, I would like to be a government official to help the people so that they don't have to work so hard. I think study is good as it helps people get better jobs than doing difficult labour.

*

Students in the Murray Bridge audience put forward ideas of how education could benefit young people like Valli, Eswaran and themselves: reading and writing, job opportunities, managing money, problem solving, communicating and negotiating, the chance to help people and the skills to change communities.

We finished the talk with questions about Bike, Trailer and the ride, during which the students showed a morbid fascination with the hows, the wheres and the whys of my falling-off-Bike statistics. At least they didn't hold my bike-riding ineptitude against me, unlike some Danes I could think of.

Monday 7 February
Southend to Mount Gambier, South Australia
84 kilometres – 4 hours 14 minutes

Today I began my media campaign.

Christine, the Adelaide coordinator of Cycle of Learning, and I had exchanged a flurry of phone calls as I made my way through the pine forests leading into Mount Gambier. "They want to meet you at the top of Hay Drive. You should see the signs just as you come into town."

"OK. I wonder why there. Do you think that's where the TV station is?"

"Who knows? It doesn't matter as long as you're getting some publicity. Remember to mention the website and that you're tax deductible."

Christine and I have been friends since the first day of primary school. Even at that stage she was outlandishly clever. Not just smart in that she knew about negative numbers and how to read and write before she started school, but clever in that she had an overflowing imagination, was braver than a five year old should probably be and, in my case anyway, was able to get other children to do whatever she wanted. This worked quite well since I was extremely timid when I was young, and needed someone to drag me along on their adventures with them. For a shy child like me, having an anarchic friend like Christine – who bit people to make a point, hit boys with chess boards when she had to, and organised secret societies that involved you breaking school rules and stealing things – was probably just what I needed to balance out my meekness.

Since primary school Christine has settled down in some ways – I haven't seen her bite or hit anyone with a chessboard for ages now. What remains the same, though, is how excited she gets by ideas. Eighteen years ago, it was excitement about how we were going to booby trap a bedroom, or about an atlas we were making for an imaginary world. Today it's excitement about any new undertaking that she or her friends are thinking of embarking on – travel, study, a new recipe. While Christine has been helping me organise Cycle of Learning, this excitement has been so valuable. Instead of falling into a pit of worrying about what I've taken on, Christine and her excitement has helped things feel positive and achievable and worth doing.

Adelaide Coordinator of Cycle of Learning is what we decided to call Christine's role for this project, which she is balancing with dashing off a PhD. She is doing all the things in Adelaide that I can't while I am on my bike and out of range of phones and computers.

For all her logistical support to me today, Christine forgot to remind me not to sweat on screen. By the time I inched my way up the hill, I was dripping with sweat and – checking in my handlebar mirror – an almost fluorescent shade of pink. It was not the image I had hoped to start my life in the media with. The interview began before I'd even got my helmet off, and was over in a few short minutes.

Perspiration issues aside, today on camera I came face to sweaty face with one of the biggest challenges of Cycle of Learning.

"So, what are you riding your bike around Australia for?"

"To raise money to help support disadvantaged young people in India through high school and tertiary education. And to raise awareness for Australian students about the role that education can play in overcoming social disadvantage … and to promote bike riding."

It's not exactly a cause that rolls off the tongue, or keeps the listener's attention past the *to help support* … part. I feel quite envious of those cycling fundraisers that can answer with "for an orphanage". Or "to stop animal cruelty". Even something like "for world peace" would be more three-minute TV interview friendly.

As well as my dishevelled brush with local TV, I had two schools to visit in town, an invitation to speak at a Rotary club and – in a departure from the caravan parks I've been staying in – accommodation with two families for my time in town. One is the parents of Christine's housemate and the other is a colleague of my mother's. It was quite lovely to have the hospitality of these families that I had never met before but who were willing to offer their support through loose and stretched out connections.

Now that I was starting to line up speaking gigs, and had people hosting me on my journey, Cycle of Learning was finally being transformed into something real and tangible. In the months leading up to the ride it was at first just an idea-seed, then an abstract future event incubating while I put in hours behind computers, sent out information, looked at maps, got advice, made phone calls and shopped for camping gear I didn't know how to use. Even once I mounted my bike and left Adelaide, I still felt like I was trying to conjure something out of nothing by claiming "I will ride around Australia and raise fifty thousand dollars". After 500 kilometres or so, I no longer felt like I was pretending. I was over the first hurdle now that Cycle of Learning had a life – albeit, a very young one – of its own. I was just not entirely sure what it would grow into, and if it would match the ambitious plans spun for it.

Wednesday 16 February
Geelong to outer Melbourne, Victoria
84 kilometres – 3 hours 59 minutes

I rode the freeway from Geelong to Melbourne this afternoon for the second time in as many days. I had been staying in Geelong with my cousin Heidi and her husband Tim. As much as they have to love me because we're family, I think I may have outstayed my welcome by a few days, half a dozen burritos and a garage break-in.

Heidi made a pre-emptive phone call prior to my arrival on Saturday to find out what I wanted for dinner. I rolled in to a Mexican extravaganza and warm welcomes from hosts I knew well enough to borrow clothes from so I could do a 99% wardrobe wash (I felt asking to borrow a pair of undies would be overstepping a certain line, even between cousins).

On Sunday, Heidi and Tim had some commitments in Melbourne so they left me alone in the house for a few hours with the leftovers from the previous night's dinner. On their return they were polite enough not to mention the large gap in the fridge where those leftovers had been, or the salsa stain on their t-shirt I was still wearing.

I could sense a renewed confidence in me when they had to leave for work on Monday morning. They must have felt it was OK to leave me since there was no opened food that I could demolish and I was back in my own clothes. Also, they knew I would be kept out of mischief since I had a visit to a school nearby which would take up much of my day.

I watched some morning television until it was time to leave for the school. It was at this point I realised I had somehow misplaced the keys to Heidi and Tim's house and shed where Bike and Trailer were safely locked away.

After a lot of general panicked rushing around followed by some inspired work on the louvred windows of the shed, I got us all to the school, but it was lucky that the police hadn't driven by while I was breaking into the shed and bleeding all over its windows. At least the visit went well with the local primary school, where I visited each of the classes. We spoke some Tamil to each other (the language spoken in Kodaikanal) and thought of lots of reasons why bicycles are a great way of getting around – not least because it's easier to drag a bike out of a shed window than a car.

Tim found another set of keys and gave them to me so I could lock up on the way out when I left for Melbourne the next day. In the morning, I waved Tim and Heidi farewell as they drove off to work and sat with the keys in my hand until my departure time. Proud of myself, I locked the doors, hid the keys in the nominated spot and headed for the highway. My plan was to stop at a school in Werribee before riding the rest of the highway into Melbourne by nightfall.

After the school visit and a photo shoot for the local newspaper, I pointed Bike north, ready to hit the bright lights of Melbourne. Luckily, I decided to check in with Christine in Adelaide first, and received instructions for a new assignment. I turned Bike 180 degrees and headed back to Geelong since the assignment involved speaking at a school there the next day.

After my unexpected return, I suspect Heidi and Tim were considering changing their locks (and if that failed, their address) to avoid the possibility of me continually turning up at their house unannounced. They may have had to change their locks anyway if they weren't able to find those keys.

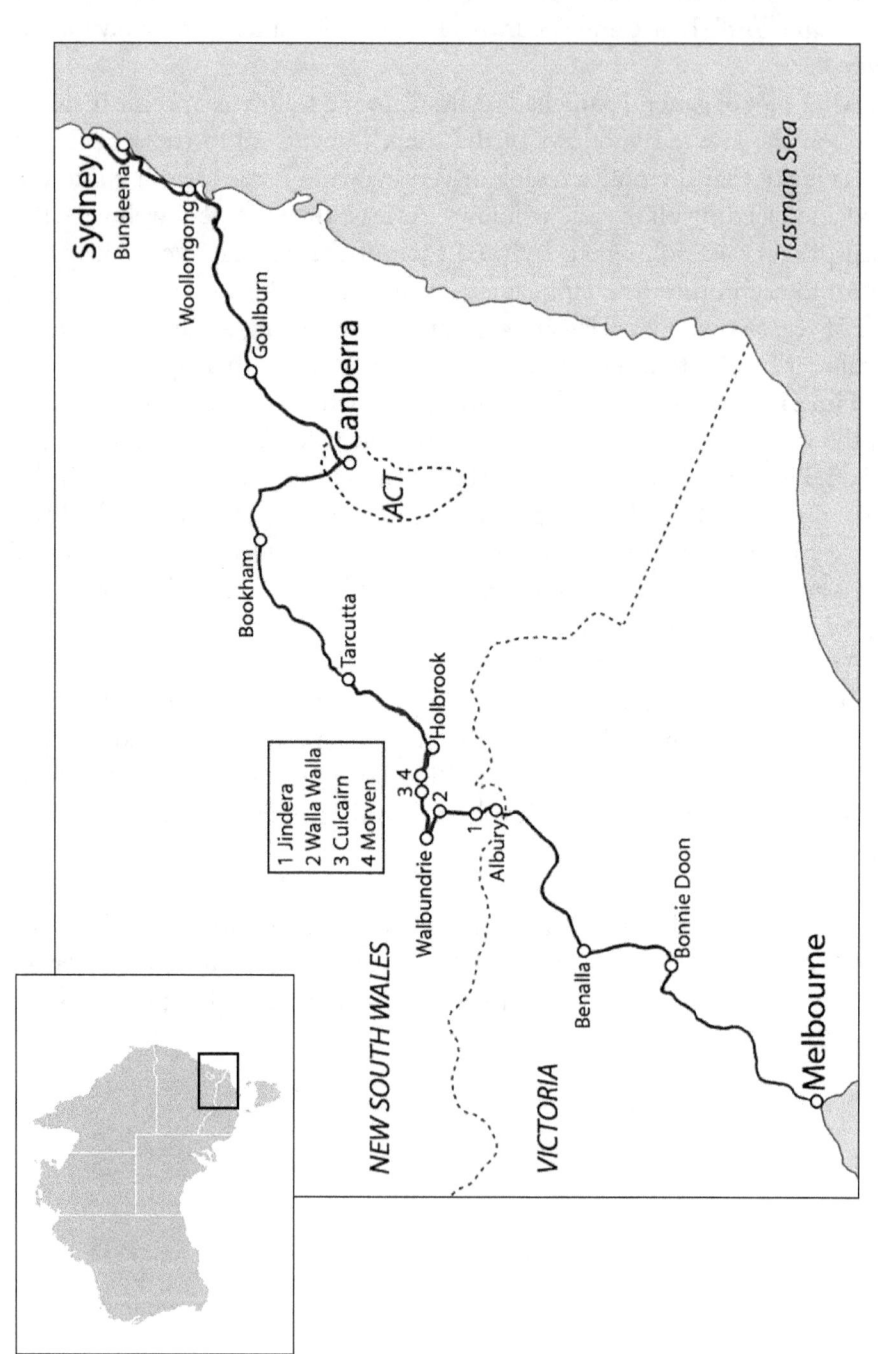

Chapter 2

Dirty and Altitudinally Challenged

Melbourne – Bonnie Doon – Benalla – Albury – Jindera – Walla Walla – Walbundrie – Culcairn – Morven – Holbrook – Tarcutta – Bookham – Canberra – Goulburn – Wollongong – Bundeena – Sydney

Totals: 2,537 kilometres – 144 hours 16 minutes – $4,197 raised

Sunday 20 February
Bonnie Doon to Benalla, Victoria
73 kilometres – 3 hours 39 minutes

I learnt a lot in the past two weeks – how to outride flies, how to eat and ride at the same time, and how to go to sleep with dirty feet – but yesterday showed me I still have some troubling gaps in my cycling know-how.

In the morning I farewelled Diane and Neil, the hospitable second cousins I had met for the first time only the evening before, packed my bags and headed for the hills. These lasted a long time but weren't too steep, and there was lush national park and forest around to take my mind off my legs.

I was feeling rather sunny and happy with my crew. In the kilometres from Adelaide to Melbourne, Bike, Trailer and I had settled into a functional working relationship and I was happy that I chose them as my travel companions. Before I left Adelaide I'd received all sorts of conflicting advice from cycling aficionados about the fancy, complicated equipment I would need. I ended up using a simple criterion for selecting my purchases: cheapness. I was lucky enough in August to meet someone who could help me distinguish between bad-quality cheap and good-quality cheap. I first encountered Harley, a raw-vegan anti-establishment ultra-athlete, working in a bike shop and he took me under his wing, psyched me up with his raw-vegan anti-establishment ultra-athletic philosophies, and led me around the displays, telling me quietly: "You won't need that; you won't need that; this bike is cheap but will get you round the country; you can get that cheaper on the internet; you won't need that ..." I left as a vegetarian, with half of my savings intact and a hope that ultra-athleticism was contagious.

True to Harley's word, Bike and Trailer were doing a fine job. Although not ridiculously lightweight or high-tech, they required minimal attention and kept me trundling along. Trailer was easy to pack and with its single wheel following directly behind Bike, I hardly felt the weight of my sleeping bag, food, paperwork, clothes and small range of tools that I didn't entirely know how to use.

While Bike marked a substantial improvement comfort-wise from the cheap, poorly-constructed bicycle that I used to own, my body was taking some time to adjust to life on the road. The first few weeks of riding were painful – in my shoulders, wrists, back, neck, legs, bottom, head, forearms, and in a spot that's near where I think my pancreas lives. I had been warned about this by other cyclists – the soreness in general, not specifically in my pancreas – but also been assured that the pain would disappear after a fortnight or so in the saddle. They were spot on, to the day almost, and by the time I was crossing the Great Dividing Range the day before, I was feeling fit and comfortable. In fact, that whole morning I had an all-pervading sense of self-assurance with the performance of my body and equipment that was probably on the smug end of the confidence spectrum.

Prior to my departure from Adelaide I had a decent level of fitness, though not quite enough or the right sort of conditioning for this sort of ride. In its place, I had a confidence in my body assuring me that I could rise to and withstand whatever physical challenges came my way on the journey. This confidence came from the ten years of martial arts training that had been a huge part of my life since I stepped into my first class when I was 15. I had trained in wrestling, capoeira, a month each of Thai krabi krabong in Bangkok and traditional karate classes in India, and the bulk of my time in a club that practised a mix of karate, judo, jiu jitsu and weaponry.

This training had given me a multitude of rewards. Through it I learnt how wonderful it is to hone skills with repetition and focus, how to teach others, how something comes alive in you when you find what sparks your passion, and what an amazing tool and instrument the human body is. I learnt that my body was not something to be ashamed of for not looking as skinny or pretty as some parts of society suggested it should be. Why be ashamed of a body that can kick high, kick hard, kick with balance and timing and accuracy? Why be embarrassed by a body that can choke and armlock and throw another person? Why doubt a body that can be picked up and driven into the mats with a crunching wrestling drive, but knows exactly how to tense up and land safely so it can jump up and do the same back to its partner? Why not be proud of a body that can figure out how to do one-armed cartwheels, manipulate nunchucks, staff and sword, and fight round after round of sparring, boxing, kickboxing, throwing and grappling?

This is the confidence that martial arts gave me. I knew from experience that my body could refine technique, build strength in new muscles, ramp up its fitness levels and adapt however it needed to ride me around Australia.

In the early afternoon, I hit my usual post-lunch lethargy. Strangely, it didn't disappear after a while as it normally did. Instead, I seemed to be moving progressively slower and slower. I thought it could be the fault of one of the small apples I had eaten from a tree by the side of the road. So, to test the hypothesis, I ate another one from the next tree to see if I felt worse. I did feel worse but not in a poisoned way, so wondered if I just needed even more energy. I ate some almonds and followed them up with a mouthful of honey, but was still struggling, so next I tried drinking lots of water.

I decided my body wasn't to blame, and became more frustrated because, by my evaluation, I was riding downhill and should be going more than the 10 km/h I was. Once I checked for a puncture. Another time I stopped to see if a dead snake was caught in Bike's chain. I'd narrowly missed running over three already that day, and one dead wombat. I figured, though, that a wombat would be too fat to get caught, so didn't bother checking for one of those. As the absence of snakes cast no light on the situation, I gave up, dismounted and started pushing Bike and Trailer along. I looked over my shoulder to check for traffic that may think me soft, and realised I had actually been riding uphill for the past five kilometres or so. I know I have a bad sense of direction, but there is something odd going on when I can be on a hill and not know if I am going up or down it. Around Australia suddenly felt like an incredibly long exercise and my position on the confidence spectrum slid swiftly to the bottom of the chart.

This morning it was only a short ride to Benalla and the idyllic scenery kept me distracted from over-analysing the gradient of the road. I passed fluffy sheep eating the grass on the hills, flocks of birds, clear blue lakes, and children being towed behind speed boats (in a recreational, fun, non-abusive way).

Tomorrow I would ride out of Victoria. I had made it through the state in less than two weeks. Thanks to minimalist results in the school-booking department, I had pushed through the quiet countryside at a steady pace with Geelong as my only extended stop. It was worrying me that a state with such a significant proportion of Australia's population wasn't interested in me; or rather, that I hadn't captured any interest.

There was not much to do though, but keep pedalling and hope that some better marketing skills developed along with my leg muscles, or that I would become more interesting the further I got from home.

Thursday 24 February
Albury to Walla Walla, New South Wales
52 kilometres – 2 hours 53 minutes

This morning's dark 6 am start for a high school in Walla Walla provided me with not only the chance to use my beloved three-function headlamp but also to ride through a breathtaking sunrise as I went up and over the Jindera Gap. I spoke during an assembly which was themed "How much stuff do we need to be happy?" I was tempted to base my talk on the fact that everyone needs a three-function headlamp to be truly happy, but instead shared some of what I had observed during my time in Kodaikanal.

On the one hand there is definitely a lot of "stuff" that most of us have in Australia that families around Kodaikanal happily do without. On the other hand, there are things that, through poverty and social inequality, some families miss out on: easy access to clean water, adequate nutrition and health care, the opportunity to go to school, political rights and, quite often, three-function headlamps. These aren't luxuries, but things that everyone should have the right to.

Wary of the fact that I was not an expert in Indian sociology, poverty or development, I tried to base the majority of my talks on information given to me by the PEAK team and on interviews I conducted with students when I returned to Kodaikanal for the second time.

Return to Kodaikanal

For this fact-finding return visit I navigated the Tamil Nadu trains, buses and sweet shops to retrace my steps back to Kodaikanal where the women wear fragrant strings of jasmine in their hair; men enquire after your "good name"; children either stare with horror at you or laugh with bewilderment; you get asked "You came here alone?" with a certain tone of disapproval, and "The food here is very pungent, yes?" with a certain smugness; and the hilly location means it is cool enough to not be sweating all the time as you do in the plains.

At Sacred Heart College, PEAK's headquarters, I was welcomed once again into the ill-defined role I had occupied three years previously: something between a student, a nun, a man, a tourist, a visiting academic and a performing monkey. As there were grains of truth in a few of those, I couldn't complain. I caught up with fatherly and brotherly friends of the Roman Catholic persuasion, and was warmly welcomed by the children in the hostels again. True, this was mainly due to my skills of pretending to eat imaginary head lice, killing real ones the kids brought to me, owning a watch with a button that lit up the screen, and singing my limited range of Tamil songs – but I still felt welcomed.

My lateral neck muscles reawakened to assist with at least 80% of my communication. I have considered compiling a phrase book with instructions for the head wobbles with meanings from "Yes, I'd love some more fried congealed goat's blood with my rice" to "Thanks for asking. My diarrhoea is now painful but not inconvenient" to "Good morning. Yes I am a strange white person walking through your village" to "Mm, that was a tasty head louse".

I wasn't entirely sure what to expect when I began conducting interviews with hostel students. With the help of staff with translating, I collected a range of stories revealing the students' love for their villages and families, the conditions their people live and work under, their hopes for the future and their feelings about living away from home and studying in the PEAK hostels.

A few students became upset while they were telling me about their families. Obviously, the children in the hostels love their families and miss them dearly. Talking about their father's illness or the abuse their family has suffered through caste discrimination brought some to tears and others close. Hearing the children speak about their hopes for the future was a mixed experience for me. Nearly every young person I interviewed had grand dreams: to become a teacher, become a doctor, get a job with the government, teach and heal their people, and free them from the suffering that exists in their villages now.

The reality, however, is that while some of these students will continue their studies and *maybe* finish high school and *maybe* go on for further training and *maybe* have the career that they dreamed of, many of them won't. Family needs will bring many of them back to their villages to work alongside their parents as coolies. Tradition often calls on girls to get married in their early teens, bringing their chances of formal education to an end. In school and college exams, these students are competing against students from literate families with uninterrupted schooling and more resources. Only a tiny proportion of the cost of education, particularly past the high-school level, can be met by the Dalit and Adhivasi families. So when the PEAK team put forward the idea of establishing a trust fund for the ever-growing number of students that finish primary school and are ready to go on to high school and beyond, I felt so excited at the thought that Cycle of Learning would contribute to something that would be sustainable, on-going and meet a real need for the people of the Kodai hills.

Back in New South Wales, I finished my talk and rode out of Walla Walla. A few minutes down the road, my Albury host – my godmother Maureen – pulled up in a ute and we surreptitiously hauled Bike and Trailer into the back to return to Albury in time for another round of school visits that Maureen had lined up for me. Not only is Maureen a fantastic godmother, she is also a hurricane of organisation and action.

I arrived in Albury on Monday to the reception of Maureen and her brother Philip (Mum's cousins) and his wife Marie sitting on Maureen's front fence cheering me in. Before I even had my gear out of Trailer, Maureen was on the phone lining up appointments with schools, church groups and newspapers. During most of the phone calls she made some sort of connection with the person on the other end of the phone – "You're a Cunningham are you? Is your family from Corowa? Oh yes, my son

Steven has been shearing in Culcairn with your father." She gave a masterclass in networking.

Maureen is one of the people I admire most. She's interested in everyone and everything she encounters, and if she notices any situation that needs someone to do something, she'll be the person to do it. A few years ago she came across some newly arrived Bhutanese refugees who lived nearby and set to giving them all driving lessons. There was no one to do the church bulletin, so she taught herself how to use the computer software and now puts it together every week. When she visits her sons' homes she'll busy herself with cleaning out the fridge or doing some ironing (whether they want her to or not). She visits her mother in a nursing home every day and usually ends up spending a few hours feeding other residents, helping organise entertainment and popping in on people who need some company. Keep in mind Maureen's mum is close to 100 and Maureen herself is 72. And chose to go skydiving for her 70th birthday.

On her trips to visit my family in Adelaide, Maureen starts chatting to people wherever we take her. She came down once for a wrestling competition I was in. I had spent the morning being intimidated by all the fit, muscly interstate wrestlers milling about waiting for their rounds. Within half an hour of Maureen's arrival at the stadium, she had got to know a dozen or so of the competitors, and decided to barrack for Bill from Melbourne (one of the more handsome, less cauliflower-eared wrestlers in our vicinity) since he had the same name as her late husband. Whenever I'm in Albury with her, given she's friends with a significant proportion of its population, a trip to the shops will involve stopping every few metres to say hello to her librarian's daughter's acupuncturist, or whoever it is that she knows.

I'm pretty sure if a neurologist did a scan of Maureen's brain, the huge overdevelopment of "thinking about other people" region would be shown to have strangled out the "self-conscious" zone. She's the sort of open woman who if conversation turns to dentists she will pull out her false tooth to give you a look, or after having a run-in with a sheep on one of her son's farms, she'll drop her trousers to show you the bruise she's got on her thigh.

She is one of the best examples I know of how to live a happy life. We had a conversation once about depression. Maureen told me that while she felt really sorry for people who suffered from it, she found the whole concept completely confusing. "Why don't they just go out and talk to people, or do something interesting … ?" Maureen has the balance right – by spending her time thinking about others and acting on their needs enthusiastically and unreservedly, she's eliminated the parts of her thinking that cause suffering to a lot of the rest of us. Ego, insecurity, self-centredness and disconnect from others do not get a look-in on how Maureen functions.

On the way back into Albury, as we barrelled through farmland with brown crops and receding dams, I saw two figures on bikes in the distance. They looked familiarly fast and unfriendly. As we neared the cyclists with their matching panniers, my suspicions were confirmed. They were the two Danish riders who had passed me on the way to Meningie two weeks ago. Maureen wanted to stop and talk to them of course, but as my pride was still wounded, I insisted that we drive past and not disrupt them from their fast and focused cycling. Ego and social disconnect is particularly hard to rid yourself of when it comes to being ignored on the road.

Saturday 12 March
Bundeena to Sydney, New South Wales
39 kilometres – 2 hours 31 minutes

In the past few days, I came to realise that there are some things I cannot do, and some places a bike should not go. The day before, Macquarie Pass earned a place high on the list of the latter. I had a few route options to get to Sydney, but this one had nice-sounding roads and towns, and the route – on the map at least – looked easy enough. There must be better criteria for navigational decision-making but I was yet to figure it out.

I began the morning meandering down the Illawarra Highway reflecting on the students I'd spoken to in a Goulburn primary school. They had listened politely to my spiel about India, discrimination, education and social change. I had my enlarged laminated photos of Kodaikanal ready for question time, but the kids immediately homed in on my personal hygiene during this trip. "How do you wash your clothes?" was the first question fired at me. I put down the photos from India and explained how I use the same bar of soap to wash myself, my hair and my clothes. I would use it to wash Bike and Trailer too, but they hadn't started smelling yet, unlike myself, my hair and my clothes.

A volley of questions followed concerning camping logistics, regularity of showers, teeth cleaning habits and, finally, a thoughtful follow-up question from a small boy in the front. "How big *is* your bar of soap?" The image of a monstrous 90 x 40 x 15 centimetre bar of soap travelling solo in Trailer was a wonderful thought, but I told him the 125 grams of truth. I rode away from the school to waves from the students who seemed relieved to be ridding themselves of their dirty guest speaker.

I had just resolved to investigate some alternative hair-cleaning arrangements when the shoulder of the road suddenly narrowed, heralding the beginning of Macquarie Pass. As I rode higher and higher, mist set in and then some fine rain which I laughed at and imagined I was getting some sort of hydrating facial treatment in a fancy beauty salon (that probably has a wide range of specific soaps for different purposes). It had been blue skied and sunny just moments ago, and the line on my map hadn't looked at all wet or slippery, so I was sure the rain would disappear soon.

With Bike and Trailer on the New South Wales coast.

Ten minutes later as I began my descent of the pass, I suddenly hoped I wouldn't literally be laughing out of the other side of my face, in a terrible-disfiguring-accident way. The minimalist shoulder had become a non-existent one. Even with my brakes squeezed to their utmost, I hurtled though the hairpin bends with the engines of a constant stream of articulated trucks in my right ear. In contrast to this clamour, the echoes of birdcalls from the rainforest-filled ravine below rang in my left ear adding to the feeling of careering, slippery, almost air-borne terror.

I squinted through the rain, which was bucketing down, now more reminiscent of falling into a swimming pool than the gentle mist of a beauty treatment. Through the litres of water, I spotted a big red sign telling cars to travel at 15 km/h because of the steep declines for the next eight kilometres. I tried to imagine what sort of sign the road safety department would construct for Bike. Following the hypothetical instructions, I squeezed my brakes even harder. The brakes shrieked at me, and Bike slowed down but couldn't quite stop. I clenched my teeth and executed a rolling dismount, thankfully finding myself on the road and not plummeting into the ravine. I walked the rest of the way, placing Bike and Trailer between the traffic and me. I exited the pass with my brakes and nerves completely worn through and mounted Bike once more, to ride with the heavy traffic headed into Wollongong.

The next morning I laid out my tools and spare parts and did my best to replace Bike's brake pads. They had been ground down to the metal bases by Macquarie Pass, and it seemed the denuded pads had also worn into the rims of the wheels. On close inspection, I found there were no actual holes in the rims, so I decided to ignore the situation. I was feeling rather proud of my mechanical victory of fitting the new brakes and didn't want any pesky wheel rim issues spoiling my mood.

I headed into Royal National Park and revelled in the absence of rain, trucks and red signs. I could look at the sparkling ocean views all I wanted without interruption. Until my gears went demented. Dropping into my lowest gear to climb a hill, cogs clicked, whirred, and refused to function. I gave Bike a lecture along the lines of "I spend my morning fixing your brakes, and this is how you thank me?" and got off to start fiddling. I pulled wires and twisted screws and managed to reduce my gear-changing capacity to half of Bike's advertised 27 speeds. After another ten minutes with a spanner and having done further damage, I gave in before we became a single speed rig.

Gears became less of an issue when I hit a section of the road that was closed for road works. I faced a choice between a 40-kilometre detour or catching a train for two stops. I decided to railroad it, to the dismay of Bike and Trailer. They resisted every step of the way as I pushed them up a near-vertical hill to the train station, let them bump and shudder down a huge flight of stairs to get to the platform and folded them into a complex origami design to fit them into the annexe of the train.

The three of us limped into Sydney and tracked down some family friends who had a pile of mail and lunch waiting for me. Col took Bike aside and swiftly sorted out the brake and gear situation. I would normally have felt embarrassed by this, but given that Pam and Col are acquainted with a few generations of my family, they are aware of the DIY genes I have to work with. The fact that I had not burst a water main, electrocuted myself or found myself stuck naked inside a newly painted bathtub while wrecking my brakes is actually impressive for someone from my family.

After lunch, Col got on his own bike and led me along his favourite route into the city centre. I soon realised we must have very different tastes. The sensations of imminent death or injury I experienced on Macquarie Pass started flashing back to me as we dodged flocks of pedestrians, hijacked escalators and sneaked into bus lanes. I summoned the calming techniques I have been developing for stressful riding situations: breath holding, brow furrowing and jaw clenching got me through some manoeuvres while humming or singing worked for others. Whenever Col turned around to check I was still behind him, I made sure I had a smile and unfurrowed brow for show.

Reaching the end of my death-defying escorted tour, I farewelled Col and found some old high school friends who live in a tall block of apartments. With some quiet words of apology to Bike and Trailer, I hauled them up the fire stairs to the roof. There I left them to recover from the trauma of the last few days with a view of the Sydney Opera House and the Harbour Bridge.

I settled in a few levels down with Rebecca and Brett. Since one is a chiropractor and the other a journalist and reiki practitioner, these two were not only providing me with a bed, meals and company for a few days, but also alignments, interviews and some channelling of universal energy. Kindly, they didn't mention my grubbiness or grimy fingernails, although a gift from Rebecca of Chanel Shimmering Décolletage Gel may have been a subtle hint not to let myself go *too* much.

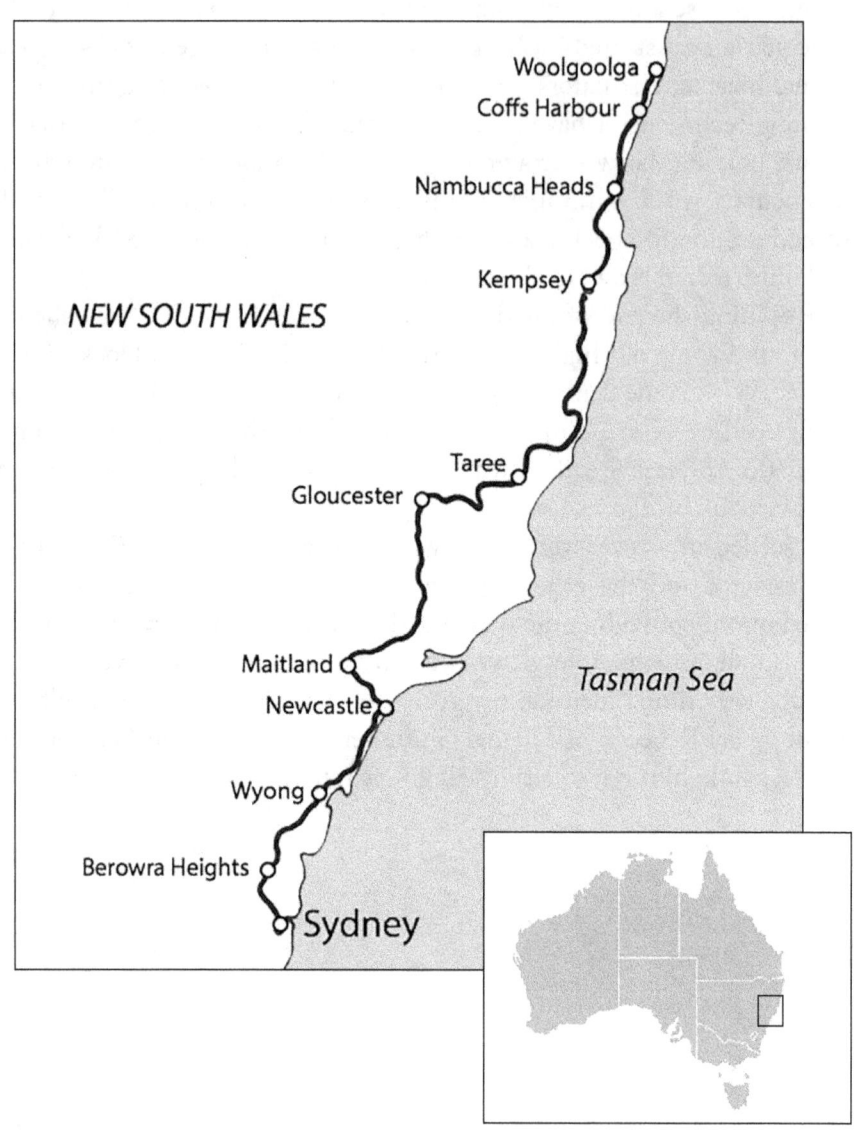

Chapter 3
Nipple Confusion and Corporate Uniforms

Sydney – Ku-Rin-Gai Chase National Park – Berowra Heights – Wyong – Newcastle – Maitland – Gloucester – Taree – Kempsey – Nambucca Heads – Coffs Harbour – Woolgoolga

Totals: 3,557 kilometres – 204 hours 33 minutes – $4,847

Friday 18 March
Sydney, New South Wales

I spent nearly a week in Sydney, catching up with friends, eating ice cream and refreshing my library at secondhand bookshops. On the down side, I had just one school visit in this time. Another school got in touch to find out if Kodaikanal was affected by the 2004 Boxing Day tsunami. I cringed into the phone as I heard myself replying, "Unfortunately, no." I paused and rephrased my answer. "Thankfully, Kodaikanal is a hill station about 200 kilometres from the coast."

This school, like a number of others I had heard from, would have liked to support Cycle of Learning but was dedicating their fundraising efforts this year to victims of the tsunami. That's the reality of fundraising, I suppose. There are so many causes and charities both here and overseas asking for support. The community has limited money and attention to give and people have to choose. There is no one to blame, but it gets disheartening when your cause is not being chosen. More disheartening was the fact I'd only raised a few thousand dollars so far.

The fundraising strategy I had been using was to notify as many schools, churches, community groups and media outlets as possible about my ride and its cause, and ask if they would like me to stop and speak to them. When I visited, after giving a talk and answering questions, I would leave them with information about how they could donate if they so chose.

The Lutheran Church of Australia's aid and development arm, Australian Lutheran World Service, had endorsed my project, and was processing donations and issuing tax-deductible receipts. I'd considered seeking corporate sponsorship before I left Adelaide, and tried approaching some companies, but the whole process terrified me and seemed to require a level of professionalism, self-assurance and persistence that I just wasn't able to muster.

Financial self-pity aside, the school I *did* visit in Sydney made me feel important. After a tour with two school captains, I was escorted to a balcony from where I addressed the entire student body who were sitting below on the basketball courts. I felt a little like royalty greeting loyal subjects. If my fundraising strategy didn't work out, maybe I could get a part-time job somewhere being a princess to raise the rest of the money.

After my balcony performance, I gave a more intimate reception to a group of student leaders from the senior school. I was glad to be able to touch on some of the more complex issues for young people in Kodaikanal, and share some other stories from Kodaikanal, including what Pandimeena shared with me about her life.

Pandimeena and the Grihini program

I work for PEAK as a nurse and am from one of the upper hill villages in the Kodaikanal Hills. About 20% of the people there are cobblers – a Dalit caste.

I am the first Dalit girl in the Upper Kodaikanal villages to finish Year 12, which I did in 1999. I was motivated to complete school by my elder brother who was the first Dalit boy in the village to finish high school. After I finished high school, PEAK provided me with financial and pastoral support to gain a diploma in Multi-Purpose Health Work. My parents, especially my father, were supportive of my training in nursing. I chose nursing because I remembered when I was a child how my mother suffered from chest pain.

I have worked with PEAK since 2001. I am in charge of the Mother and Child Health Program, which assists six Adhivasi villages in the lower Kodaikanal Hills. I also take care of the health needs of students at PEAK's hostels, villagers that live nearby, and girls from the Grihini program.

I have seen first-hand the violence, exploitation and discrimination arising from caste issues in the villages. In my village, there are five dominant, so-called higher-caste, groups and one cobbler group. I have at times seen four families living together in one small house, with the result that the families suffer from many diseases.

At least half the Dalits in my village are dependent on the landowners who belong to the dominant caste. Because of this situation, the Dalits' wages are very low and they are unable to educate their children. Once the Dalit boys finish Year 5 they are forced to tend the cattle belonging to the so-called higher-caste people. This is a form of bonded labour.

My vision is to get a further two years of training in a hospital, then start a clinic in my village. I would like my clinic to help my own community, which is poor and under-privileged.

I am particularly glad that as well as looking after the health needs of the girls in the Grihini program, I am living closely with them. These girls can be motivated by seeing what I have accomplished, and they, in turn, will educate their children right through high school.

This Grihini program that Pandimeena spoke of was the reason I first came to Kodaikanal. I'd been backpacking through India when a family friend, Norm, invited me to travel with him to Kodai, where he was visiting Grihini. In 1988, Norm, with his wife Jan, a Jesuit Father, Arokiam, and two teachers from a local school, Dency and Ruth, set up Grihini for local girls and young women from marginalised communities who were not in formal education. Grihini gave girls skills in health, income generation, literacy and numeracy, and awareness of social issues, as well as the tools to be part of social change in their villages and wider community by returning to their villages as "animators", to educate others in health, hygiene, finances and liberative social action.

The 28 young women I met in the 2001 batch of Grihini welcomed me into their close-knit and vibrant fold. Most days I would make my way to their space at the back of Sacred Heart College, which, being on the side of the hills, was a secluded, grassed area with a handful of buildings opening onto it. A few girls might be in the open kitchen preparing the next meal on a big fire that needed firewood constantly fed into it. One room held most of the classes – literacy, or instruction on crochet or macramé basket-making. The writing slates or craft materials would be cleared away for tutorials on caste issues, human rights and gender. The girls would have debates, devise street theatre, sing awareness songs and meet Grihini alumni who were now working in their home villages to share awareness of health, hygiene and human rights.

Another room had a bank of foot-pedalled sewing machines for learning tailoring skills on. I could never figure the machines out, and was content to sit with a group on the floor sewing buttons onto shirts while chatter flowed around me. I gave self-defence classes to the Grihini group, one of the only skills I'd brought with me that had any potentially practical use there. It was a wonderful sight – seeing their strength and power physically manifest as we practised getting out of grabs, protecting from strikes and delivering punches, kicks, head-butts and eye-gouges. Without the kick bags I used in Australian classes, I made do with bringing the pillow down from my room for the girls to practise on. My plan for them to each bring their own pillow never transpired since, as I soon realised, the girls slept in the usual Tamil Nadu way – lined up in rows with nothing beneath them except the thin mats rolled out over the concrete floor of their classroom.

This constant togetherness – when at home being with family always, and in Grihini, continually in the company of their peers – contrasted sharply with my independence. The girls questioned me about the travel I had done and couldn't get their heads around it. They liked the idea of seeing different places, but were baffled as to why I would do it by myself. It sounded like some sort of punishment to them.

The times I loved the most with the girls was Sunday mornings. It was their day off from study, and they took it in turns to bathe, wash their hair, and then sit on the side of the hill combing coconut oil through each other's long tresses until they were glossy. A group of girls would make idli – steamed rice cakes – and a chickpea curry for the special breakfast of the week. Normally breakfast was a nutritious but plain bowl of rice porridge with a dab of lime pickle in it for flavour. These idlis had the girls grinning in anticipation, and they devoured serve after serve of the heavy cakes. They were making up for lost nutrients. Coming from families with limited access to health care or adequate food, these girls were small, under-developed and only one or two stood taller than my shoulder. When I met some of their parents who had travelled down for an agricultural workshop I saw what the future might have in store for these beautiful girls, so full of life and energy now. The parents seemed even smaller still than their daughters – scrawny and worn down from hard manual work in the home and fields. Even though the mothers would have had their children at a very early age, I initially mistook them for their grandparents. They had wizened wrinkled faces, gnarled and calloused hands, and a certain tiredness in their eyes, which I later recognised in the faces of some of their daughters when they spoke of a family member's death, illness or abuse.

I don't know all of the trials that these families had gone through. Some stories I heard from the staff. Female relatives that had been set on fire for not bringing a large enough dowry to the husband's family. Siblings dying from asthma because the village had no clinic. Suicides to escape from shame or abuse. Parents tricked and betrayed in village politics. Family members beaten and insulted for their status as Dalits when accessing village resources.

For all this real hardship that they lived with, I felt humbled at the apparent eruption of grief they farewelled me with when it was time for my departure in December. Along with me, they were in tears, squeezing my hands and, in a regional show of affection, stroking the length of my face with a hand on each side, and then pushing their knuckles with a "crack" against their own heads. As I got in the jeep that was taking me to the bus stand, Vimala, one of the older girls who taught me how to dance, pushed something into my hand. It was the necklace she always wore, a heart-shaped pendant with green glass around it – a precious item for her, I knew, so I tried to put it back in her hand. She wouldn't take it, and I left with that necklace as a physical reminder of what had happened in Kodaikanal. I came to Kodai thinking I could contribute something to needy people. However, for all my English speaking and first-world experiences, I had nothing to offer. Regardless, the Grihini girls, like everyone else I encountered there, bestowed me with friendship, affection and understanding.

*

Sunday 20 March
Ku-Rin-Gai Chase National Park to Berowa Heights, New South Wales
54 kilometres – 3 hours 42 minutes

Saturday marked my exit from Sydney. As much as I had enjoyed being in the hub of a big city and having easy access to friends and ice cream, I felt my lungs were asking for a break from all the car exhaust fumes I'd been inhaling. Bike and Trailer also seemed to be tired of being dragged up and down stairwells and getting caught in automatically closing apartment block doors.

We took the scenic route out of the city via the Harbour Bridge and caught a ferry across to The Basin in Ku-Rin-Gai Chase National Park. We stopped here for the night in a camping ground that had no showers, and was hosting what seemed to be a festive father–child camping event. I didn't want to investigate too thoroughly though in case Bike or Trailer started feeling sad that they don't have dads.

This morning I conferred with a ranger and some maps and planned a route through the national park. Just getting out of The Basin was a challenge however, since it ended up to be not so much riding terrain, but hauling Bike and Trailer up vertical inclines of loose gravel terrain. When we finally hit ridable road there was some ominous rattling from Trailer, maybe from the gravel cliffs or maybe from when he fell down some stairs getting off the Harbour Bridge the day before. Or maybe because of his father issues.

We kept riding, but I kept my ears open for any developments. Halfway through the national park, I heard a sharp "ping" not from Trailer but from Bike's rear wheel, and discovered one of its spokes had snapped off at the base where it was attached to the rim by the metal rivet called a "nipple".

Unsure what to do, I took the wheel off, ate some sultanas, and waited for expert advice. I knew this would arrive soon as the area was a popular cycling route for proper cyclists who ride fast and eat special energy bars that they store in the pocket on the back of their riding shirts. I was confident they would know more than I did about broken spokes.

I soon managed to ambush a trio of cyclists who didn't seem too happy to be interrupted midway speeding down a hill. They reluctantly pulled over and I did my best to impress them with my recently acquired bike part knowledge. I informed the pack that I'd "broken a spoke, which I have spares for, but I don't have any nipples." "No WHAT?!" was the reply. I started worrying that the bike mechanics I'd befriended just before leaving Adelaide had played a nasty trick on me. After clearing up our communication difficulties, they told me to keep on riding, as there was a bike shop located close to the national park. I made it out of the park, found the shop and pointed out the spoke that had broken off inside "… this part here". "You mean in the nipple?" clarified the bike shop owner and set to the complicated task of replacing the spoke with just the right amount of tension. I took a number of good lessons away with me: don't think someone's better than you just because they have a pocket in the back of their cycling shirt, don't talk about nipples to strangers, and always break spokes near a bike shop.

I headed down a side road into a valley that, according to my map, had a camping ground in it. It was a careful descent as Bike and my pride still felt injured. Despite the extra care, halfway down, Bike's rear wheel produced an exciting popping noise. This time it was a puncture caused by the tyre itself wearing through. I dismounted and walked us all down to the banks of a small river at the bottom of the valley. There was no sign of the camping ground that was clearly marked on my map, but there was what appeared to be an old, weathered sailor sitting quietly by the water smoking his pipe. (This pipe, plus his proximity to the water, was how I knew he was a sailor.) I followed my new resolution and refrained from any mention of nipples, but asked him if he knew a place to camp. He nodded and pointed his pipe in the direction of a walking track along the side of the river, which I followed and found a small campable clearing.

The sounds of the lapping of water on the bank and the occasional fish frolicking in the shallows were soothing background music as I patched the punctured tube and replaced the tyre with the spare I carried strapped on top of Trailer. I felt so relaxed that even when I realised I'd messed up my gears again, I just smiled and took it as a good excuse to plan a walk back up the massive hill we had come down that afternoon, instead of riding it. I'm sure some cyclists would eat hills like that for breakfast, but I'm quite happy with muesli and going by foot sometimes.

Monday 21 March
Berowra Heights to Wyong, New South Wales
95 kilometres – 6 hours 24 minutes

I spent nearly two hours this morning walking Bike and Trailer out of the steep valley where I'd camped the night before.

By the time we emerged from the valley, I decided it was time for Bike to do his job again, so I squatted down to look at his gears with new resolve. Somehow, by gritting my teeth and muttering "Imagine you're Col, imagine you're Col", I restored the gears to their pre-valley, functional glory.

I had three schools to visit in Newcastle on Wednesday and plenty of time to ride the 200 kilometres there, so I hopped on Bike and headed north, not exactly sure where to aim for by nightfall.

The Pacific Highway route I took to get there was beautiful, with lush greenery and blue skies. Beautiful, but with a generous supply of wind, hills, and motorcycles. I sweated a lot and got repeatedly distracted by the regular appearance of bakeries.

Carbed up, I made it to Wyong. Following the town map toward a caravan park, I stopped off at a deli and discovered a large bag of very, very ripe bananas. They were six for $1 and came with a warning: "For cakes and muffins ONLY". Ignoring the warning, I started dreaming of what I could create with these bananas and the just-add-water custard powder I'd purchased that afternoon, and about how I would eat this custardy, banana-y creation after a long, hot shower.

Discovering a "Manufactured Home Village" sign out the front of what was marked on my map as a caravan park, I asked around and was soon informed that it was *not* a caravan park for camping, but a place for people to live in manufactured homes.

Confused, I picked up my rotten bananas and cruised the streets until I found a petrol station to ask for directions to a "proper" caravan park. Following these led me to another Manufactured Home Village. The manager informed me that I wasn't allowed to stay there either, unless I was retired and willing to book in for a lot longer than one night.

I began to suspect that my problems were originating from conflicting definitions of the term "caravan park". I explained the concept of temporary accommodation, grass to put a tent on, and surrounding caravans in a park-like setting, and the manager gave me directions to *another* caravan park. "Go to the end of the street then go through the scrub to Johns Road."

I got to the scrub and decided to stop there, before I found myself being the Manufactured Home Village Idiot. Feeling content at the good fortune of finding a secluded, free and pretty location in which to set up camp, I sat on a log, and opened a tin of baked beans for dinner. After the first bite, I realised I was covered in mosquitoes. I killed six with my first slap, put down my baked beans and set up my tent as quickly as possible, only stopping to flick massive orange and black spiders off my feet occasionally. It seemed that while my campground was entirely unmanufactured and free of retirees, it was, instead, full of over-friendly insects.

I managed to throw all my gear, my tin of baked beans and myself into the tent without spilling anything, and finished off my first course while squashing the few rogue mosquitoes that had snuck in with me. I was alone by the time it finally came to mix up a huge mug of custard and overripe bananas. I'm not sure if it would have tasted better after a shower. Somehow, being coated in a fine but visible layer of squashed mosquitoes, blood, sweat, old sunscreen, banana and bicycle grease, lets you enjoy a meal in a heightened, uninhibited way.

Monday 28 March
Taree to Kempsey, New South Wales
120 kilometres – 6 hours 6 minutes

I spent a few nights and a quiet Easter in Taree. I celebrated the holiday with what seemed to be a never-ending bag of carrots and a change in my choice of condiment. I had made liberal use of honey over the previous two months: in muesli, on banana sandwiches, and, whenever an inconvenient low blood sugar situation arose, taken straight from the bottle. As useful and tasty as it was though, I'd been considering my finances over the past few days, and decided to use a cheaper honey-replacement as part of a strategy to tighten my budget.

After my fact-finding trip to India the previous year, and then the necessary purchase of equipment, I started my ride with just a few thousand dollars in the bank for living expenses for the year. I also wanted to use any funds raised purely for the Kodaikanal trust fund, not for my own costs. My solution was to take up my mum's offer to borrow some money from her when I inevitably ran out of my own savings. Sometimes I had no option but to pay for an unpowered spot in a caravan park, so food was the only area over which I felt I had any control. Unfortunately, I eat a lot even when I'm not riding around Australia, so I was going to have to target quality, not quantity. The cheap bottle of home brand golden syrup at a discount shop probably only saved me a few dollars compared to honey, but it did make me feel financially back in control.

I packed the rest of the carrots into Trailer and coasted further north along the refreshingly flat Pacific Highway and reached Kempsey by mid-afternoon. This gave me time to try to reduce my accommodation costs by visiting all four caravan parks in town and selecting the cheapest one at $11 for the night. For this bargain price, I enjoyed an impressive lack of facilities. It took me 20 minutes and a few trips to the front desk to procure a functioning shower, and since there was no communal barbeque, I had to eat raw zucchini and tomato with my cold baked beans.

There was also a visit from the local police. I don't think it was for me personally, although I had been smelling a bit offensive due to recent experimentation in saving money by not owning deodorant.

When I was finally showered, fed, and not arrested, I settled down with my safety vest and a permanent marker I'd bought that afternoon in a flash of inspiration. I wanted to increase the exposure of Cycle of Learning to people I passed on the road, as they could be potential donors. I already had a fluoro workman's vest that I wore for visibility whenever I was riding and, because I kept forgetting to take it off, quite often when I wasn't too. I thought I might as well exploit my visibility and use the vest not just for safety but also for publicity.

Half an hour later, I had a vest covered on all available surfaces with the project website address and "CYCLE OF LEARNING" written in large black letters.

Tuesday 29 March

Kempsey to Nambucca Heads, New South Wales
74 kilometres – 4 hours

My target for the day was Coffs Harbour, 130 kilometres away, and a longer ride than I had attempted for a while. After spending a few hours in the Kempsey Library seeing to some correspondence and my blog, I made a late getaway. Once I was on the road though, I made good time thanks to a gentle breeze at my back and plenty of muesli energy in my legs. Fifty or so kilometres down the road, I stopped when I came across someone I am not sure whether to refer to as "a colleague" or "the competition".

I realised that I had passed this man, Colin, the day before when he was on the other side of the highway but, assuming from his three-wheeled cart that he was selling ice cream, I had not stopped. If it had been any other day, this assumption would have led me immediately across the two lanes of traffic to buy a cone with one scoop of chocolate and one of mint. I was still in money-saving mode though, and felt the responsible thing was to find another three highway vendors to compare prices, so didn't end up meeting Colin that day.

This time, when I approached Colin on the same side of the road, I got close enough to read the signage on the converted three-wheeled pram he was pushing and realised that no ice cream was involved. Instead he was walking around Australia to raise money for children with cancer. I stopped and we had a short chat on the side of the road. He was friendly, polite, and interested in my ride, but the more I talked to him, the more overwhelming my sense of inferiority grew.

Colin had spent three years planning his walk around Australia, completed a wide range of other fundraising activities previously and established a foundation for his cause. He had numerous corporate sponsors, a network of Lions service clubs, and what sounded like a team of staff behind him. In only the third month of his walk, he had already raised an incredible amount of money. Apparently, he had had drivers stop him on the side of the road to donate four figure sums to his cause.

I felt an unprecedented level of amateurness as I talked with him. I wasn't even able to eat my golden-syrup-and-banana-pita-bread-wrap in a dignified way as I waited for Colin to finish fielding phone calls from his agent, who was setting up a parade for his arrival into Brisbane.

I rode away with a rotten feeling in my gut that had nothing to do with the cheap golden syrup that I was not at all enjoying. Colin represented everything that I was not and everything I had not done. My bike ride and speaking to small school groups and the odd church or Rotary club had been well within my comfort zone. Emailing places inviting them to invite me to speak was much easier than developing contacts and networks and pushing my cause into the public eye. Buying my own gear was less painful than approaching businesses for sponsorship and support. Waiting for donations was a lot more comfortable for me than asking for them.

My planning had been rushed and haphazard. I'd fitted it in between completing my studies and working part time. Depressingly, I reflected that I could have worked this year as a graduate teacher and probably saved more from my wage than I was going to make in fundraising.

The heavy feeling in my stomach travelled down to my legs and I ended up finishing my ride for the day earlier than planned. I pulled over at a supermarket in Nambucca Heads and bought a large bottle of turpentine. I spent the evening trying to remove the black marker that I'd graffitied over my vest last night. Did I mention that Colin was wearing a nice, neat polo shirt embroidered with his logo and catch phrase "Dream. Believe. Achieve."?

After an hour of soaking, scrubbing and rinsing, the writing on my own corporate uniform was faded but still visible. The vest was now scruffy enough to be even more unprofessional, yet legible enough to indicate which charity never to donate to. Plus, it now stank of turpentine.

Friday 1 April
Coffs Harbour to Woolgoolga to Pacific Highway, New South Wales
71 kilometres – 3 hours 55 minutes

I soon learnt to leave my vest outside my tent, after spending Tuesday and Wednesday nights haunted by unsettled sleep and bizarre dreams brought on by the turpentine fumes. I tried to brighten myself up by going on a sightseeing trip to Muttonbird Island. It didn't work, as I spent the excursion plodding miserably through the rain across a scrubby island that was a good match for its grey, greasy, old-sheep name.

However, nothing cheers me up more than fruit, and after the morning's stop at the Big Banana on the way out of Coffs Harbour, I finally started feeling a bit better. Even my rain-soaked bike seat stopped bothering me as I rode north, admiring the plantations of normal-sized edible bananas lining the highway.

The town of Woolgoolga improved my spirits further and pushed all concerns of mediocre fundraising performances and stinky vests from my mind for the majority of the day. The school I visited was in a beautiful location: the sound of the sea drifted through the grounds, and there were stunning views of rolling grassy fields and woods right down to the sparkling Pacific Ocean. The idyllic setting permeated the entire school with teachers and students relaxed and friendly in a way that is only possible when you've got a view of the ocean from every part of the property.

I was thrilled to discover that Woolgoolga is home to a large Indian community and a beautiful Sikh temple. This meant that among the students there was a lot of knowledge about Indian geography, languages and culture.

After lunching on piles of fresh bananas and crunchy watermelon next to the ocean, I stopped by the home of the editor of *Australian Cyclist* magazine. After an interview and a cup of tea, she generously gave me a copy of a book that I probably should have invested in a year ago: *Around Australia by Bicycle.* Now, if I could just find an edition of *How to Gain Media Attention and Be in Demand as a Guest Speaker and Raise Huge Amounts of Money and Fix Gears and Eat Honey (or Golden Syrup) Without Getting Sticky* in a light paperback version with easy to follow diagrams …

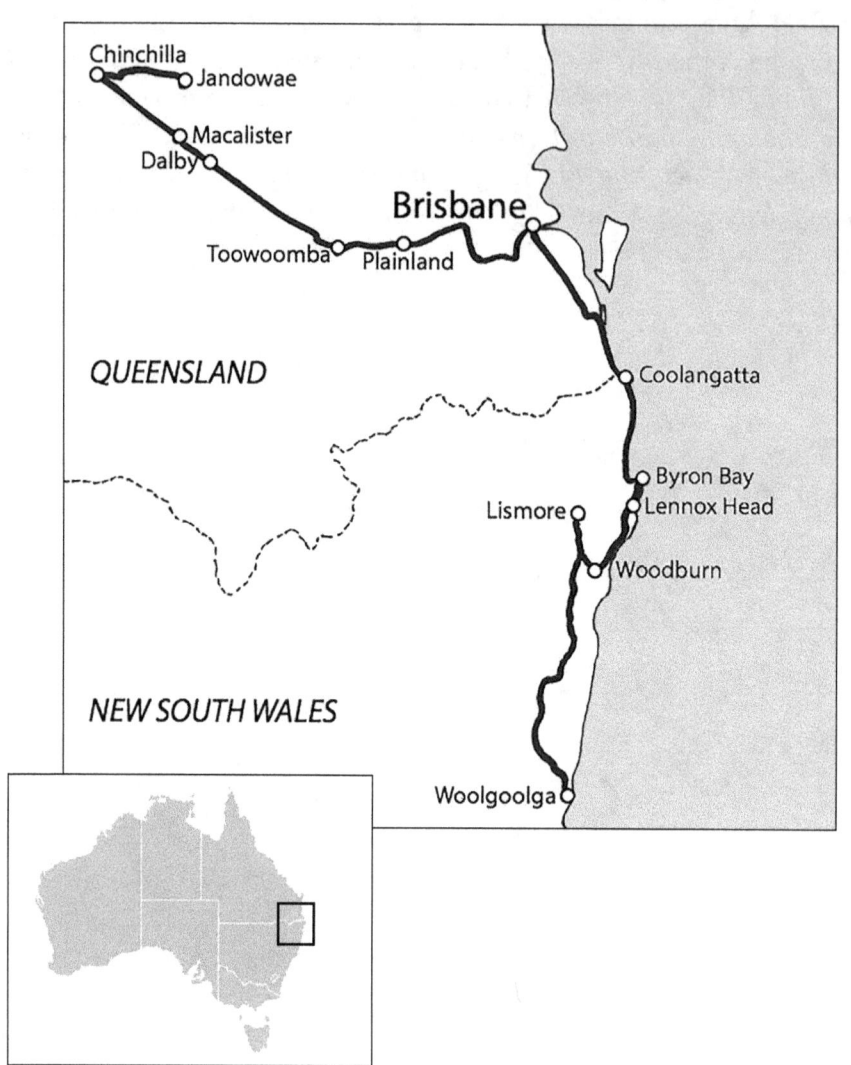

Chapter 4
Thighs of Mass Destruction

Lismore – Woodburn – Lennox Heads – Byron Bay –
Coolangatta – Brisbane – Plainland – Toowoomba –
Dalby – Macalister – Chinchilla – Jandowae

Totals: 4,622 kilometres – 263 hours 22 minutes – $5,432

Saturday 9 April
Coolangatta to Brisbane, Queensland
122 kilometres – 5 hours 46 minutes

I spent a large part of the day riding up the M1, the motorway between the Gold Coast and Brisbane. While there was a generous shoulder for a lot of the way, there were a few sections of roadwork where I had to take it upon myself to reposition the barriers. My main concerns, though, were the numerous exits and entrances that needed to be crossed without getting in the way of the high velocity traffic entering or exiting the freeway. The mirror on my right handlebar helped a lot in these situations, letting me keep an eye on what was happening behind me. I quite enjoyed utilising this mirror as every time I finished with it and turned it back and folded it down, I saw myself as Luke Skywalker turning off his targeting computer before blowing up the Death Star.

Heading into Brisbane, I felt rested and ready for a new state, which already had filled my diary with more engagements than any other. I'd originally planned to only ride as far north as Rockhampton before heading west, but my "Don't say no to a school" policy threw that plan out the window. Over the previous few months, as people from each new school – of increasingly northerly location – phoned to ask if I could visit, I had to sit back down with my maps and sums and plot new daily riding itineraries of greater and greater distances and correspondingly less rest. I was at the stage where it should be just physically possible to make the extra 1,000 kilometres to get up to Tully and still reach Darwin by the end of the second school term.

With this tough riding schedule ahead of me, I was glad of the mini Gold Coast holiday I'd just indulged in. I tried to be a tourist by visiting Tropical Fruit World, a tropical fruit-based theme park, and dutifully took a photo of the ambiguous-looking giant fruit at the entrance. I stayed with Rod, a friend I know through wrestling, who took me to the beach in the mornings to try and teach me how to surf. Rod is a very tactful guy and kindly blamed the weather for my dismal performance. He also provided a computer for me to work at when I wasn't being a tourist or almost-surfer. I sent off a few dozen emails and got the Cycle of Learning website up to date. This side of things mostly consisted of me emailing my volunteer IT-support officer, Bonnie, with requests. Bonnie is an amazing friend who stepped in after a mini-meltdown I had in December. Things were falling apart with my plans for web page design and I had spent a few days storming around home, throwing things and yelling at the world. Bonnie and I had been friends for five years and I already knew she was a proficient composer, pianist and percussionist, as well as being an officer in the navy and a final year medical student. I had no idea that she could also design web pages, write programs, and speak binary, but when she heard of my problems, she stepped up to the plate and sorted me out. She was updating things and adding more nifty functions to the website while I was on the road, and I harboured a secret dream that she would invent a virus that could ask for donations better than I could.

That Saturday morning, before farewelling Rod, I sorted through my possessions. When I left Adelaide, Trailer was carrying 30 kilograms of gear. I'd already been shedding things I hadn't been using (astronomy almanac, extra shoes etc); after a heart-wrenching hour, I whittled my equipment and supplies further down to 18.5 kilograms. I don't think our overall weight was reduced though: I had made up the 11.5 kilograms by the impressive expansion of my thigh muscles; the grime embedded in my hair, skin and clothes; the biomass of accompanying microorganisms that made this grime their home; and the weight gain from my on-the-road appetite.

I finished my cull by handing over two bags to Rod. One had stuff to be returned to my parents via the little-known National Wrestlers' Delivery Network; the other bag was given as a "gift" for Rod. He went above and beyond his hostly duties and pretended that the soap holder, pegs, and pre-owned vitamin tablets were just what he needed to cheer himself up after having his surfing reputation destroyed by association with me.

For all the emotional trauma of deciding what to keep and what to shed of my equipment, there wasn't a noticeable change in the effort it took to tow Trailer. He did seem easier to navigate, though, around the twists and turns of shopping complexes and narrow streets I encountered once I left the motorway to find my way to my next hosts.

After getting lost a few times and dropping my map in a public toilet, I finally found my way to the home of the next family putting me up for the night. Like all good Cycle of Learning hosts, they live at the top of a ridiculously steep hill, and have a spot in the sun to dry out wet maps.

Wednesday 13 April
Brisbane to Plainland, Queensland
94 kilometres – 5 hours 31 minutes

Brisbane kept me busy for the three days I spent there. The school, church, radio interview and two homes I went to in that time were all just a few streets apart with one five-way roundabout in between. Somehow, though, every trip I took between them ended up taking at least half an hour, a dozen wrong turns and a shirtful of sweat.

I made another round-Australia friend in Brisbane who I found a lot less intimidating than Colin the walker. Also from Adelaide, Paul crossed my path online a few weeks before, and figured out that we would be in Brisbane at the same time. We caught up, shared some cheap chocolate and discussed important round-Australia cycling things such as the price of caravan parks, how to carry water, and what foods can be "cooked" by soaking them in warm tap water.

I stayed a few nights with another old wrestling friend, Madeleine, who took me along to her local training night. Given that I'd busted my only pair of shorts while fighting with Rod's surfboard on the Gold Coast and didn't trust my repairs, I borrowed a pair of Madeleine's. Somehow, I managed to destroy these as well and decided to call an end to my travelling wrestling career for the year. Obviously, my thighs were out of control. Madeleine was very understanding, being a seasoned bicycle tourer herself. Madeleine spends her holidays navigating the outdoors by bike, foot, canoe, and sometimes even hand – every mountain she summits she likes to do a handstand upon. I first met Madeleine at a wrestling camp. We matched up very unevenly. She was about half my size, but exuded approximately five times the energy of most people. Between throwing me from fireman's carries and flipping me over with hip heists, Madeleine – being a scientist as well as a wrestling whiz – had my head spinning with explanations of the structure of her favourite organic compound, and how electron microscopes work. After teaching me a few moves and answering my amateur science fan questions, she rushed off a few hours later to attend some sort of conference that was going to involve her speaking German.

Staying with Madeleine in Brisbane, it was wonderful to observe at close quarters a person who has got their priorities in the right place. I particularly appreciated Madeleine's focus on waste. Besides the normal responsible round-the-house actions such as collecting food scraps for compost, and making sure rubbish is recycled properly, Madeleine aims to create as little rubbish as possible from food and other purchases. In a previous share-house she participated in a year-long, no-waste-creation experiment. Besides what they could compost in their own yard, the housemates aimed to not buy anything that created rubbish. Even in my current simple cycling lifestyle, I accumulated a bundle of rubbish each day, which would be strapped to Trailer in a plastic bag when I was away from the city and the convenience of rubbish bins. Maybe I should have dedicated part of Trailer's surface to a small vegie patch.

In the morning, I made an early getaway from Madeleine's inner-Brisbane home to speak at a high school on the outskirts of the city. En route, I was surprised to bump into Paul who was heading north out of town. It probably would have been a bit less surprising for me had I realised we were in a unisex, not female, public toilet at the time.

After my school visit, I pushed on, as I needed to be in Toowoomba by the next afternoon. I'd been hearing scary things about the steep climb up the Toowoomba Range, so was hoping to get close to the foot of the range by evening.

As the sun moved lower in the sky, I started looking for camping options. There was no open scrub around; everything was fenced off. I reached a small town and sat myself on a petrol station veranda to weigh up my options. I had the following choices:

A. Carry Bike and Trailer over a barbed-wire fence into the property of someone who may very well own a shotgun and large dogs.

B. Take up the offer of the seemingly friendly motorcyclist I met inside the petrol station to camp in his front yard.

C. Sneak behind some abandoned shops down the road and hope that no one noticed me spending the night there.

D. Ride fifteen kilometres out of my way to a caravan park.

Pondering these options, I realised what was missing from the list:

E. Go back inside and buy the huge bag of reduced-price muffins on sale for $1.20.

Feeling emotionally and physically renewed after taking up Option E, I decided to head down the side road to the caravan park. I had only turned off for a few metres when I spotted a school with a big empty lot full of long grass next to it. Perfect. I had myself an Option F.

I waited out the remaining daylight hours back in the main street watching the low, thick clouds with evening sunlight breaking through, and munching on muffins.

Under the cover of darkness, I moved back to the vacant lot and started setting up camp. When my tent was only halfway up, a motorbike roared into life across the street and headed my way with its headlamp blazing. The only thing I could think to do was duck down behind the long grass and pretend that I wasn't there. Then I remembered: Bike and Trailer were covered from top to bottom in reflective tape and I was still wearing my fluoro vest. As hard as we tried, we could not become invisible.

The motorcyclist drove straight over to us and turned out to be the school caretaker. Instead of sending me to jail for trespassing and possessing indecently cheap muffins, he offered me the use of the school showers and toilets. I was relieved, although arrest could have provided valuable publicity for Cycle of Learning.

Tuesday 19 April
Chinchilla to Jandowae, Queensland
76 kilometres – 4 hours 10 minutes

I was particularly excited to ride into Chinchilla on Monday afternoon. Chinchilla State High School was the very first place to book me in to speak. The principal had called me the year before, just hours after I had sent a pile of emails out. He'd been so friendly and enthusiastic about Cycle of Learning that I'd imagined that within days I would have hundreds of similar invitations from around the country pouring in. That did not happen; but my entire itinerary had been planned around this small town that I'd not heard of until that first phone call. I should have been aware of it though, as it is the capital of my favourite food: watermelon.

I can still remember how I felt, around the time of that phone call from Chinchilla. I'd just started my planning, I was full of ideas and excitement and I was sure Cycle of Learning would be massive and awesome. My massive and awesome vision was hazy around the edges, though. The vague images included the army of people I would have helping me deal with logistics; newspapers and TV stations following my every move around the country; businesses trying to outbid each other to have me accept their sponsorship; teachers planning units of work based on the resources from my website; and school children across the nation logging onto my web forum to send messages and questions to students in Kodaikanal. I just wasn't sure exactly what I would need to do to reach these massive and awesome heights.

Before my first visit to Kodaikanal in 2001, I had a similarly hazy and quixotic image of the time I would have "volunteering" there.

The Road to Kodaikanal

I had been backpacking through Asia and was looking for some volunteer work to do before I returned home. When Norm suggested that I join him on his trip to visit the Grihini program in Kodaikanal I was thrilled. On the long train trip from Calcutta to Chennai, I thought how good it would be to actually be useful and finally contribute something. If there is any emotion I am good at, it is guilt. I'd spent nearly eight months travelling through Thailand, Cambodia, Laos, Vietnam, China, Pakistan, Nepal and northern India. Like most people who visit these countries from a wealthy nation, I was struck by the poverty of many people I saw. I was also hounded by the disparity of my trip and their lives. I had worked a part-time job through three years of university and saved enough to travel in relative comfort through these countries for a year. I had the freedom to go where I wanted, buy food, pay for clothes and accommodation, and spend time reading, sight-seeing and wandering around because of the luck of where I was born.

I remember sitting at the top of a temple of Angkor Wat in

Cambodia one evening, when a wave of guilt-ridden nausea overwhelmed me. From the pure, logical facts of the matter, I should not have been sitting there watching street kids run (or limp, if they were missing a limb from landmines) from tourist to tourist selling postcards. I had done nothing to deserve this position of privilege. Logic told me that I should return to Australia immediately and devote any earnings or resources I had, or gained in the future, to people who deserved neither the poverty nor the hardship into which they had been born. But, of course, as the sun set and I climbed down the temple ruins, I managed to push the logic aside just enough to return to the first-world mindset that let me justify my indulgence and privilege.

As my travels continued, I kept feeling guilty. Despite the friendliness and hospitality of local people I met along the way, I felt as if I were intruding and imposing myself on all the communities I visited. "Volunteer work" seemed like a perfect solution. I thought three months of being useful and helping people in Kodaikanal would settle the score for the year. That was not how it worked out.

*

Chinchilla surpassed all expectations I had of it. Besides the watermelon, there was also an information centre where they tell you about the free campground at the picturesque weir. The library had free internet and friendly librarians and there was a fish and chip shop called Salty's. The bank tellers called all their customers by name, even me – but only after I'd filled out my details on a deposit slip. The warm and enthusiastic welcome I received at the school was exactly what I'd come to expect from Chinchillans and most people inland from Brisbane.

Since meeting the friendly caretaker on his motorbike, I had been looked after by a bevy of friendly Queenslanders. A family had me stay for a few days in Toowoomba; in Dalby, one couple invited me into their kitchen to cook myself a vegetarian lunch. A chatty cyclist I met coming up the Toowoomba Range asked me into his bike shop for a cup of tea and offered to have a look over my bike. When he saw the amount of gunk in my chain, his jaw dropped and he spluttered, "You've ridden how far without cleaning that?" I'd always thought that cleaning bike chains was one of those things that people talk about but never do, like defragmenting computers and dusting. But after he'd spent a few minutes cleaning it out for me and I rode away from the bike shop using a third of the effort I had ridden there with, I realised that a clean bike chain has certain advantages.

The latest fabulous Queensland person I met was Fiona. I have to admit, when I first made contact with Fiona, the inexplicably large amount of similarities between us and the synchronicity of our meeting made me a little suspicious. I wondered if she was actually an undercover slave trader in the market for stock with high-quality thigh muscles for an important grape-crushing operation or running a leg-powered pirate ship. I first heard from her in a friendly email out of the blue telling me of her own project, five years previously, very similar to Cycle of Learning, but raising money and awareness for a poverty-alleviation project in Indonesia. It was the first time I'd encountered someone who'd done not just the same sort of Around Australia fundraising cycling thing, but had done it in a similar way – low key in the publicity and fundraising arena, with a big focus on connecting with schools and communities to share information. And we both obviously liked countries that start with the letter I. After an email or two, it came to light that I would be riding right past Fiona within a few days. It wouldn't have been so strangely coincidental if she lived in a big city that I couldn't have avoided, but she was on a farm in the middle of south-Queensland-nowhere. A nowhere that I happened to have planned in my itinerary in a few days' time on my way to Chinchilla.

Accordingly, I headed out of a small road from Dalby, dismounted Bike at the entrance to a dirt track disappearing into a cotton field and waited for the designated time. The expected ute arrived, a shout from the window instructed me to load myself and my gear onto the back tray, and I prepared myself to be driven to the beginning of my life in the grape-crushing slave trade.

It turned out Fiona wasn't luring me to her farm for my awesome leg muscles; she was entirely who she had said she was, and the exact person I had been needing to meet. Over a vegetarian stir-fry (we were even gastronomically kindred spirits) I shared all my fundraising, organisational and bike-riding worries with her, while Fiona made me feel better with stories of her own similar struggles and reassurances that the way I was going about things made sense. It was a wonderful relief, and encouraging to meet someone who had come out the other side of a project like mine, relatively unscathed. Fiona had taken a few bizarre turns since her circumnavigation, firmly establishing herself in the field of philanthropic consultancy while simultaneously moving onto this cotton farm to be with her partner, vast fields of cotton plants and what seemed to be a small army of green frogs (who appeared at various times of my visit when I least expected them, and screamed at me if I accidentally squashed them in sliding doors).

In a final demonstration of deep understanding of my present condition, Fiona served me the most comprehensive breakfast I had encountered so far that year – complete with two types of chocolate – before I headed off into the wee hours of Monday morning.

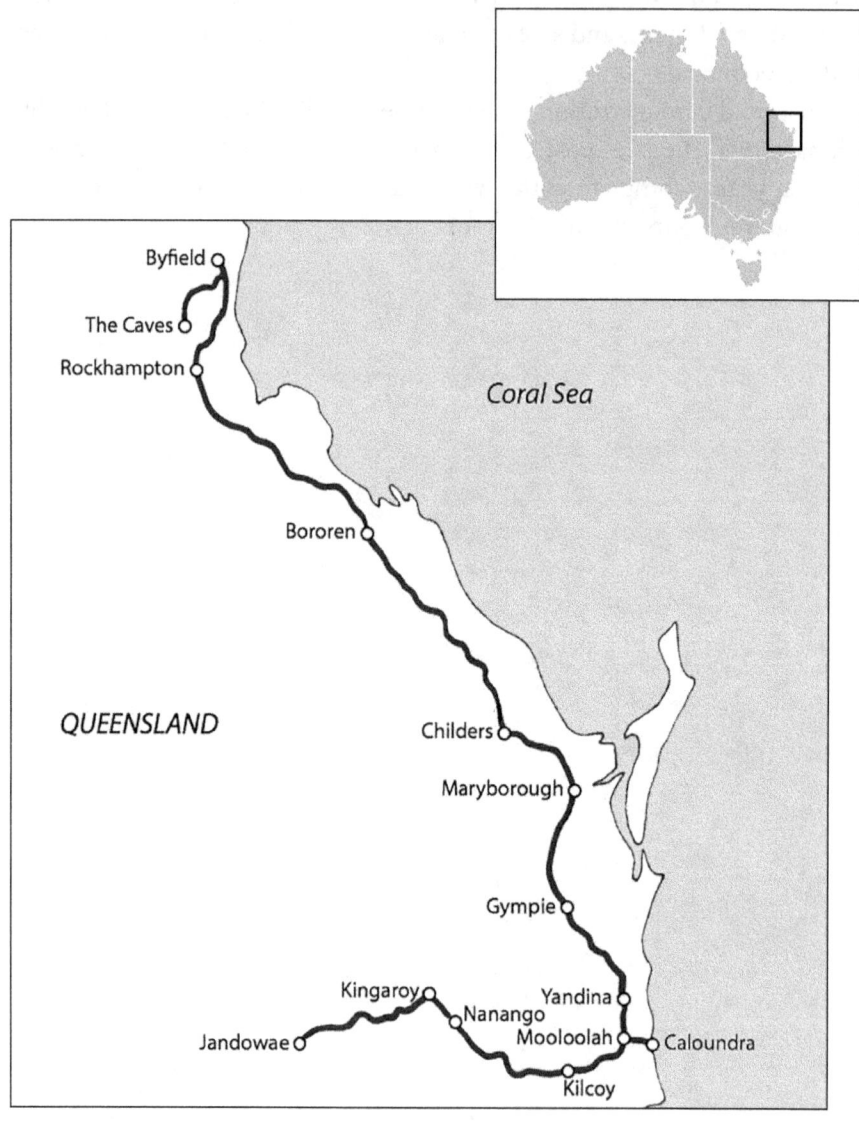

Chapter 5

Lost and Found

Jandowae – Kingaroy – Nanango – Kilcoy – Mooloolah – Caloundra – Yandina – Gympie – Maryborough – Childers – Bororen – Rockhampton – Byfield – The Caves

Totals: 5,817 kilometres – 331 hours 13 minutes – $7,314

Thursday 21 April
Kingaroy to near Nanango, Queensland
27 kilometres – 1 hour 34 minutes

Heading back towards the coast brought a change in scenery. From flat, dry, brown farmland with occasional fields blackened by fire, I was riding into hilly browny-green bush, views of the Bunya Mountains, and an increasing number of dead kangaroos in various stages of bird-assisted disembowelment.

I'd hit Kingaroy on Wednesday. Like Chinchilla, Kingaroy is also a national food capital, this time of peanuts and navy beans. I investigated the local peanut brittle and salt-and-vinegar peanuts, and felt some twinges in my mouth that reminded me to buy some new toothbrushes, one each for me and Bike. Trailer doesn't have teeth or a chain, so he made do with a new octopus ("ockie") strap to keep my gear lashed on tightly.

On the way to the supermarket, I ran into Jeremy, a wonderfully friendly journalist from Radio National who had interviewed me about Cycle of Learning in Brisbane. Jeremy was in town because Kingaroy was where every self-respecting reporter was at the time, waiting for the imminent death of Sir Joh Bjelke-Peterson, a former Queensland premier. Jeremy introduced me to some of his colleagues who, given the lack of news until Sir Joh passed, asked me for an interview. I headed down to the local hospital with them where the media camp had been set up. The radio interview involved having various recording paraphernalia strapped onto Trailer to capture authentic bike riding sounds. I rode more carefully than usual, as I wasn't keen on having to do a second lap around the country to pay the ABC back for their ruined audio equipment.

As soon as the other waiting journalists saw me being interviewed, they rushed over thinking I might have a good story. Once they realised I wasn't that interesting, most of them wandered off. I ended up doing only one additional radio interview and one newspaper interview that probably didn't get printed, but these journalists were as close to paparazzi as I'll get in my life. Thanks, Sir Joh.

The afternoon saw me taken for a ride (in the literal, not figurative, sense) by a group from the local high school. They were in training to do a seven-day bike ride to raise money for a charity supporting children with cancer. I had a depressing moment when their coordinating teacher asked me if I had any fundraising suggestions for them. My initial response was almost "Don't be me", but I restrained myself and suggested approaching local businesses and writing letters to philanthropists – two things I had not had the guts to do myself for my own fundraising, hence I was sure they would be effective. Once we got riding I was a little scared by the riders' aerodynamic lycra; Bike was intimidated by their fast-looking machines; and Trailer was concerned that all they were carrying were pumps in their back pockets. However, Bike, Trailer and I held our own once we hit the open road. We even made it up the enormous hill that the Kingaroy lads found for us, without getting off and walking – prospective shame is a wonderful motivator. We said goodbye once we reached the highway, and I told the squad I would be riding on to Nanango. As soon as they disappeared from sight, though, I found a private patch of scrub and collapsed into it for the night.

Tuesday 26 April
Yandina to near Gympie, Queensland
93 kilometres – 5 hours 10 minutes

I was sad to leave Mooloolah yesterday as I'd made myself at home with Janet, the daughter of my Albury godmother Maureen. One of the unexpected joys of the year turned out to be how much I was enjoying spending time with distant relatives. Some of them, like Janet, I had only met previously when I was a lot younger, and some, never before at all. It is interesting that at all the relatives' homes I'd visited so far, I had almost immediately felt relaxed and comfortable, and experienced a tangible sense of being with family. At this particular home, I think I felt even more part of the family than usual due to the red hair that Janet, Janet's daughter Milly and I share. There's nothing nicer than sitting around a kitchen table, chatting, with cups of tea, a plate of Anzac biscuits and some shared genetic material. I feel very lucky to have such widely dispersed, friendly and hospitable relatives.

Like her mother in Albury, Janet had been busy organising appointments for me. After two interviews with local newspapers, Janet booked me in with two church groups to speak to on Sunday morning – with ten kilometres between them. The pastor (who used a car to travel between the two congregations) calculated that if I left straight after my talk at the first church, I would make it in time to the second. Knowing that my poor sense of direction can add hundreds of kilometres onto a ride on a bad day, I got some detailed directions from a gentleman in the congregation. I've committed them to memory to use whenever I don't know where to go in the future: "Keep riding until you think you're lost, go through two roundabouts and then you'll be there." Surprisingly, they worked perfectly and got me to the church on time.

A minor compensation for leaving family was the new mobile phone holder attached to Bike's handlebars. Janet's husband, Robin, had poked around in his shed to find some spare brackets to go with the hose clamps I'd been carrying for a fastening emergency, and we put them together in such a way as to have my mobile phone close enough that I could now answer it easily, without jumping off Bike and rummaging through my backpack when I heard it ringing.

I called into North Arm to visit a school, and then headed up the Bruce Highway. After a few hours, I stopped at a rest area complex with petrol station, cafe, information centre, and general rest stop facilities, to have a look in the public toilets to see if they had power points. One major problem with camping by the side of the road is that you don't always know when or where you can charge up your phone. Since I was not really in a position to play "hard to get" with any interested media or schools wanting me to visit, a phone was essential, whether placed on an ingenious phone holder on the handlebars or in the depths of a backpack. I found a power point next to the hand dryers and, as discreetly as possible, plugged my phone in. With time on my hands I wandered off to look at magazine covers outside the newsagents and to eat carrots – two things you either can't or shouldn't do in a public toilet.

Half an hour later, I returned to find phone and charger gone. Had I been so discreet in my stealing of electricity that even I couldn't notice where I'd plugged in my phone? Luckily, my gasps of shock attracted the attention of another public toilet patron who told me that my things had been taken to Lost Property.

I wondered why someone would think a charging phone classified as lost property. Do people normally lose their electrical goods in such a way that they are misplaced into power sockets? Maybe it's a Queensland thing. Then I started wondering if it might also be a Queensland thing that people who steal electricity from public toilets are breaking the law.

I fronted up to Lost Property unsure of the best way to present myself: apologetic, sheepish, grateful, embarrassed, relieved or guilty. After briefly wondering if a limp might help, I decided to play it cool, poised and a little confused. Thankfully, I didn't have a problem getting my possessions back. In the end, I think my success was due to the authority that a fluoro visibility vest brings.

Camping at Yandina, Queensland.

Friday 29 April
Childers to Bruce Highway, Queensland
20 kilometres – 1 hour 20 minutes

I stopped worrying that I was on the police "most wanted" list for trespassing and electricity theft, and turned my concerns to the military. On the way to Childers it started raining, so I took a quieter back road to avoid having cars spray muddy water at me. I hadn't counted on the fact that, it being a quieter rural road, there was plenty of horse manure to mix with the muddy water I now sprayed on myself as I rode. I distracted myself from the regret of leaving my front mud guard in Rod's bin in Coolangatta, by taking advantage of the lack of traffic and singing my heart out.

I'd just moved from the slightly clichéd "Singin' in the Rain" to a *The Sound of Music* medley when I noticed a tank rolling through the scrub next to me, complete with camouflaged commandos carrying guns. I fell silent and hoped that my voice wasn't considered a threat to national security. The soldiers gave me a wave, and then rolled out of sight, but the whole incident gave me a shock. Would I be spending the rest of the year checking over my shoulder for submarines surfacing at beaches or paratroopers landing around my campsite in the night?

My subconscious must have concocted a plan to shake the military from tailing me. The next morning I packed my campsite up and made my way back to the highway. When I reached the road, I spent a few minutes looking at the nondescript scenery and then realised I couldn't remember which way I'd come from the night before. I tried using the logic that Steph, my old travelling partner, employed whenever we got lost. "Anne," she would say to me, "which way do you think we need to go?" I would tell her and then she would take us in the opposite direction. Fool proof.

This method didn't really work solo: without Steph there to enforce step two of the system, I only followed step one. By the time I realised that I needed to turn around, no doubt the military personnel following me would have been convinced that I had given up my bike ride and was heading home, and would move on to another operation.

Today's speaking event was something different for me. I was booked in for four sessions as a "motivational speaker" for a Year 8 Development Day. Even now, after the event, I'm a little unsure what they expected of me, or if I was going to be held responsible for any unmotivated Year 8 incidents later on in the year.

I tried to remember that quote about jumping for the moon and reaching the treetops, or maybe the stars. Unable to recall which one you jump for and which one you reach, I stuck to my own material: some information about Cycle of Learning, thoughts on taking paths less travelled, advice on organisation and goal setting, and reflections on my experiences this year.

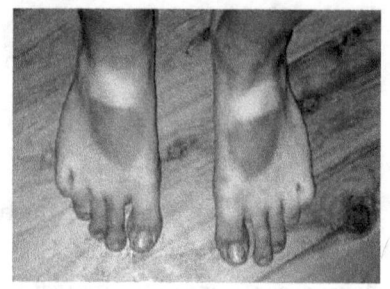

My foot tan.

The most well received part of my sessions ended up being me showing the classes my foot tan. Since I owned and wore only one pair of shoes, I had a sharply defined brown pattern, starkly contrasting with the pasty whiteness of the sections of my feet under my sandals. By the end of the day, audiences were asking me for a look at the feet they'd heard about from their friends. I never knew being a motivational speaker was so easy. It just takes the flexibility to get your feet to eye height.

I had been given a generous amount of time with each of the groups, and was able to field lots of ideas and questions from the Year 8s. While most were similar to others I'd had – questions about day-to-day life for kids in Kodaikanal, riding times, puncture statistics – there was one particularly insightful query regarding the relationship between the long distances I had been riding by myself, my sanity, and my method of public speaking.

One of the teachers at the final session asked about what I did in the three months of my first visit to Kodaikanal. I'd had this question a few times, and I suspect the answer was usually expected to involve straight-forward and heart-warming activities such as teaching, looking after orphans, building schools, or maybe even digging a well or two. I generally skimmed over my answer because "I just hung around" isn't that impressive. But as I'll explain, "hanging around" describes best what I did in Kodaikanal.

Kodaikanal Welcome

When Norm and I arrived at Sacred Heart College to meet the PEAK team at the beginning of Norm's two-week monitoring visit, we had a warm welcome. My preconceptions that I would be "volunteering" were initially shaken when the director of the PEAK program, Father Kulandai, politely asked if I was Norm's secretary. He seemed to deal well with the fact that I wasn't and my subsequent request to stay on with the program for three months.

I generally like to be in a situation for a reason, with a well-defined role, and hate to feel that I am bothering someone or making a nuisance of myself. In Kodaikanal, at Sacred Heart College, I got three months' practice at having no reason for being anywhere, while being looked after and playing no particular role except that of guest – guest of PEAK, their hostels, the associated Grihini program, the religious community at the college and every one of the Kodaikanal locals that came across me during my time in the area.

I paid a minimal amount for my board and meals in the college. Besides the two priests and two priests-in-training of the PEAK team and various other Jesuits who passed through for retreats or workshops, Sacred Heart was a more permanent home to a small flock (or whatever the appropriate collective noun may be) of older monks and priests. They spent their days quietly: reading, in prayer or at work in the gardens, libraries, archives and their natural history museum. I'm not sure what these more senior Fathers and Brothers thought of my presence, but I ended up quite enjoying the atmosphere: the routine of the solemn, shared meals in the dining hall; the echoes of services drifting through the hallways; silent nods to the Father who seemed to be permanently installed in the newspaper room; the restrained festivity of breakfast on the feast day of a member of the community; the sight of bent figures strolling the gardens in their white cassocks. By the time I left, I wished there was some way I could sign up to become an honorary Jesuit to live in that kind of place back in Australia.

Right next door to the college was the Inigo Siruvar Ilum, translated as "St Ignatius Children's Home". I felt most at home here, where the children always welcomed me with an excited "Anne Sister! Anne Sister!" as they took my hands and pulled me over to the current game or chore they were involved with. I often went over in the evenings with one of the four PEAK team members. The children were generally sweeping up from dinner, washing plates, hands and faces or gathering mats and blankets to sleep in the hall. When all these jobs were done, a prayer was led by one of the older children. It was a reminder to work hard and take care of others and was not specific to any particular faith. If there was time after prayer, I sometimes got story-telling duty. With the help of whoever could translate, I created a serialised drama, shamelessly plagiarised from Harry Potter, Narnia, the Magic Faraway Tree and a mish-mash of fairy tales. When I didn't have anyone to translate for me, the stories became even more bizarre as I cobbled together my sparse Tamil vocabulary and physically acted them out as best I could.

During the day, I'd often visit the four Ackaas (Tamil for "big sisters") who cooked meals, helped with homework and looked after the hundred or so children. As they prepared vats of rice and curry for the evening meal, we would sit around and chat. Whenever one of the Fathers came over, the Ackaas became quiet, shy and reserved, as most women are in male company in India. As soon as the men left, the women would be back to their gossiping about the Father who'd just departed, interrogating me about life in Australia, telling me about their families, teasing each other and complaining about work that had to be done. I developed just the right tone and intonation for two of the most useful Tamil responses for these conversations: "paavam" – that's a pity, and "custum" – that's difficult or hard to bear.

We had become friends in the space of an afternoon on only my second day in Kodaikanal. I had wandered over to the sports field where some of the children were playing. The Ackaas were sitting on a bench overlooking the field next to the stone steps that led down to the corner where a group of girls were playing hand-clapping games. On the far side was a rough game of soccer and groups of kids skipping or doing amateur acrobatics around the edges of the ground. The women smiled at me and made room for me on the bench. I didn't speak any Tamil at this point, and they weren't game enough yet to use the bit of English they had. I put a smile on my face, while behind it ran a stream of thoughts along the lines of: "What do they think of me? I don't belong! I'm going to be getting in everyone's way for the next three months!"

We kept watching the children play, the odd boy or girl running up the stairs to tell the Ackaas something before running back down again, while the women chatted now and then in Tamil I couldn't understand. After a while the woman who was sitting next to me, the tallest of the four, took hold of my hand. Once some time had passed, still holding my hand in hers, she introduced herself as Gomathi and the other three women as Chandramathi, Chandrakala and Sumaetha. They had me practise getting my tongue around all of their names, and before I knew it we'd somehow understood each other and shared laughs about small things, and the worried thoughts had stopped marching through my brain. Connecting with other people and feeling a sense of belonging, however tentative, makes such a tremendous difference.

From the sports field, a 20-minute walk down the hill, through paddocks and alongside forest, takes you to the Boys' Home. This is smaller than the Siruvar Ilum, with just a few dozen boys studying at high-school level. A similar hostel for older girls operated further up the hills near the town centre, but this was run by a group of nuns and didn't require the same level of input from the PEAK team. The boys, for all their English textbooks full of complex grammar, were

The sports field next to Sacred Heart College where
the hostel students come to play.

initially shy and greeted me with a salute and no more English than an earnest "Good afternoon, sister".

Some evenings, when the Jesuit Brother who normally supervised them was away, I was allowed to take on the job of Warden. I would sit with the boys on the floor as they studied, reminding them to "padipoo" ("study!") when they got distracted from their work. They got half an hour of recreation at 7:00 on the dot, when I would be invited to a game of chess, carom (a game where you try and flick small discs into holes in a square board), or maybe to join the group of lads dancing if they were feeling bold. Books and games were put away to make space for dinner. Often, one of the older boys would call me into the kitchen to see Rakkammal, their Mami (Auntie), who cooked for them and was a beloved maternal presence in the place. She and the boys looked after me well. She usually cooked up something especially for me; the boys would insist on pouring a generous swirl of costly ghee over my rice.

Such generosity was impossible to refuse, even though I squirmed inside. This was hospitality to the extreme: feed the chubby tourist with fancy food and butter, while the boys eat white rice and plain curry. Some boys still suffered from the effects of inadequate nutrition in childhood, and took vitamin tablets from a communal jar each evening with their dinner. I encountered this sort of embarrassing but astonishing generosity nearly every day while I was in Kodai. Once, an old lady at a function tried to give me her seat when she saw me sitting on the ground. Walking past a wedding of a neighbouring family that I hadn't met before, I got invited in to be served lunch with their guests of honour.

The person who gave me some of my most challenging experiences was PEAK's second in command, Father Prem. "Come," he'd say, and he'd invite me on a jeep ride to the lower hills. On the way, he'd tell me we were meeting with a men's group and I could give them a talk on how to be good fathers, or he'd have me give a class on marriage to a group of young women. He brushed off my concerns about my lack of experience in any of these areas; his attitude made sense after I saw him deliver a thorough lecture on family planning to a huge village meeting.

Father Prem would drop me off at various hostels and community groups and have me stay with them while he did his work in the villages nearby – anywhere between a few hours to a week. These people had no idea who I was or what they were meant to do with me. We would end up breaking the ice by sharing some songs and dances with each other. Then I might give an impromptu English or martial arts class, or join in on their daily activities. At other times, Prem encouraged the workers employed by the college to invite me over for dinner or took me along to his own family functions.

Throughout my three months in Kodaikanal, I got a running commentary from the four PEAK team Jesuits on what I was seeing and experiencing. They filled me in on individual stories of family hardship, the intricacies of social issues, and global factors such as trade agreements that were influencing the Kodai agricultural communities. I was introduced to the religious and social philosophies that drove their work and allowed to sit in on their meetings where they had heated debates over the best course of action to take for various issues. While the children and staff in the hostels gave me boundless warmth and friendship, the Jesuits gave me an education. No one I met in Kodaikanal expected anything in return, but I left feeling I had so much that I owed them.

Wednesday 4 May
Byfield State Forest to The Caves, Queensland
103 kilometres – 5 hours 55 minutes

I hightailed it out of Byfield State Forest in the afternoon, bloodied and vowing never to return.

I had spent the previous morning in Rockhampton completing a long list of chores and being told by all the locals how lovely Byfield is. I stopped first at a bike shop to sort out my backside. Things had been OK down there for a long time, but recently I'd been increasing my mileage. To get into Rockhampton I set a personal record of 162 kilometres in one day, and as the bike shop attendant sympathised, "After 150 kilometres in a day, things are going to start to tear." He showed me some high quality "knicks" that had at least three times the padding of my old ones, and I happily parted with the money for them. In fact, I would have signed a family member or two over for medical research if that was what he'd asked for. (For those who are not up with bicycle accessory lingo, "knicks" are lycra shorts with padding in the seat. The only other thing you need to know about knicks is that you're not allowed to wear anything underneath them. It's something to do with physics.)

After a string of other jobs around town, I was left with one final mission: a search for some drinking-quality tubing. I had an idea for an engineering project involving an extremely long drinking straw to encourage a better relationship between me and my water bottles. I followed directions from the camping shop to the hardware store to the irrigation specialist to the refrigeration outlet, with no luck at all. Realising that I was thinking about the problem in completely the wrong way, I finally went into the homebrew shop.

It took more than ten minutes trying to explain that I was not planning on attaching a keg to Bike, but finally I walked out with two metres of perfect tubing that did not involve any industrial chemicals.

By this time, the afternoon had well and truly set in, so I headed out of town to Byfield. The last part of this ride was along the coast and through state forest, giving me dusky hills and serene forest to roll through. It looked all the more beautiful because of my comfortable backside. I pulled over to set up camp in the national park, only to engage in what is now officially known as the Battle of Byfield.

I should mention that earlier in the day I had said to the lady waxing my legs (not all chores involved bike-riding equipment), "Mosquitoes don't bother me so much anymore." It seems that a challenge spreads quickly in the insect world. The swarms of mosquitoes came fast and furious as I was setting up camp, so I focused on pitching my tent and throwing inside everything I needed, then diving in and zipping up the door. I wasn't too worried. Hadn't I emerged unscathed from a similar situation in Wyong?

I enjoyed the victory of having made it inside the tent for a few moments before realising that dozens of mozzies had come in with me. I went about killing the intruders to the accompaniment of a hum outside, rapidly getting louder, signalling an ever-increasing number of insects trying to find a way into my sanctuary. I started panicking as I realised the numbers inside were increasing exponentially. I thought there must have been a hole in the tent, but then realised they had Trojan Horsed it in by hiding in my bag. I cursed myself for being fooled by such an archaic ruse as they launched wave after wave of attacks. The pile of mosquito carcasses grew and I thought I'd won until I had to open the tent door to put some stuff outside and face the swarms that had been waiting for me by my tent door.

After another half an hour of killing, smeared with blood and black gunk, I fell asleep hoping the army outside would get sick of waiting for me to reappear, and go away.

They didn't. In fact, the mosquitoes had such a good time during my night-time toilet break, biting my backside and sneaking back into the tent, that they'd invited even more friends for the final offensive at daybreak.

I waited in my tent until the sun came up, hoping the light would send them away – which, since my muesli was outside, meant that I had to go without breakfast. It was a clever strategy: they'd cut off my supplies so I was weaker for the morning's skirmish.

The sun didn't worry them, so I finally leapt out of the tent and packed everything up as quickly as possible, simultaneously jogging in circles trying to outrun the cloud of mozzies that surrounded me. I tried yelling at them, bargaining, begging, crying, and swearing, but they wouldn't leave me alone. It made Wyong seem like the ideal location for a nudist colony.

I formally declared mosquitoes the winners of the Battle of Byfield and rode away as quickly as I could.

The day improved dramatically with my visit to the primary school located in the town in the heart of the forest. We had a good discussion about whether or not going to school is important, and the kids had an inexhaustible supply of questions about Bike and Trailer. The questions became quite complex: how exactly did my odometer work, and what were the various parts on Bike. By the time I had to start answering, "That bit … is just part of the bike", I felt it was time to wrap up and say my goodbyes.

I lost no time in retracing my steps to get out of the forest, accumulating a few more bites for old times' sake.

Finally, well out of Byfield, I ended up in a confusing camping ground as pleasant as last night's was bloody. The only sign I could find labelled the site as "The Caves". There were no caves to be seen, likewise no staff either, but full facilities including toilets, showers, empty cabins, and only a few mosquitoes. However, from the erratic way they were flying it was highly likely that they were from Byfield, and had spent the day rolled up in my tent.

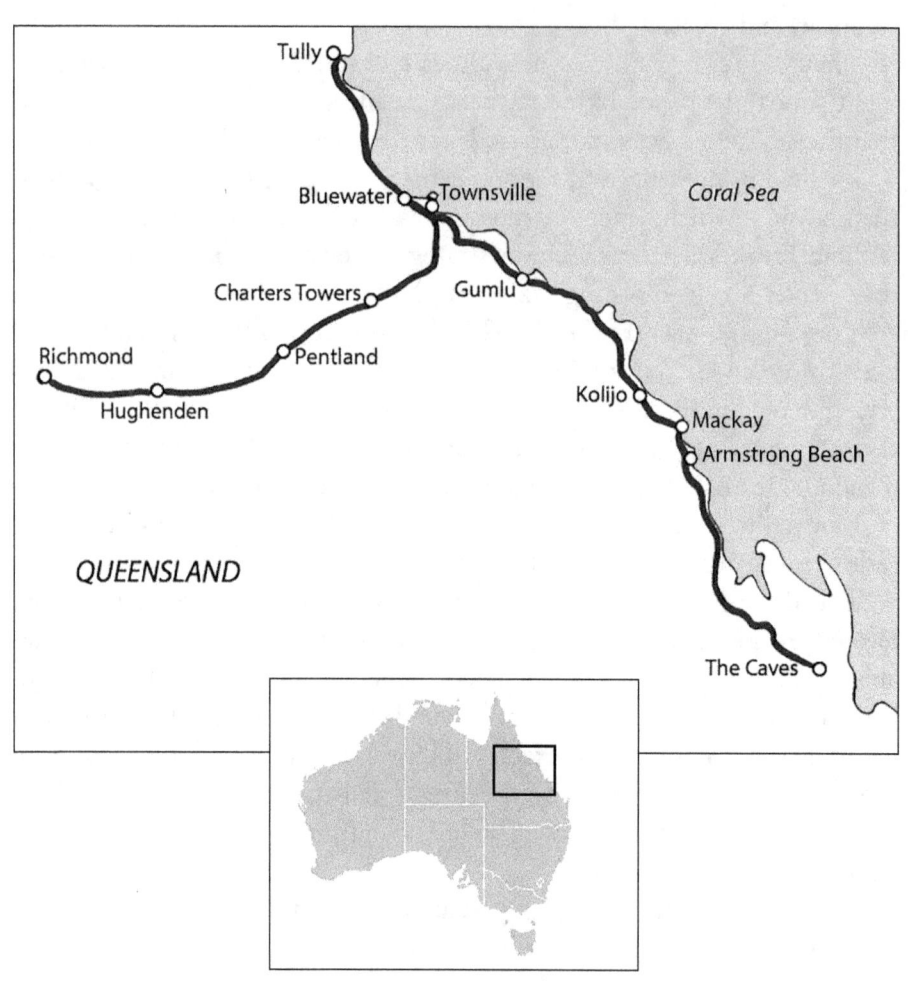

Chapter 6

Gender, Bottoms and Nudists

The Caves – Armstrong Beach – Mackay – Kolijo – Gumlu –
Bluewater – Townsville – Tully – Charters Towers –
Pentland – Hughendon – Richmond

Totals: 7,455 kilometres – 414 hours 42 minutes – $5,597

Monday 9 May
Mackay to Kolijo, Queensland
55 kilometres – 2 hours 42 minutes

I have a great aunt who lives in Lakes Entrance, Victoria. Even though I'd only met Auntie Glen once before, she took on the Cycle of Learning cause like none other. I'd been receiving wonderful letters of encouragement and praise from her and she had been enlisting everyone she knew or met to get involved. She'd even found a cyclist at her local supermarket, brought him home for lunch and put her hand to some match-making on my behalf.

A less romantic contact she made for me was with the family of Sally and Robert who live in Mackay. I stayed with them for a few days and Sally was amazing. She'd lined up numerous school and church visits and was following my blog closely. She knew all my stories so well, that I didn't have any good tales left to tell around the kitchen table.

There were some interesting dinnertime conversations still, thanks to my parents. My mum called the family's landline one evening and, before I knew it, the question "How's your bottom going?" was relayed via Sally, across the table to me and the answer back again, much to the amusement of her sons. I didn't mind too much, particularly as I had good news to report, thanks to the new expensive knicks.

A question I was less happy to receive was from a youngster at a youth group I spoke with on the previous Friday night. During the post-talk supper, she walked up to me, looked me up and down and enquired, "Are you a boy or a girl?"

I have encountered this question too many times in my life. In the year I spent travelling through Asia, I managed to collect it at least once in each of the countries I visited, every time in a new and unusual way:

- After striking up a conversation with a Lao Buddhist monk who said, "I thought you were a man until you spoke!"
- A Thai army officer who thought my friend Steph was beautiful, and asked if I was her boyfriend.
- Ditto in Indonesia except it was a man in a soup shop and he thought I was Steph's brother. He, too, thought Steph was beautiful, and that was when she still had scabies.
- The woman giving me a Thai massage who didn't have the English to ask, so just felt for herself.
- A man in a train in China who wanted to know if Julia Roberts was my girlfriend.
- A teenage girl in Vietnam who at least did it politely: "Excuse me; are you a man or a woman?" That was a day I was wearing a skirt too.
- A priestly member of the PEAK team who looked at one of my passport photos and asked if it was my brother.
- The woman in the Indian beauty parlour waxing my legs, who did know I was a woman but still took great joy in informing me, "You are hairier than a man."

I stared back at the girl who was waiting for an answer and ran through my mental checklist of excuses for the question. Do I have short hair at the moment? No. Does she have poor English? No. Are we in a country where the majority of women are delicate, long-haired and beautiful? No. Do I have visible leg hair? No, not since Rockhampton. Is she a Buddhist monk or Jesuit priest, and therefore has had limited contact with women? No.

Damn. I must just have looked like a man. "Girl," I told her, and went and ate more pizza.

Between all the engagements that Sally had lined up for me, I was able to fit in some serious remodelling of Bike and Trailer. I had the help of Robert and his shed full of tools to create an engineering masterpiece. I used the homebrew shop tubing, some extra water-bottle cages, hose clamps and plumber's tape to create extra space for bottles on either side of my front wheel-forks. With the tubing, I could now sip water at my leisure, without removing the bottles. In fact, with this new design, if a person with no hands was riding my bike, they too could stay hydrated.

My favourite visit in the area was to a Year 4/5 class who were doing a unit on Exploring Australia. On request, I concluded my talk with a 15-minute summary of my route from Adelaide to Mackay. I may not have improved their geographic knowledge, but by the end of it they all knew exactly where to go to get good bananas, peanuts, watermelons and pineapple fritters.

Sunday 15 May
Ingham to Bluewater, Queensland
82 kilometres – 4 hours 4 minutes

It was a weird evening in Bluewater rest area. I was enjoying the last hour of daylight as I taped spare spokes to Bike's frame and sewed up my sleeping sheet. I interspersed the handiwork with mouthfuls of my dinner – a can of creamed corn and a packet of rice crackers.

As I was tinkering, a couple came along, introduced themselves, and gave me some information about joining the local nudist community. I'm not the biggest fan of clothes and although being nude could have been a solution to recent gender confusion issues, I decided this wasn't the best stage of my life to be considering such options. I racked my brain for an appropriate excuse. The cost of sunscreen? The widespread following of my foot tan pattern? The reflective superiority of my vest compared to my skin? I finally told them that I was just passing through town and wouldn't be able to join up and they politely moved on to the grey nomads to my right. Only after they left I realised I should have told them about Wyong as a good retreat location.

I would normally be surprised by an encounter of this kind, but that week it didn't seem at all unusual. It seemed to fit in with the slightly loosened hold on reality I'd been experiencing lately. I blamed the large distances and small amount of sleep for my altered mental state. I had recently had a number of 2 am starts and my first 200-kilometre day. This was to fit in all of my engagements up the coast as far as Tully and then back to Townsville again. The school and church visits I had on this route were all small, but wonderfully welcoming in a northern Queensland relaxed way.

I wish I'd had more opportunity to enjoy the landscape. For a start, some of my riding was in the dark of early morning or night-time. During daylight hours, I did notice things becoming increasingly lush and tropical the further north I rode. Given that I'd had some sessions on the road when I found it difficult even to understand the concepts of gear changing, I had little more detail on the scenery to report. The memories I do have are of trees that looked like they belonged in a Doctor Seuss book, and the constant presence of birds. One type was jet black with a brilliant daub of red on its tail. There were flocks that kept me company, flying parallel with me for a kilometre or so. There was a lone cheeky bird in Ingham who sat on clothes that were hung out to dry and watched me finish off a packet of Weetbix. From the look on his face, I think he somehow knew it was only my fourth sitting to get through the box. Near Cardwell, there were also a few small, perfect, birds dead on the side of the road. I think they might have been struck by little bird heart attacks or something else fatal mid-flight.

The only bird I didn't see was a cassowary, but I'm not sure if I was meant to or not. People kept asking me if I had seen one, but it could have been in the same way that Scottish locals ask visitors if they've seen the Loch Ness monster.

In the midst of my weird, bird-motifed fatigue, I got disconcertingly geographically confused too. When I started seeing signs for the Whitsundays, I couldn't figure out what was going on, as I had been sure they were located somewhere exotic overseas. It just got worse with advertising for the Great Barrier Reef, since I'd always thought that was on the western side of Australia.

I credit two things with getting me through this challenging stretch of riding. One was my brilliant new water bottle access system, which made it easy to keep up my fluids while the country was rearranging itself. While riding in the night, even when cars refused to dip their high beam as they came towards me, so that I couldn't see where I was going, I could still sip water in a stylish manner.

As well as my revolutionary hydration system, bananas kept me on the road. I found buying bananas deeply reassuring in times of physical challenge. Eating them was nice too, but there was something about buying bananas from a roadside stall that made me feel invincible. I'd found no fewer than a dozen in my bag some nights before and managed to get through them all; I'd since made an effort not to get quite so carried away.

Fatigue had one benefit, which I discovered in a Cardwell youth hostel. I was sharing the camping space on the lawn with another cycling fundraiser. His mission was to help homeless people and apparently he had a book and movie deal lined up, hundreds of sponsors, media commitments every day, and a special contraption on his handlebars that enabled him to lean forward onto his forearms as he rode. Having had only three hours' sleep the night before, I listened to how much better a fundraiser he was than me, ate some bananas, then went straight to bed, much too tired to bother feeling inferior.

Friday 20 May
Pentland to Hughenden, Queensland
148 kilometres – 6 hours 55 minutes

It seemed my profile had become considerably more public since I'd hit the outback. When I was still pre-outback in Townsville, I'd remained unobtrusive enough. I got around town and went about my business inconspicuously, visiting some schools and Rotary clubs. One of the Rotarians, Tony, and his wife Helen hosted me for my time in Townsville. They showed me an unprecedented level of gastronomic hospitality. On the first night of my stay, they offered me the last ice cream in their freezer, and somehow made me still feel comfortable while I ate it in front of them. Then a few days later, when Tony dropped into conversation that he was from Chinchilla, and I paid homage to the fruits of his home town, he nonchalantly pulled out an organic Chinchillan watermelon from the kitchen and let me loose on it. Double hosting points. It would have been triple if they'd sold me some bananas as well.

One of the Rotary clubs I spoke at – a Daybreak group that meets over breakfast – gave a very generous on-the-spot donation, but I was a little concerned I scared them into it. The member who greeted me at the door seemed taken aback when she saw me, and gushed, "Wow, you're like an Amazon." This was a nice way of phrasing it. A lot of people expected me to have the physique of a Tour de France competitor, but given my genetically sturdy frame, indomitable appetite and shoulders wider than any I got to ride on, my body just doesn't "do" skinny. I liked the Amazon comment though, and it might have added an extra swagger and touch of aggression to my speech. Even if they were scared into their donation, they hid their fear well, with friendliness and piles of toast.

Bike left Townsville with extra zing in his step, thanks to a stop at a bike shop. I spoilt him with a new chain, cassette, front hub, water-bottle cage and the same fancy device to lean my elbows and forearms on that I had seen on my colleague's bike in Cardwell. I also found a new flag for Trailer, since he'd rather carelessly lost his old one somewhere up near Tully.

The three of us rode out of town on Wednesday, headed for Charters Towers, the Start of the Outback and the Beginning of my Lack of Privacy.

In Charters Towers I found a copy of the local Townsville newspaper at a petrol station and flicked through quickly to see if the interview I had done the previous day had been published. It had, and I read that "Ms Fitzpatrick claims the only downside of her journey is a sore bottom." I swear I just mentioned that in passing, after the reporter had packed up her notepad.

I received a phone call a few days later from a school in Darwin inviting me to visit. Before we'd even finalised a time, the teacher asked about the state of my backside. Either the *Townsville Bulletin* had a wider circulation than I'd realised, or there'd been a national press release that my bum has officially become property of Cycle of Learning, and normal anatomical discretion no longer applies to it.

I accidentally transgressed as well, when a police car pulled over to check that I was OK while I was taking a break by the side of the road one afternoon. I reassured the officer immediately without pausing to self-censor. "I'm fine; I'm just resting my bottom." I can't really complain about journalists.

It goes further than my backside though. On the road to Pentland, I was stopped at a rest area, enjoying a banana sandwich, when two couples in a four-wheel drive pulled up to have a chat. I did appreciate these interactions. The amount of traffic in an area seemed to have an inverse relationship to its friendliness. Since I'd been north of Brisbane, people were becoming increasingly sociable and ready to have a conversation. They'd tell me where they were from, I'd tell them about my ride and often they liked to have a look at my rig. I always did my best to feign modesty when they commented on the mechanical hydro-masterpiece on my front forks. There had been even more comments on this system lately since I'd incorporated a refrigerating function. I put each of the water bottles inside a damp sock before loading them onto the front forks. The socks not only kept the sun off, but the resulting evaporation cooled the water inside. When we got to the back of Bike, I was never sure if I should feel embarrassed or not when people saw my bright orange spade. This was a spade to dig holes for toilet-type activities and bright orange in case I ever needed to signal someone searching for me from a plane. I liked that it had two functions, but it did seem to be broadcasting the fact that my life involved pooing in the outdoors.

To add to my embarrassment, midway through this particular tour of Bike and Trailer, I realised that I hadn't brought in my washing yet. A few things, mostly underwear, were not yet dry after being washed the night before, so I'd lashed them on top of Trailer with ockie straps before leaving Charters Towers. I rushed through the rest of my commentary, "... and my trailer just hooks on to the rear axle of my bike. And that's it." The gentlemen had a long list of questions for me though, and I was relieved when they finally left without asking about the tensile strength of my underwire.

In Hughenden's main street, I had a truck driver ask how my tyres were going. I wasn't sure whether he'd passed me the day before while I was mending a puncture or if the bike shop where I bought a new tube had put out a bulletin on my shopping. I was quite surprised the truckie didn't ask about my leg temperature as well, since the other purchases I made in town were to deal with a fall in night-time temperatures I had not anticipated. Since I'd come inland, it was getting really cold when the sun went down. For each of the previous few nights, I'd woken up with my legs aching from cold, and would rock myself back to sleep regretting my decision to donate my one pair of socks to my water bottles. So, after the bike shop, I went to the general store and invested in a pair of tracksuit pants that weighed more than all my other clothes combined, but were wonderfully warm.

During the day's ride to Richmond, I pondered whether this new-found openness in my relationship with the world was a negative or positive turn of events. I am quite a candid person, and have never minded discussing diarrhoea or telling people about the time I nearly was eaten by a shark while swimming naked at the beach. Maybe the fact that all of Queensland seemed to know the details of my life was saving me time, and helping other, more reserved, people feel comfortable talking about their nether regions and letting people see their underwear. And then, 30 kilometres out of Richmond, I had one more incident that confirmed the constructive nature of this whole lack of privacy.

Around ten o'clock that morning the flies arrived. They'd been hunting me for the past few days, and I realised they were only going to increase in number as the weather warmed up and I rode further inland. At this point they'd reached the stage where they easily dodged my swats and kept walking right on in to my nose, mouth and eyes. If I sped up to 28 km/h or more, most flies got blown off, but I couldn't keep that kind of speed up for long without the assistance of a tailwind. I stopped, rummaged through my gear and put on a bandana, legionnaire's hat and sunglasses, then resumed riding, breathing in a particular way to try to avoid fogging up the lenses. This stopped the fly issue in a few ways. Firstly, I looked and sounded like Darth Vader, and so scared them away with the dark side of the Force. For the flies that hadn't seen *Star Wars*, I looked like a giant fly myself, thus gaining their respect so they left me alone. Lastly, I was so preoccupied with trying to get oxygen, seeing through the fogged-up sunglasses and not having a panic attack from the claustrophobic head conditions, that I didn't have time to worry about those flies that made it through my headgear and were still crawling on me.

For distraction, I started playing the "what would I swap for a fly net?" game. I'd got up to my new tracksuit pants, my extra-padded riding shorts,

Attempting fly deterrence between Hughenden and Richmond, Queensland.

my nearly full packet of ginger nut biscuits, my supply of lanolin (which had special anti-chafing powers that my backside was a big fan of), the pair of socks I planned on buying in Cloncurry, and any family members not already being experimented on in Rockhampton.

I was just about to add the much-loved green beanie that my much-loved aunt had knitted for me – which is the best place to hide when the world is treating you badly – when I pulled into what proved to be an auspicious rest stop. A middle-aged couple were already there, and they plied me with vast amounts of coffee and biscuits. During our conversation, the woman casually pulled out a selection of fly nets and asked if I needed one, as she had bought too many just a few days ago. This was an extreme, slightly spooky example of the world knowing my business. If it meant, though, that the world would also intercede and sort some of my business out for me, I was not going to complain any more.

Fly net joy, Richmond to Julia Creek, Queensland.

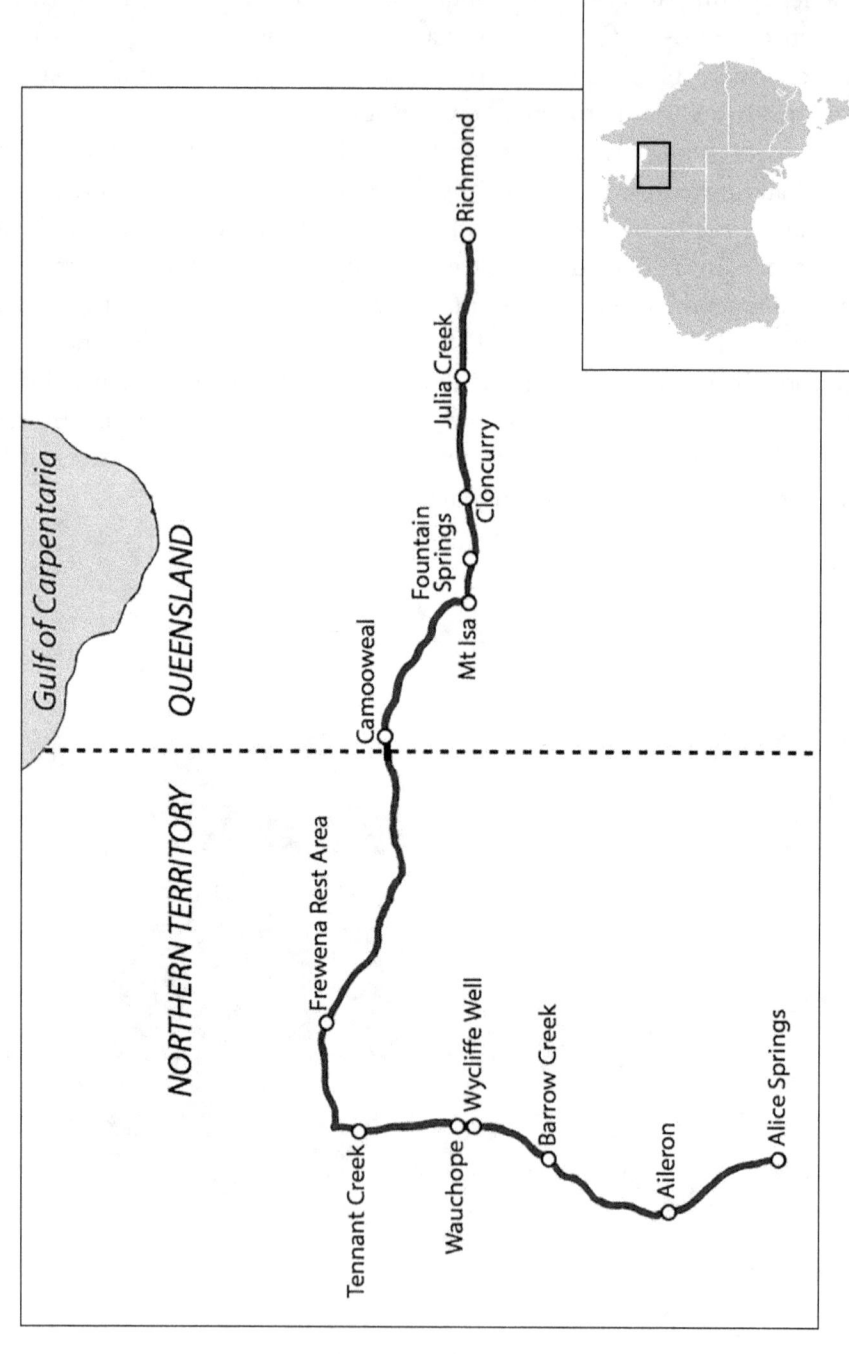

Chapter 7

Desert Craziness on a Bike with No Name

Richmond – Julia Creek – Cloncurry – Fountain Springs – Mount Isa – Camooweal – Frewena Rest Area – Tennant Creek – Wauchope – Wycliffe Well – Barrow Creek – Aileron – Alice Springs

Totals: 9,230 kilometres – 506 hours 54 minutes – $9,315

Sunday 22 May
Richmond to Julia Creek, Queensland
156 kilometres – 6 hours 55 minutes

Today's ride was a milestone for me. For the past few weeks, I had been closely following *Around Australia by Bicycle*, the book I was given in Woolgoolga. It has routes with distances between food and water access marked in to the metre. In more populated parts of Australia, you don't need this sort of information, but in the outback it is vital to know these things to plan your riding. Yesterday I had come to the end of one of the chapters and turned the page to the next section – Richmond to Tennant Creek. This chapter, and a number after it, begins with an opening statement written in capitals in a large bold font: **WARNING – FOR HIGHLY EXPERIENCED CYCLISTS ONLY**.

After reading this I had a restless night, with an uneasy feeling in my stomach. I was not highly experienced at anything, except maybe eating large quantities of fruit. I worried that these daunting "for highly experienced cyclists only" routes were going to be some sort of *Survivor* challenge crossed with *Indiana Jones and the Temple of Doom* crossed with *It's a Knockout*. Would I have to ride across a beam between quicksand and crocodiles? Be able to spell deraileur/derailer/derailier? Locate and remove my rear hub? Explain the physics of a slipstream? Fix a puncture with nothing but dead kangaroo liver and some barbed wire? Know why Stuart O'Grady was famous?

I set off with trepidation, but by the time I rode into Julia Creek seven hours later, I felt much less concerned. There were no obstacle courses or riddles to solve. It seemed that this rating just meant that it was a long ride with nothing around. To be fair, not nothing: there were lots of roadkill and birds of prey and fences and scrubby bushes and big blue sky. But nothing in the way of water, food or companionship.

I celebrated another milestone that same evening. It was now nine days since I had washed my hair. A personal record.

Wednesday 25 May
Fountain Springs to Mount Isa, Queensland
69 kilometres – 3 hours 48 minutes

The Queensland outback was throwing a wonderful number of friends into my path. This could have been because there is only one direct route from Townsville into the Northern Territory, so it is a lot easier for Queensland to get its aim right. It could also have been because, in the outback, there is always plenty of spare space and time to have a proper chat to someone without getting upset and letting loose with a bottle of turpentine on your belongings afterwards.

Speaking of the man with the ultra-professional corporate uniform, I ended up crossing paths with Colin another three times, which says a lot for his walking speed but probably more for my own slow riding speed and navigational difficulties. Once I got over my fundraising-envy issues, I realised there was a lot I could learn from Colin's control of his mental state. We both had been finding that in the more isolated areas, without the distractions of people or cities, it was easy for negative thoughts to hijack one's frame of mind. Colin, however, used this knowledge to pre-empt cycles of negativity, and to be prepared to limit the damage that they could have to his physical performance, decision-making and the success of his project. His approach made sense to me, although I knew that it was something that would take me a lot longer than this year to master – even when things were going well, to remind myself that I would feel down at some stage in the future to take the potency out of the despair when it occurred. Also, to be tough on negative thoughts when they came along and not let them take over rational thinking. I'd be reminding myself of Colin for inspiration for mental resilience in the coming outback months, and was glad to have his mobile number stored in my phone for times that I might need to call on someone that bit older and wiser who knows what it is to be at your physical and mental limits on a highway in the middle of nowhere.

In Julia Creek, I met another highway traveller, Andrew, for the first time. Andrew was also riding around Australia, but with his family travelling "alongside". Andrew would ride off in the morning while his wife Kate and their kids did some schoolwork and packed up the caravan. They would meet up for morning tea together, and then the non-cyclists kept moving to set up camp at the next stop, ready to do family things when Andrew arrived. Andrew and I rode together to Cloncurry for about one hundred kilometres, swapping notes on towns, roads and interesting characters we'd come across so far.

Time flew by, especially with the pace Andrew set, but I eventually had to admit defeat and tell him to go on ahead for the final 30 kilometres, while I finished at a pace that I and the flies trying to catch me were more comfortable with.

Yesterday morning, on the way out of the Cloncurry caravan park, I stopped by Andrew and Kate's site to say good morning. A disturbingly pale-looking Andrew, who I learnt had been sick all night, opened the caravan door. The extent of his pastiness was matched only by his determination to make it to Mount Isa that day. I had suspicions that I might be following a trail of vomit for the next few days if he kept riding ahead of me.

My own plan was to split the ride into two legs, so I stopped in the late afternoon at a rest area where I was met with beer and a waiting chair by a duo from a project called Handcycle Oz. Mark and Andreas were raising money for children's charities by doing a Guinness World Record hand-cycling-round-Australia type trip with Andreas on the hand cycle, and Mark as support crew driving the car and towing the solar-powered caravan behind. They'd been expecting me, thanks to a semi-conscious Andrew who'd let them know I was on my way before he lurched off to Mount Isa.

Handcycle Oz were so hospitable, sharing drinks and fold-out chairs and conversation with me, that I thought I'd take the liberty of borrowing their support crew when the world delivered me a broken spoke in Mount Isa the next day. Mark did such a wonderful job of replacing the offending spoke (no nipples were involved, thank goodness) that I started wondering if I should place an advertisement in the Mount Isa newspapers inviting support crews to apply. They would have to be small enough to fit on Trailer though, so I may have had trouble finding someone before I left town.

My guest appearance at a Rotary club tonight was overshadowed by a rugby league State of Origin game. I worked the crowd well by wearing my maroon trousers (the Queensland team colour) and cutting my speech down significantly so as not to interfere with the broadcast of the kick off. In return, they let me sneak off before the end of the game so I could get an early night in preparation for my bid for the Northern Territory border the next day. Within my truncated speech, I told Kalaivani's story.

Kalaivani

I am 14 years old and in Year 9 at school. The road to my home village is not good, which makes it hard to get there. The caste people in the village treat the Dalits as slaves. The Dalits do jobs such as sweeping in front of caste people's houses, and beating the drums for people's funerals. In shops, two sets of cups are kept: one for Dalits and the other for higher-caste people. The caste people do not show respect to the Dalits, and call them by their caste name as an insult. I think that the people in the oppressed classes in my village must study so that they can come up in life.

My father ran as secretary in the last three local elections, but was never successful. The so-called higher-caste people promised him they would get him the position, so that he would encourage others to vote for them – but then they didn't vote him in. My family lost a lot of our money in these elections. My father has also spent a lot of money travelling to a distant temple to pray for his painful leg to be cured.

I want to study well so that I can go back to my village and be respected. I want to be a teacher to educate Dalits. At the school in my village, the education is poor – since the school is far from the city and doesn't get inspected, the teacher often won't attend.

*

Sunday 29 May
Frewena Rest Area to Tennant Creek, Northern Territory
162 kilometres – 8 hours 43 minutes

From Mount Isa to Tennant Creek, only the tiny town of Camooweal and one lone petrol station break up the 680 kilometres of Barkly Highway. It was a new sort of riding for me. If I ever write my own manual for cycling this part of the country, I will put in a warning that this route is **FOR CYCLISTS WITH LOW STANDARDS ONLY**.

The first standard that I dropped was that of drinking water. There are windmill-generated bores regularly placed along the Barkly. This is good because it means you won't die of thirst, but bad because the water is warm and has a slightly salty taste. It's therefore remarkably easy to choose mild dehydration over drinking as much of it as you should. When I reached the petrol station midway between Camooweal and the Stuart Highway, the litre of fresh cold milk I bought was the best thing I had tasted since the watermelon in Chinchilla – and worth the small fortune I handed over for it.

400 kilometres left of the Barkly, and its bore water, until the Stuart Highway.

My food standards dropped significantly as well. I blame most of this on the fact I'd chosen to store my peanut butter and sultana sandwiches in a carrot bag instead of a bread bag. A key component of a carrot bag is its holes: holes big enough to let flies in and become quite intimate with your bread. It was multigrain bread too, which made it harder to be 100% sure there were no insect corpses or larvae within it once you'd brushed off all the live adults. I then accidentally dropped my very last sandwich in the dirt, just an hour away from expensive new bread at the petrol station. The grit complemented the potential insect infestation nicely.

My personal hygiene took a dive as well. I had become used to being unshowered and grimy, but after a few falls off Bike I was also bloody and oozing stuff from my knees and elbows. My first high-speed crash that week was due to Bike's new handlebar attachments that let me lean forward on my forearms, and so become more aerodynamic. The other factor in the crash was the fact that all year Trailer had been tricking me by making the rattle of his single wheel sound exactly like a truck approaching from

Just outside of Camooweal, I picked up a handy piece of
carpet to give my backside a bit of variety.

behind. Even though I knew it was him, I'd still find myself checking for the elusive truck following me. This time I turned around to check while leaning forward on my handlebar attachment. I encountered a completely new centre of balance that I didn't know how to deal with, and ended up veering off the road and into the bushes at 27 km/h. Bike and Trailer pulled up fine (though Trailer did seem a little sheepish and less truck-like afterwards), but my hydration system suffered some damage and my right knee and elbow lost a few chunks of skin and flesh.

The next day I balanced things up by falling on my left side while trying to get onto Bike. This time I didn't have the privacy of the bushes to lie around in afterwards, since I was right in the middle of the highway with a car speeding towards me. I jumped up, hopped back on and gave the driver a nonchalant glance as if to say, "Oh, that's just how we Highly Experienced Cyclists entertain ourselves. You should try it sometime."

A day down the road, I stopped at a rest area and had a chat to a middle-aged couple, Susan and Terry. They were currently caravanning around the Northern Territory, and had spent years cycling through Europe, Asia and North America. We had an animated debate about whether or not helmets should be mandatory on bikes. They thought helmets discourage people from riding, but I'm all for them. In fact, I think I would support mandatory helmet wearing for everyone regardless of the transport they use, because then people might think, "My helmet clashes with my car; I might ride my bike instead."

I was just about to make this point, when Susan looked down at my leg and said with visible horror: "The flies are ... ah ... they're feeding on your legs." This upset me a lot, not because there was a swarm of flies gorging themselves on the wounds on my knees – I had been well aware of their presence for the last few days – but because until then I had thought it was normal for a cyclist to have her legs fed on by flies sometimes. I decided not to mention any of the problems I'd been having with carrot bags and sandwiches, and bid farewell to them instead.

At another rest area, I spent an evening with some other, less fly-judgemental caravanners. After a while, one of the men quietly got a few cans of soft drink from the car and put them in front of me as I chatted with his wife.

This sort of quiet giving continually surprised me throughout the year. The backpackers who "knocked" on my tent with a donation, saying, "This is for the kids in India"; the teenage offspring of the family I stayed with who found me as I was packing up, and said, "I know it's not much, but ..."; the Rotarians who quietly passed me some money on the way out; the student who came up after the assembly and gave me twenty cents; the five-minute conversations that left me with some fruit, a fly net, or a piece of cake. It is a wonderful side of human nature to experience.

Through spending time with Mark and Andreas, I had seen a much more direct and efficient way of being a fundraiser. At each place they got to, they found the local council office, shops and caravan park, explained what they were doing and raising money for, and asked what could be done to support them. People and businesses were usually more than happy to provide food, accommodation, fuel and donations. When they were in a town, they would rock up at the local school, and often ended up giving an unscheduled presentation to the kids, with the likelihood that the school would do some follow-up fundraising for them.

Mark gave me a pep talk in Mount Isa. He reminded me that the best way to get anything (donations included) is just to ask. And the louder and more clearly you ask, the less likely people are to refuse. I nodded miserably into my stale peanut butter sandwich while he tucked into his donated roast lamb dinner. I knew he was right. If I waited around for invitations to speak at places, and for people on the road to ask me what I was doing, my fundraising was going to continue at its current slow rate. I felt queasy inside though, just thinking about asking outright for donations. Being already on the receiving end of so much generosity and quiet giving made it hard to start asking loudly.

I made it to Tennant Creek just in time. That morning I woke up at Frewena Bore, after a night of disturbing dreams about bore water. I got up, ate a mug of muesli mixed with the dead-tasting water and a touch of golden syrup, and glumly packed my tent up. I was sick of the Barkly, sick of not being able to quench my thirst properly, and sick of not having a proper fundraising temperament. I made the 60 kilometres to the next windmill/rest area/bore water supply in a relatively rational state of mind and took a short break, then headed out on the final leg of my trek along the Barkly Highway. A dozen or so pedals in I was already wishing that Tennant Creek would shuffle itself a few dozen kilometres east, to get the ride over and done with.

I realised, in retrospect, at the end of the day, snug in my tent with water bottles full of lovely tap water, that what happened next was inevitable. No travel story is complete without a "Going Crazy in the Desert" incident, and the last section of the Barkly Highway was mine.

I'm not sure if it was because I was a bit dehydrated, or had been looking at the same scenery for too long, or because the bore water had changed my body chemistry, but within the space of a few kilometres, something inside me snapped. I lost the part of me that was meant to remain patient and reasonable, and spent a few hours as a bellowing, frothing-at-the-mouth, crying, shuddering wreck. Ideas about smashing Bike against a tree or lying in the scrub for the indefinite future ran through my mind. All I wanted was to *not* be there, *not* have to ride my bike, and *not* have to be me. It was a new sort of scary feeling when, with only yourself to rely on, yourself has cracked the shits and walked off the job.

Twenty kilometres out from where the Barkly meets the Stuart Highway, I finally wore myself out enough to calm down, and even managed to smile nicely for the German couple who wanted a photo of me. They stopped in their four-wheel drive, wound down a window and shouted, "Take photo!" They captured a beautiful shot of me and my cloud of flies. The fellas on my knees had called in their friends to make the most of my stinky clothes and body, and to be around in case I went insane enough to remove my fly net. At least it made for an interesting photograph for the Germans.

Thursday 2 June
Aileron to Alice Springs, Northern Territory
145 kilometres – 8 hours 10 minutes

I had encountered head winds before, but riding into the southerly that opposed me the entire 500 kilometres from Tennant Creek to Alice Springs was a completely new experience. In the past, headwinds had been annoying but relatively minor players in a day's ride. Over the past few days however, on the Stuart Highway, the wind had become a tyrannical main character in my life. Every time I tried to defy it by pedalling harder, clicking up a gear or yelling, "I'll get to Alice Springs eventually. Just you wait and see!", it taunted me by getting stronger. As a cruel joke, every time I stopped it would slow down enough to let the flies find me. Each food break, I would have to perform a special dance to try to keep the flies at a reasonable distance from my face, scabby knees, and peanut butter sandwiches, all the time begging the wind to come back and do one nice thing for me. It wouldn't, but as soon as I started riding again, it would pick up strength, blowing just as hard as before, and slowing me down to a lethargic trundle.

By the time I reached Wycliffe Well Roadhouse, I was so worn out by the wind that I barely paid attention to the UFO and alien-themed statues, murals and souvenirs displayed in and around the roadhouse. Wycliffe Well may be the UFO capital of Australia, but all I had the energy for was buying a litre of UHT (long-life) milk. As I left the shop, already opening the lid of the carton, ready to sit in the morning sunshine and scull the lot, I realised I might have a problem. I needed to admit something. I had become a milkaholic.

When I left Adelaide, I was a soy milk "I-don't-handle-dairy-too-well" kind of girl. In the next few months though, things changed. It started with being polite and accepting the bowl of cereal and cow's milk I was offered at friends' homes for breakfast. Then I began experimenting with small amounts of condensed milk. Soon this just wasn't enough and I found myself stopping at petrol stations for 600 ml cartons of full cream milk. And now, given half a chance, I would down a one-litre carton of warm UHT milk, sometimes a few times a day. I should have been riding a cow around Australia.

The milk and my supply of Nutella sandwiches kept me going through the steadily warming headwind for most of the morning. However, by early afternoon I was completely drained of energy. I reverted to a head down, bum up, creep along the road, with the riff "I've been through the desert on a horse with no name" running through my head on repeat.

My target for the day was Barrow Creek Roadhouse, which allegedly doubled as a pub and a caravan park. It was quite a run-down looking place, but nevertheless came good on my mumbled request for a litre of milk and a glass, once I got through the door and propped myself up at the bar.

I asked about their camping facilities and was informed that, since they currently had no running water, I could camp for free in their caravan park. Since the main reason I liked caravan parks was for their running water, I turned down the generous offer and bought a loaf of bread and a ten-litre cask of drinking water instead. Outside, I dispersed the contents of the cask into my water bottles and found myself with a surplus of three litres of old, warm bore water. Too fluid-obsessed to throw anything drinkable away, I drank the lot – which was as much fun as eating a three-course meal of Brussels sprouts. I suspected that by the time I returned to Adelaide I would have an obscure emotional disorder that would manifest itself by the compulsion to carry at least 15 litres of water, two cartons of milk, and a bottle of golden syrup with me everywhere I went.

The next morning I emerged from the bush with a thick layer of red dust over me, and the uncomfortable knowledge of just how much muesli is too much for my stomach. I rode for half an hour, fending off the cold in my Hughenden socks and tracksuit pants, before stopping to admit defeat in the foot department. My stylish second-hand Mr Men socks were just not up to the job. So, on top of them I added my old, holey pair that had been moonlighting as insulators and refrigeration systems for my water bottles, and occasionally as medical swabs for my knee injuries.

Ten minutes later, my toes were still numb to the point of eliciting uncouth words from my normally civilised mouth, and I had to stop riding again. Not only was all of my non-essential blood supply being kept busy with the mug of muesli in my stomach, but also my old friend, the wind, was directing its entire force directly at my toes. It was no longer a headwind, but a toewind.

I briefly considered the logistics of cycling while inside my sleeping bag. Then I remembered the empty and almost-clean bread bags I had kept stashed away, a result of my recent very un-Atkins-like consumption of bread. They perfectly complemented my outfit, sitting snugly between my dusty sandals and two layers of socks. Eventually I warmed up, and was able to return the bread bags to my backpack (making a serious effort to remember which ones they were, for future food-storage decisions).

This morning was even colder than yesterday. I sat inside my sleeping bag, in my tent, listening to the headwind that was already up and waiting for me. I didn't feel like getting up. I didn't feel like taking off my warm sleeping clothes and putting on my cold and clammy riding clothes. I didn't feel like getting cold fingers while I packed up my tent. I didn't feel like playing today.

Still inside my sleeping bag, with my cosy beanie on, I rocked backwards and forwards with my eyes half closed. Maybe if I went on strike for long enough, the world would give in and provide me with a lazy Saturday morning at home reading the paper, and going to the Central Market for a coffee with friends. Or at the very least, maybe it would give me a tailwind and a rise in temperature by a few degrees.

I eventually conceded defeat and got most of my packing done as the sun was coming up, but when I reached the point in my routine where I should pack my incredibly warm down jacket and green beanie in Trailer,

I started crying at the thought of being cold again. The trouble was that, even when I was cold, once I started riding for a few minutes, I would start sweating. In a bid to keep just a few items of clothing sweat-free and pleasant to wear at night, I had forbidden myself from wearing my beanie or jacket while riding Bike. Instead of making the executive decision to break with routine and wear my warm clothes for the first part of my ride, I went for option two: wandering over to the caravan park shop, buying some hideously expensive chocolate (which was also hideously out of date), and phoning home to my parents.

Nothing raises the spirits like opening the foil of a new – well, maybe not new, but at least unopened – bar of chocolate and hearing your mother tell you that she got word that donations had reached the $9,000 mark.

My improved mood was not even broken by a few rounds of flat tyres and a late start on the road to Alice Springs. The distance left to Alice was 130 kilometres, and I hoped the thought of a warm bed and a good friend at the end of the day would be just the motivation needed to get me there relatively unscathed, both emotionally and physically. Forty kilometres down the road, however, Desert Craziness returned.

Something cracked inside me again and I desperately wanted to lie down in the red dirt and sleep for years, or burn Bike until it was ashes, or find a big red Abort Mission button on a tree stump somewhere, and press it yelling "I GIVE UP!!!" Did anything really exist besides this long road with its caravans appearing and then disappearing into the distance? Ninety kilometres more riding seemed too much to bear.

Singing wasn't helping. All the pleasant thoughts I tried to conjure up had been conjured up too many times before, making them as tedious as the landscape; a nasty, helpless feeling started spreading from my brain towards my legs.

I stopped at the green 80-kilometre marker and slowly and firmly told myself that THIS WAS JUST NOT ON. Having gained my full attention, I then invited the Voice of Reason to speak, and I let it explain to me how to remain sensible and in control for every metre of the next 80 kilometres. "Get on your bike." "You can do it." "Just take your time." "You've ridden this far before lots of times." "You're doing well." I got back on Bike and listened to the Voice of Reason for the next few hours as I got myself within reach of Alice Springs still relatively sane. In my battle with Desert Craziness, the score was one all.

With only 15 kilometres to Alice Springs left, the hills began closing in, making for an exhilarating ride: I was weaving left and right, up and down, riding faster and faster as the sun started setting behind me. Every corner offered the possibility of a glimpse of the town and every hillcrest held a glorious view.

I knew I must nearly be there when I met a team of lycra-clad cyclists riding in single file, heading in the opposite direction. I did my best to muster a smile at them, and was met by looks of what could have been either jealousy or contempt for my legionnaires hat/helmet amalgamation. Whatever the look, it was fast and in formation.

I finally made it into Alice Springs as the sun went down, and made it to the sanctuary of my old friend Olivia's home. Reaching a friend on a day like that one brought an amazing feeling. Even more amazing was the realisation that I had broken my own record: I had gone ten days without washing my hair. I suspected Olivia would insist I rectify this. She always has lovely clean hair.

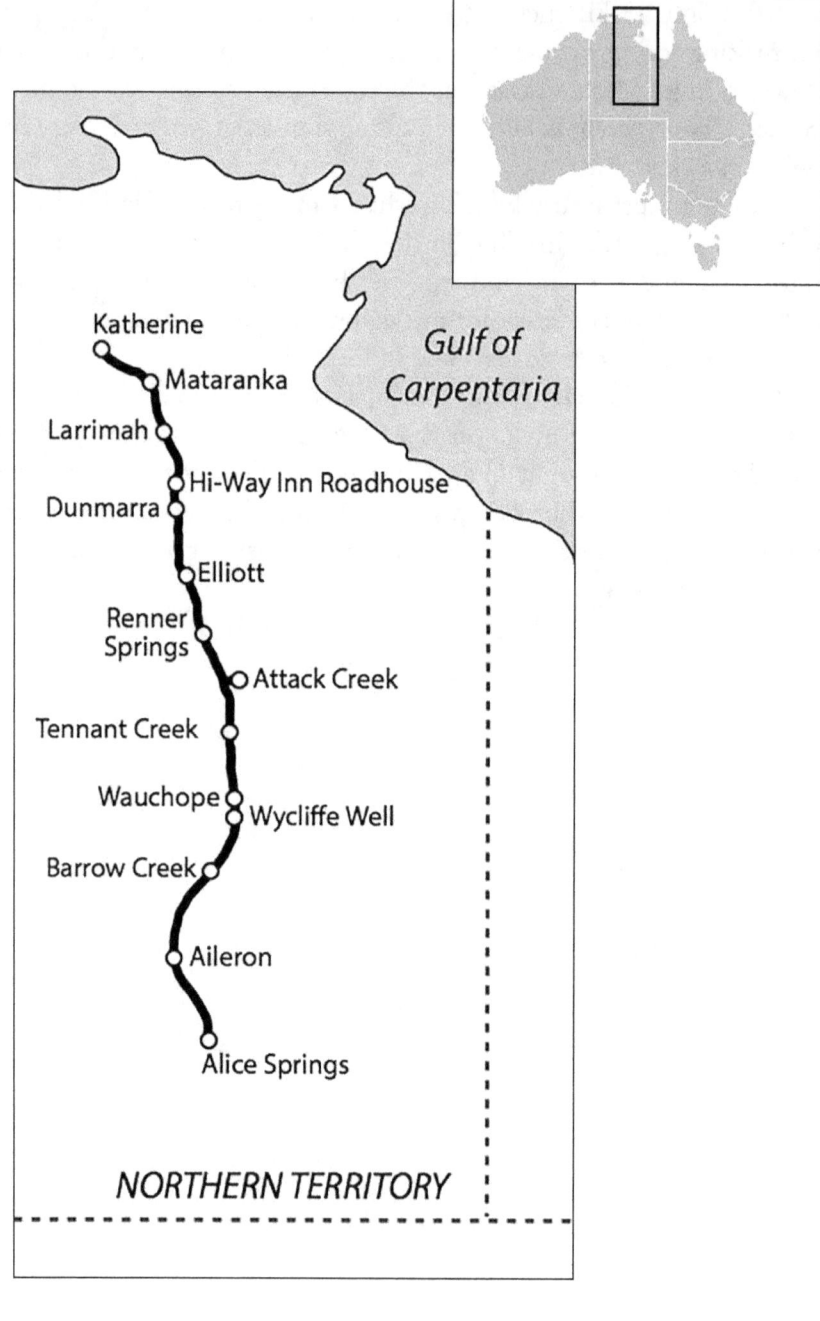

Chapter 8

The Wondrous Glory of the Everlasting Stars and the Vomit that Missed Banjo Paterson

Alice Springs – Aileron – Barrow Creek – Wycliffe Well – Wauchope – Tennant Creek – Attack Creek – Renner Springs – Elliott – Dunmarra – Hi-Way Inn Roadhouse – Larrimah – Mataranka – Katherine

Totals: 10,547 kilometres – 581 hours 45 minutes – $9,856

Friday 10 June
Stuart Highway Rest Area to Attack Creek Rest Area, Northern Territory
166 kilometres – 10 hours 18 minutes

The headwind I'd endured last week was made bearable by just one fact. I knew that when the time came for me to ride back up to Tennant Creek in the opposite direction, the headwind would then be a tailwind for me. My plan to ride the 500 kilometres from Alice Springs to Tennant Creek in two days would be a lot easier with a tailwind than without it.

I monitored the wind during my time in Alice Springs as I found my way to churches, dinner invitations and all sorts of schools. Of the schools I visited, I had some variety. One was a Steiner school, another a boarding school for Indigenous students and one was a run-of-the-mill primary school, but with slightly morbid students. Among other questions they fired at me was: "What would you do if you fell off your bike, hurt your arm and couldn't reach your phone?" And I'd thought a roadhouse without milk was something to worry about!

When I wasn't being asked scary questions, one of the stories I shared in Alice Springs was that of Rajkumar.

Rajkumar

My name is Rajkumar. I am 15 and in Year 9. I am from a village that is five and a half hours from the hostel. There are about 30 families in my village. We are from the Pulaiyair tribal group. When I go back to my village, I work on the land my father leases, where we grow beans. I also play games such as kabadi. [Kabadi is a team game that is a mixture of chasey, wrestling and a breath-holding competition.] There is a balwadi [kindergarten] in my village, but there is no school. My village has a water tank, a well and a community television. Children of my age are the first generation to study at high-school level – my father only studied up to Year 5. People in my village live under constant fear that the person that owns the land my village is built on will make them move away.

I hope my education will help me to get a good job: maybe working with computers. They are the way of the future. My hope for my village is that all children will be educated, since once people are educated, they become leaders who do good for people and help them rise up in life. If I were a leader, I would get the government to build houses and build roads for my village, and help the people find jobs. I believe that a good leader serves the people, doesn't cheat them, and doesn't take part in bribery.

*

Staying with my old friend Olivia was just what I needed during my time in Alice Springs. I could feel my brain release the tightness and tension that came with constant new encounters and new acquaintances on the road. Even better was letting go of the loops of self-analysis that came with extended solitude. In Olivia's company I could fall into the familiar conversations, common reminiscences and easy jokes that come from a shared history. I also loved hearing about Olivia's time in the Territory over the past few years. I first met Olivia during her time studying in Adelaide, but seeing her back in her home town of Alice Springs made me realise how much of what I like about my friend is innately linked to her roots in the NT. Olivia, like the Territory, has an unpretentious appreciation for style, socialising and festivities, complemented with a passionate pride in and love of the bush. Olivia is the only friend who I can call on to help me choose what shoes to wear to a formal event and also suggest what sort of knife to take on a week-long camping trip. Olivia will be first onto the dance floor at a wedding reception, and also first to sort out how to move a four-wheel drive bogged in a riverbank.

I had my last school visit in Alice Springs on the Wednesday morning, and left straight after since I had a school visit booked in for Friday afternoon back in Tennant Creek. As I rode out of town and got my bearings, I noticed something wrong. The seasonal, cool southerly that had been the bane of my existence riding down here, but a symbol of hope for the rushed return I knew I'd have to do over the next two days, had somehow swung around, becoming an unseasonal hot northerly and was blowing in my face just as strongly as on my ride down.

I spent a few minutes sulking and threatening the wind with a formal complaint, but realised there was no time to waste. No time to waste going crazy. No time to waste feeling sorry for myself in my tent in the mornings. In fact no time to waste doing anything but riding.

I got as far as I could that evening and rose at four o'clock the next morning with a plan to ride until I hit 300 kilometres or midnight – whichever came first. I have little memory of the day, but can report with some confidence that I definitely stopped at Ti-Tree Roadhouse. While I was there, I'm pretty sure that I stole a piece of toast left on a plate at a vacated table.

Besides falling into unsavoury eating habits, my massive ride passed in a hot, windy blur. Some time after 11 pm I was chatting away to myself to stay awake, when I came across a rest area. I finished my conversation in case I woke up someone in one of the parked caravans, and then noticed an empty picnic table. It was just too inviting, so even though I'd only done 279 kilometres (21 kilometres short of my target), I decided to stop there, throw my mattress and sleeping bag on the table and drift off into a starry, exhausted sleep.

When I woke the next morning, it was a mere 90 kilometres into Tennant Creek from my picnic table, and I assumed that, since I was only aiming for double figures, the ride would be easily knocked off before the school visit that I had tentatively lined up for the afternoon. I was sure that, compared to yesterday's hard slog, the morning would be a pleasant, leisurely ride.

And so it was for about 23 minutes. Then the headwind picked up again. It was so strong that even though I was using every single muscle in my body to defy it, I was still only moving at 12 km/h. After an hour or so, my spirits were already shattered by the wind, when suddenly I had a shooting pain in my right Achilles tendon that forced me to gingerly dismount onto the side of the road. I swore at my leg, regained my composure, and lowered my seat so I could change my pedalling style to accommodate my throbbing Achilles.

By the time I wobbled into Tennant Creek, the rest of my body also felt well and truly wrong. I think it was a combination of being tired, under-hydrated and un-stretched. I made it to the supermarket and, once I had paid for my things, found a corner near the bags of fertiliser where I could covertly make use of the air-conditioning and drink litres of cold fluids. I was found, luckily not by the anti-loitering brigade, but by a caravanning couple, Lars and Ruth, whom I'd met at the Alice Springs church as well as on the road before that. Even after they'd been nice to me and left, I still felt quite out of sorts. The tentative school visit for which I had rushed up the Stuart Highway hadn't eventuated after all, and it was still only the early afternoon, so I decided to keep riding. This may not have been the best of ideas, but I knew Mark and Andreas of Handcycle Oz were somewhere close up the road. I thought I might as well be hot and sore and wrong while covering some distance towards friends, instead of hot and sore and wrong sitting around Tennant Creek.

I stocked up with supplies, including liquorice bullets for comfort food, and hit the road again. The last 70 kilometres of the day was superb. The wind had died down, my ankles felt better with my new asymmetrical riding style, the road was smooth, and the liquorice in my top pocket tasted delicious. I looked out over the landscape and felt impelled, between mouthfuls, to recite Banjo Paterson's lines from "Clancy of the Overflow":

> He sees the vision splendid of the sunlit plains extended,
> And at night the wond'rous glory of the everlasting stars.

Saturday 11 June
Attack Creek Rest Area to Renner Springs Road House, Northern Territory
103 kilometres – 7 hours 16 minutes

I probably should have listened to my body when it was feeling wrong yesterday.

I rose early again in the morning, with the town of Elliott in my sights: 180 kilometres away. I didn't actually need to get to Elliott urgently but I had entered a new physical and mental realm that was calling me to push on up the road as quickly as possible. I had been riding like a machine these past few days: early rises, big distances, heat, sun, late nights. The last few nights when I lay in my sleeping bag, my body didn't seem to understand what resting was. It was wound up, ready for action and wondering what the point of this lying down business was.

A part of me enjoyed this machine-like state and wanted to push my limits further than I'd pushed them before. And today I pushed things further on the Stuart Highway. The road was windy, hot and hilly. The queasiness I'd felt for the past few days, and put down to being tired, turned into downright nausea. I added to my graceless riding style by periodically leaning to the side, so that if I did indeed vomit, as I felt I was going to, I would not damage any of Bike's components or the book of Banjo Paterson's poetry strapped to the handlebars. I sipped sun-warmed water and managed to keep the morning's muesli down, even throughout a few dry-retching sessions. For some reason, I didn't feel too concerned. I was physically and mentally absorbed in my riding, however uncomfortable; the idea of stopping didn't enter my mind.

I got to the halfway point, Renner Springs Roadhouse, where I worked my way through a few cold drinks, doused myself with bore water from the hose out the front, and forced myself back on Bike. I made it five kilometres down the road and peered up from my miserable haze at the long gradual hill rising ahead of me. At that moment I realised I was not a machine. I could die on that road. If I kept riding much longer, I would pass out; I suddenly appreciated the fact that the middle of the Stuart Highway, hundreds of kilometres from a hospital, is a dangerous place to collapse.

Even after I realised this, I still didn't care and might have kept on riding. But then I remembered my family. It wasn't the thought of never seeing them again – I was too exhausted to feel emotional about that; it was the memory of my promise to them to "be sensible". I took one last look at the long hill ahead, executed a slow U-turn and sensibly made my way back to the roadhouse.

Once there, I stumbled off Bike and into an outside seat next to a phone box. I wasn't able to move for half an hour, instead choosing to cry. Then I noticed the phone next to me, so used it to cry at people: first Christine, then my sister. I finally pulled myself together to go inside and organise a campsite, but made it just a few steps to the big 49-gallon drum doubling as a bin next to the door, and promptly threw up what looked to be about five litres of fluid into it. I had reached my limit.

Unfortunately, the bin was rusted through at the bottom, so my special gift was leaking all over the forecourt. I apologised to the staff inside, who took one look at me and put me in a cabin with bed, fridge, shower, air-conditioning, and a supply of rehydration formula.

Thursday 16 June
Mataranka to Katherine, Northern Territory
113 kilometres – 6 hours 5 minutes

Little did I know that while I was being so well looked after in Renner Springs, the phones were running hot in Adelaide as my family started getting nervous about my well-being. It is true that I may have used the phrase "I feel like I'm going to die" to my sister, but I also had assured her I would phone back if I didn't feel any better. Had I been in a better state of mind, I would have realised the poor logic in that proposition. Unfortunately, Renner Springs was not in mobile phone range, so my family could not call me to check if I had indeed died or not. I might have kept to my "being sensible" promise by not collapsing on the Stuart Highway, but I didn't do so well in the not-letting-them-worry department.

While they were worrying, I spent the day wallowing in air-conditioning, drinking cold water, and trying to figure out what food I could stomach. The thought of any of my staples (baked beans, peanuts, dried fruit, muesli, golden syrup) made me feel as nauseated as did the thought of cycling. I was not sure how to fix my body after what I'd put it through in the last few days. Obviously, I was dehydrated, and I knew that if I didn't look after myself I would mess up my schedule for Cycle of Learning.

I ended up seeking advice by phone from my former travelling buddy Steph. After our time at high school together, then at university and, finally, travelling overseas for the trip where Steph was always declared more beautiful and feminine than me, Steph and I have a friendship that involves an in-depth understanding of how the other operates – perfect placement of jokes to appeal to our mutual sense of humour; insight into one another's bowel habits; and an ability to know exactly when an iced coffee is required to cheer the other up.

Steph is just the person you need for decision-making or looking at things from a fresh angle. She has the ability to examine any situation with rationality and logic. Sometimes this can be frustrating and damaging to any nearby egos but it's usually enlightening. Discussions about anything remotely supernatural or based on common assumptions get shut down as Steph requests the randomised double-blind study to prove what you're saying or outlines the scientific process that explains away what you're basing your whole argument on. Sometimes Steph uses her power of scientific thought for slightly dubious purposes though, such as the time she showed me a chemical cascade hypothesis establishing that lots of salt in your diet is actually a healthy thing. This was at a period when Steph was a huge fan of fetta cheese and other salty foods, so I took this one with a, pardon the pun, grain of salt.

Our friendship had been cemented one lunchtime, a few months into the undergraduate medical degree we were both studying, when Steph confided in me, "So, I still don't actually understand what a cell is." I'd nearly burst into tears of relief that there was someone else who had no idea what had been going on in lectures all year. We both ended up doing OK academically, with the same approach to our study – fitting in as much part-time work and outside activities as possible during the semester and then cramming before exams. We shared a lack of certainty about our career choices, which made us feel somewhat alien to the rest of our self-assured and professionally ambitious cohort. We shared a solution as well – deferring the fourth year of study to travel overseas. We spent the first few months in south-east Asia together, with mixed results. There were moments of harmony – mostly when we were eating and Steph couldn't finish her food and I was extra hungry so ate her leftovers. There were moments of tension, as can be expected when two people spend nearly every moment of every day together and begin to take offence at the way the other brushes their teeth, or how they insist on walking for three hours to find a particular coconut drink. There were moments of being mutually naive enough to find ourselves handing over most of our money to a scam artist and his two armed guards. The majority of moments, though, were of good companionship thanks to our shared travel priorities – spending as little money as possible, eating interesting food, and getting a feel for local, everyday life.

Knowing the sharpness of Steph's scientific mind, her medical knowledge (much improved from first year uni – and not just because she now knows what a cell is) and that she knows how I tick and has my best interests at heart, Steph was just the right person to consult about my Stuart Highway medical situation. Her love of salt also came in handy. Besides loving to eat salty foods recreationally, she knows how to use it therapeutically too. Since the time Steph worked in remote Pakistan, educating women about how to rehydrate their babies in times of dysentery, she has been a big advocate for the use of table salt for getting a person's electrolytes back in whack. Since I was as likely to spend money on expensive sports rehydration formulas as would a rural Pakistani woman, Steph was just the girl to call. She instructed me to put a small scoop of sugar and a pinch of salt in the water I drink to keep my fluids better balanced. Steph's knowledge of salt is amazing. It is also the key to her very tasty Greek salad.

The conversation finished with Steph telling me she'd seen a patient the previous week in Darwin hospital whose brain had nearly exploded (this was not the exact terminology she used, but the meaning was close) because he was dehydrated, and asking me to please stop riding; I assured her I would take it easy from then on.

And take it easy I did, with my new riding strategy. Come five o'clock in the afternoon, I loaded Bike up with bottles of salty cordial, dropped a home-made thankyou card in for Judith, the wonderfully considerate operator of the roadhouse, and headed down the road feeling much better than the last time I'd tried.

Riding through the evening and night went well. I sipped my fluids regularly and made myself stop every 20 kilometres or so. It was cool, and the wind had died off almost completely. The other bonus I discovered was that there was much less traffic around at that time of night, and when anything did come along you could see it from miles away. There was plenty of time to get off the road completely if traffic came from behind, although this led to a few road trains stopping in confusion thinking I needed some help.

I got into Elliott by 10:30 pm and decided to blow my budget and lash out on the money for a cabin so I could rest through the remainder of the night, and during the following day before the next leg. Just as my luck would have it, the one time I was willing to part with money, the caravan park was completely locked up. I couldn't even sneak in to set up camp, since it was equipped with barbed wire and guard dogs. I made do with the picnic table 50 metres down the road.

Meanwhile, back in Adelaide, my mother had finally tracked down a phone number for Renner Springs. She reached Judith, who told her, yes, I had vomited there, and for some reason I had pedalled off late in the afternoon. And yes, there was more news: a bus coming from Elliott had seen me at 8:30 pm, when I was pulled over by the side of the road, a long way still from Elliott, and my lights were very dull. And yes, Judith, the bus driver, the passengers on the bus, and now my mother were all very worried. In fact, Judith had called the Elliott police to ask them to keep an eye out for me.

Oblivious to the drama I was causing across Australia, in the morning I booked an unpowered campsite in the caravan park. I set my tent up for the day and tried my best to get some sleep. A hot tent in the middle of the day is not very conducive to sleep, so I soon gave up and went in search of food instead.

In the morning, my mum decided to phone Judith again to find out if she had any news; not getting any from her, she then thought she would give my phone a shot. I happened to be in a roadhouse eating hot chips when she called. By chance, the roadhouse was one of the few spots in Elliott that gets reception, and I took my mum's call, nonchalantly telling her I was fine, eating hot chips, and would take it easy from then on.

Relieved, my mum phoned back Judith to tell her the good news, but dialled one number wrong and ended up talking to the Elliott police. They had indeed been looking for me, and were also glad to hear I was alive. In fact, if I was eating hot chips and had phone reception, they knew just where I was and would go have a chat with me.

Luckily, I had no knowledge of this conversation, and left before I got myself a telling off for wasting police time and riding with weak headlight batteries. I made my way back to the caravan park, packed up, had a pre-ride swim in my clothes to cool down, and farewelled Elliott and its massive peacock population.

True to my promise of "taking it easy" I again planned to ride at night, this time to Larrimah. The less easy side of things was that Larrimah was 245 kilometres away.

By 11 pm I had reached Dunmarra Roadhouse. It was closing time, and I had the good fortune to score three free muffins. I ate two, stashed the last one for later, and pushed on, worried that if I dawdled too much, Desert Craziness would find me again. Instead, through the night I discovered a new companion: Deep Night Serenity. Without the distractions of flies, heat, or the sight of the metres clicking over on my odometer, the minutes and kilometres slipped past quietly. I sang and sang, not the hearty bellowing needed when hurtling down hills in the rain, but quiet songs that didn't disturb the night too much.

Soon it was 5 am and I was getting tired. I'd consumed two cans of caffeinated multinational beverages, but the effects had worn off and I was resorting to dousing myself with water and slapping my cheeks to stay awake. When a face full of water was only providing a minute and a half of alertness and a slap only 30 seconds, I decided I could probably do with a short kip.

I parked Bike off the road and lay down in the dirt, out of sight, for an hour or so of sleep. I'm sure that there are long lists of reasons involving snakes, murderers, spiders, dingos and dignity that make sleeping in the dirt by the side of the road not a good idea. None of them seemed very important at the time though, so I set my alarm for an hour and went under as soon as I closed my eyes. I woke with a rotten feeling in my stomach and fiery heartburn, and lumbered the last 60 kilometres into town with occasional breaks to stop and stand, mentally turned off but propped up by Bike, for ten minutes or so at a time.

I pulled in by 11 in the morning, and spent a few hours chasing shade around a tree with my tent and pretending to sleep, but really just slowly stewing in my own sweat. I gave up after a while, and joined what became the Larrimah Cyclist Convention of 2005. First up, Mark and Andreas of Handcycle Oz pulled in. They played postie, giving me a card from a couple working at Daly Waters Pub whom I'd met back in Hughenden. While we were all whinging about headwinds, another cyclist rolled in on a home-renovated bike. Hubert was an interesting mix of German, Canadian and Australian, and soon busied himself starting a fire on the caravan park lawn in an old car hub he found. The next morning, two new convention members cycled into town. Leonard and Tina had been riding around the world for the past few years, sometimes with a foldable canoe. The final convention member pulled in and circled round my tent in the early afternoon as I was having a swim. An Austrian gentleman called Tobias, he brought good wishes from Judith at Renner Springs. He then informed me that we would ride to Mataranka together, taking it in turns to be in front, so as to block out the wind.

Obediently, I packed up and hit the road with Tobias. The lead-sharing plan worked for about 30 minutes until Tobias got a two-kilometre lead on me, which didn't really do much to cut down the effect of the wind. We tried again, but my busted Achilles, tired body and intrinsic slowness just couldn't hack the pace, so we rode into town separately and caught up over dinner (in my case, a litre of milk). Tobias informed me he was a retired tax consultant and grandfather, but I think he may have forgotten to mention the highly-trained-Austrian-sprint-cyclist part of his bio.

I got up the next morning with only one dry outfit left. During the night, I had woken up three times in a cold sweat, needing a shower and change of clothes. I suspect my body was still not too happy about its current work contract. Even though I was sticking to riding in the evening and night-time, I think it would rather have had a bike-free environment for a while.

I had to vacate my campsite by 10 am, and so packed up and lounged in the rest area on the edge of town eating dried biscuits and Vegemite. I sipped on a large carton of juice, too, since Mataranka's bore water was not that tasty.

A few months before, someone had asked me if I was "over it" yet. The answer was a definite "No". However, at this point, in Mataranka, I had to admit to myself that, thinking of all the organising I still had to do for Western and South Australia, the riding ahead of me, the fundraising that needed to happen … I felt over it. Things were moving slower than expected. I hadn't turned into the self-promoting, event-seeking, hat-passing, media-savvy cyclist I should have been, and my body seemed to be falling apart. Even my hair was protesting, though that could have had more to do with the brand of soap I bought in Alice Springs than with my competence as a cycling fundraiser.

At least, sitting in the rest area, I was in a prime position to simultaneously wallow in gloom and be sociable at the same time. I chatted with a few locals and some of the caravanners stopping over, including Lars and Ruth, my personal cheer-up squad. Since Tennant Creek when I'd last met them, we'd again crossed paths while I was eating my hot chips in Elliott. They seemed to be on hand whenever I was feeling a bit low.

After Lars and Ruth moved on, I got back to my brooding until Handcycle Oz arrived. We caught up in the pub with an enthusiastic couple from Germany on a tandem bike with trailer. We swapped cycling statistics, and I was disheartened to find out that I seemed to be the slowest cyclist in the Northern Territory.

Bearing my new title, I farewelled the troops in the pub, filled up my bottles with the hideous Mataranka water, and headed for Katherine. It was one of those evenings where it seemed a whole lot easier to stop and eat ginger nut biscuits, baked beans or peanut butter than to ride a bike.

I eventually pulled into Katherine after 11 pm and couldn't find a caravan park with anyone on duty. I finally found one that didn't require a key and set myself up. The best part of the night was when I tasted the water from the taps, and nearly cried with joy at its sweet, un-borish taste.

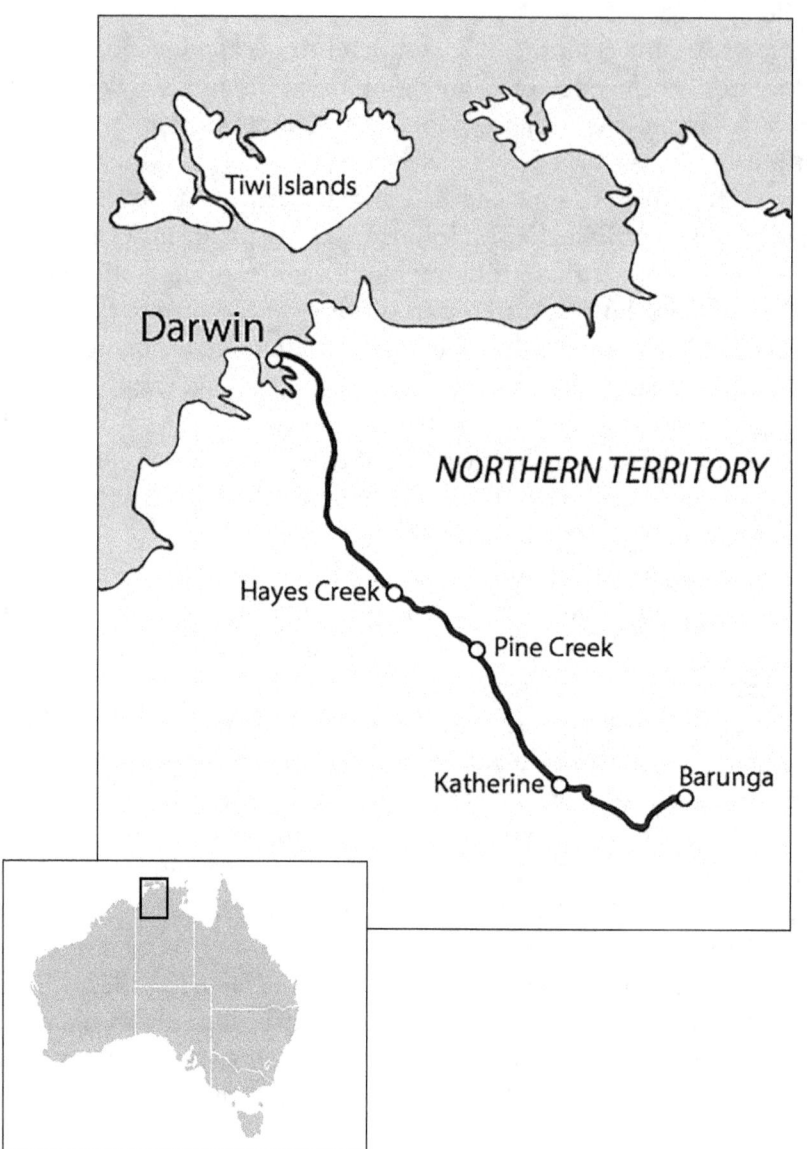

Chapter 9

No Fire-Twirling Inside

Katherine – Barunga – Pine Creek – Brooks Creek – Darwin – Hayes Creek

Totals: 11,488 kilometres – 630 hours 20 minutes – $12,937

Wednesday 22 June
Stuart Highway to Darwin, Northern Territory
155 kilometres – 7 hours 52 minutes

I spent three days in Katherine, enjoying the town's water supply and various other cyclist-friendly services. These included:

- Library: perfect for spending air-conditioned time plotting routes for Western Australia, and, when that got too tiring, reading John Marsden books.
- Op-shop: where I found a replacement long-sleeved shirt for riding in. (My old one had begun releasing the odour of the previous owner out of the collar. I also had some negative gastro-intestinal associations with it since I'd been wearing it during my vomiting episode at Renner Springs.)
- Supermarket: a refuge from heat and boredom when the library was closed. They also sold a product that I had never come across before. Some genius baker had bred finger buns with hot cross buns, producing a delectable combination of two of my all-time favourite bakery products. Even when the supermarket wasn't selling the Hot Cross Fingers, I liked to loiter in the air-conditioning, looking at different brands of cereal and thinking about which shape of water bottle would fit best for my next water-carrying project.

Between loitering sessions, I fitted in a few school visits and, in a first for the year, I was on the receiving end of a visit: from my cousin Heidi and her husband Tim, from Geelong. I was very excited to see them and wished I could repay their hospitality by letting them lose my keys and eat all my leftovers, if I'd had any of either. Instead, I played host by showing them around the supermarket and pointing out the library. We pitched tents next to each other in a caravan park and had a cousinly meal of barbequed vegie burgers.

I must have spent more time than I realised moaning about my lack of assertive fundraising skills because Tim felt the need to help me out in the morning. We were eating breakfast when he noticed a tourist bus parked nearby, and sprang into action. He grabbed Trailer as proof of my ride and charged off to the bus to elicit donations from the passengers. He was gone a long time and returned a hero in my eyes, even though the driver hadn't actually let him on the bus. It could have been because he thought Tim was wielding Trailer more as a weapon than as a prop for a fundraising presentation.

A week earlier, I had made plans with Steph that she would pick me up from Katherine after my visit to Barunga and drive me up to Darwin. That way, she could make sure my brain didn't explode from dehydration and I could ride that section only once – from north to south – next month.

Since Larrimah, I had been counting down the hours until I would see my dear friend, load my gear into her car, be driven to Darwin in air-conditioned comfort and relax in a house that wasn't a hot, cramped tent. I could picture it perfectly, down to which mix tape she would be playing for the drive and the jokes she would make about the broadness of my shoulders.

However, on the Monday riding back into Katherine after a visit to a school in the Barunga community (home of the famous Barunga festival), I realised that I just couldn't go ahead with our arrangement. No matter how "over it" I felt, the whole point of the year was to be riding my bike. I had two full days to cover the 300 kilometres and I had drunk enough of the lovely Katherine water by then to be fully rehydrated. I sent a text message off to Darwin to cancel the plan, stopped into Katherine for supplies and kept heading north.

Once I was in Darwin, I realised what a wise decision it was. I would be staying there for three weeks, and if I'd finished on a negative note it would have done some chronic damage to my morale over that time. The extra two days I had on the road turned things around for me, and pulled me out of the malaise that the heat stroke, long distances, exhaustion and bore water had dragged me into.

The kilometres between Alice Springs and Katherine had seen me grumpy, unappreciative and despondent. I became worried that the rest of the year would be the same: six months of sulking in shopping centres, dreading getting on Bike and then riding with my head down and a frown on my face.

The last two days of riding had been a wonderful relief. I found myself enjoying the bush scenery and the rise and fall of the hills. My body was feeling better and I had plenty of petrol stations on the way at which to fill my water bottles and drench my hair and clothes with water to cool down. I was waving at caravans again instead of raising one glum forefinger off the handlebars while glancing up, hoping that they'd pick me up and take me back to Adelaide, or at least knock me off Bike and put me out of my misery.

The run into Darwin aroused all the excitement that I felt each time I rode into a capital city. The bush slowly gives way to more and more houses, the traffic starts accumulating, factories and businesses appear, shops of increasing variety present themselves.

I eventually made it to the centre of the city and found my way to the flat of Steph and Nicole. My two old uni friends were my halfway respite hosts. It was almost school holidays in the Territory, so I planned to settle in for a while, catch up on admin duties, rest my body and eat enormous quantities of high quality food. I had already started on the perfectly salty Greek salad, quiche, pavlova, and chocolate swirls that Steph prepared for my arrival when the girls sat me down to fill me in on the house rules:

1. There is a toga next to the front door for anyone who arrives inappropriately dressed.
2. The eastern alcove is the "naughty corner" for anyone who behaves badly. (This is where my mattress was located; I'm not sure what that implied.)
3. No fire-twirling inside the house.

It was going to be a great stay.

Tuesday 12 July
Darwin to Hayes Creek, Northern Territory
178 kilometres – 9 hours 41 minutes

My time in Darwin passed at a frantic pace. Between tasks to organise the next leg of Cycle of Learning, my life was largely based around eating and socialising, and sometimes socialising while eating.

Darwin was truly a happening place. First, there were all the cyclists. I had managed to time my entry into Darwin in the same week as Andrew and Kate, Mark and Andreas, and a recumbent cyclist I had heard about but not met until Darwin. Over a few beers, we all got together and swapped notes, including our deep-seated hatred of the northerly wind blowing down the Stuart Highway, our run-ins with an unfriendly cyclist dubbed Mr Cranky, and the fact that the others had been told by numerous caravanners that the person riding my bike was a man.

I came across two other cyclists the next day in the heart of Darwin. Actually, it wasn't so much coming across them as spotting them whilst in the middle of my ice cream break, sprinting a few kilometres after them, ice cream in hand, and telling them how excited I was to see other people with BOB trailers, while I got my breath back and mopped up my melted ice cream. Simon and Jack didn't seem too bothered at being chased, and showed their trailer modifications off to me, including solar panels and extra water-bottle storage areas. They were the most dusty, dishevelled, bearded cyclists I'd met, and had true spirits of adventure. They'd started in Sydney and had been riding on the outback dirt tracks where very few cars pass by, but those that do are likely to stop and offer you a hunk of road-killed goat meat. They were headed "to Asia" and who knew precisely where the winds would take them.

Life at Steph and Nicole's was always interesting. If they'd charged as a hotel, they could have hung up their stethoscopes and retired, thanks to their steady procession of house guests. We were constantly reorganising our sleeping arrangements. I was grateful to be considered well behaved enough to transfer from the naughty corner and out onto the balcony in my tent. Steph was even the ultimate hostess in actually moving out for a while so everyone would fit. Among the visitors were Steph's sister, Bronwyn, who had put me up in Canberra, Olivia who'd hosted me in Alice Springs, and my very own sister, Claire, from Adelaide.

I also used my time in Darwin to catch up on some of my healthcare needs. My teeth had been playing up over the past few months. It had reached the stage where I had to buy smooth peanut butter instead of crunchy to avoid sending shooting pains through my head whenever I bit on something with any amount of resistance. I visited a local dentist while in town, who diagnosed me with sensitive teeth and attempted a desensitisation procedure on me. I lay back in the chair and decided that if I started being rude and not noticing when people were upset with me, then I'd know who was to blame. The other possible outcome was that the procedure would not work, in which case I was advised to chew on the other side of my mouth until I got back to Adelaide, but could continue to enjoy being a sensitive person.

I was also informed that I had an incorrect brushing technique. I elected *not* to reveal to the dentist that my toothbrushes this year had been chosen based on their weight and price. One was from a pack of three that cost me $1.50. The other two were used to clean Bike's chain. The next one had approximately six bristles. If I could have read the Thai writing on the back of the packet, I may have discovered that it had been endorsed by the International False Teeth Promotion Society. The toothbrush I was using in Darwin had been bought at an op-shop. I'm pretty sure it wasn't second-hand, though.

I had hoped that a three-week rest would fix up my Achilles tendon, but by my last day in town, I was still hobbling around without much improvement. I found a physiotherapist in the morning who showed me some exercises to strengthen my tendon, gave it some massage, and shared a biomechanical laugh with me about my literal Achilles heel also being my figurative Achilles heel. While I was explaining my situation to the physiotherapist (including why I might find it hard to have access to ice at the end of each day's riding), a voice piped up from behind the dividing curtain: "I know that lady. She's raising money for children in India." It was none other than one of the boys from a school I'd visited a few weeks ago, before school holidays started.

During my presentation there, I had tried to slip in a section on nutrition and healthy food choices by showing them the range of fruit, vegetables and nuts I was carrying with me while riding. There were a few lads with very good eyesight sitting in the front though, who'd asked why I hadn't also shown them the packet of seven finger buns they could see in the bottom of my bag.

Luckily, I didn't have any unhealthy snacks on my person for the young man to spot and point out to the physiotherapist during my consultation. I'd have hated to find out they'd be bad for my rehab.

Darwin also gave me the opportunity to lavish some attention on Bike and the rest of my gear. I decked Bike out with new water bottle holders and new handlebar grips, and stocked up all my food-based supplies. In addition, my sister gave me a new pair of cycling sandals. They were exactly the same design as my old ones, so I could continue working on the incredibly well-defined tan on the tops of my feet. In nearby Palmerston, I also found a new pair of shorts for $3 in a discount shop that I decided would be joining us around the west coast. I couldn't believe they were so cheap, until I realised that they were made from a very rare fabric that can make you sweat at any time, even while giving a speech in a well-ventilated church hall.

The other purchase I made was at an electronics shop. Before I left Adelaide, I made the decision not to bring any musical-entertainment-type devices with me. Besides the fact that I didn't own anything (except a transistor radio that has trouble picking up a signal at the best of times, let alone in the middle of the outback), I thought it would be good for my soul. I figured that it would be productive to travel around Australia fully conscious and not "switched off". If I spent all of my time switched on and thinking, maybe I would figure out the answers to the big questions (meaning of life, existence of God, how to abandon all of life's attachments, and how to eat a honey sandwich without being disturbed by flies) or at least save on a bit of thinking time later on in life. So far, I had got some very intensive thinking done, and felt I had become a stronger person for not having music to fall back on when things got tough in my head. However, 11,000 kilometres was getting near the year's quota for thinking time. I was worried I would go insane if I had to reach 12,000 kilometres without any distractions.

After a lot of deliberating, I bought myself an MP3 player. Although it cost the equivalent of quite a few bottles of golden syrup, I figured it would save me in psychiatric bills later on. It was an impressive machine, having 20 gigabytes of storage, radio, and voice recorder, maybe for those times I would need access to the Voice of Reason at the push of a button. In hindsight I think, like my Palmerston shorts, it was on sale for a reason. It didn't make my legs sweat, but all the instructions were in some eastern European language and the only station that I could tune it into was in Hindi. For all of its operating challenges, at least it was a multicultural MP3 player.

By the morning I left Darwin, I felt refreshed in many ways. I had enjoyed a depth and breadth of social interaction that I'd missed on the lonely roads. I'd fire-twirled – on the beach, so without breaking any house rules. I'd worn the emergency toga on more than one occasion. I'd accidentally won a bottle of wine while visiting a Darwin Rotary Club. I'd cooked to my heart's content, although I suspected Nicole and Steph were a little sick of my one-pot surprises – cous cous surprise, pasta surprise, rice surprise, to name a few.

But it was time to hit the road again: Western Australia awaited. Also my leg and foot tan were starting to fade, although this could have had something to do with the multiple daily showers I had taken while in Darwin. I was worried there was a direct correlation between my leg strength and my foot tan, so it was time to get moving.

It was interesting packing all my gear back into Trailer the morning I left. For the last three weeks, my stuff had been sitting around the flat, useless. Not just useless, but in the way. Or, in Nicole's words, "taking over the house". Now, all of a sudden, every object seemed vital again; playing its part in keeping Cycle of Learning and me on the road – except maybe for the two hankies that I'd bought in Alice Springs. They had so much starch in them that they were stiff and slippery and made blowing my nose a socially awkward and messy operation.

Once I was loaded up and pedalling out of town, I savoured the feeling of being on the road again. A large part of the past 21 days had been spent organising things: contacting schools and community groups, making phone calls, attending to emails, and compiling lists of things to do. However, as soon as I got back on Bike – rather unsteadily, thanks to my break – I felt all the administrative concerns, social flurry, city life and bustle slip away, and all of my riding thoughts come back: turn off my lights, check the direction of the wind, stop and stretch, assess my fruit supplies. I realised I had lost track of what phase the moon was in at the moment. It's so easy to get detached from the natural world as well as from my own body.

I enjoyed the ride to Hayes Creek. I drank heaps, didn't have to eat as much as on a normal day on the bike because I was running off the city fat that I'd accumulated, binged on music from my MP3 player, and treated myself to one of my older and more pliable hankies as I dealt with the tail end of a cold that I'd picked up somewhere. I rolled into Hayes Creek Roadhouse as night was falling, and behaved like the model cyclist. I stretched thoroughly, did all the exercises the physiotherapist set me, drank two bottles of water with cordial powder and salt to rehydrate, and even sought out some ice from the bar for my Achilles tendon. I deserved a gold star.

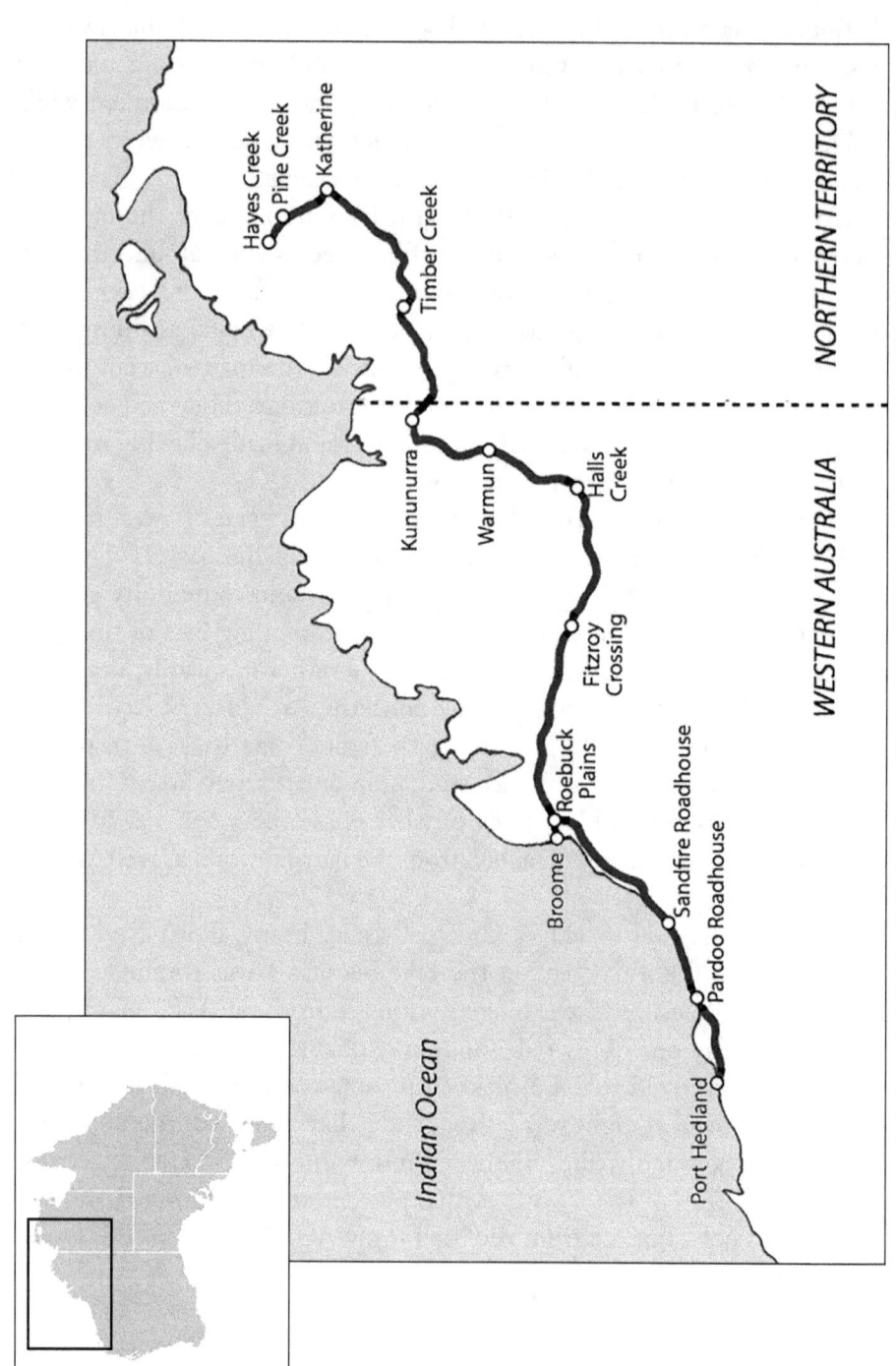

Chapter 10
Liberating the Sock

Hayes Creek – Pine Creek – Katherine – Timber Creek – Kununurra – Warmun – Spring Creek – Halls Creek – Ngumban Cliffs – Fitzroy Crossing – Broome – Roebuck Plains – Sandfire Roadhouse – Pardoo Roadhouse – Port Hedland

Totals: 14,002 kilometres – 758 hours 1 minute – $13,552

Sunday 17 July
Victoria Highway to Kununurra, Western Australia
71 kilometres – 3 hours 25 minutes

I headed back down to Katherine, then west, which took me off the Stuart Highway at last. It had been a challenging road: the vomiting, the desert craziness, the constant headwind no matter which way I was riding, the cold toes, the grumpiness ... but there had been positives too: the middle of the night serenity, the milk, the people, the convenient lack of rain.

I noticed a change in scenery as soon as I turned off onto the Victoria Highway. During my riding on the Stuart Highway, the continuous low scrubby landscape had slowly taken me over, until I could feel the almost hostile intensity of the bush beating its silent rhythm through my veins. But the Victoria Highway was lined by taller, more majestic trees. As I cruised between them, I felt like an acknowledged visitor to a softer and more welcoming land.

The vibe of the people travelling through each area felt different too. Previously, when I was travelling up and down the Stuart Highway, there seemed to be quite a few cars with lone men. I had a few dodgy encounters with drivers who had pulled over, one wanting my help in checking out his car's engine, another offering me a beer from his esky. Now that I was off the Stuart and into Western Australia, there were mostly road trains, grey nomad caravans, or cars filled with friendly families. I did have one odd confrontation with a driver, but it was more insulting than salacious. One morning a man stopped his caravan by the side of the road and purposefully hailed me down. I pulled over, wondering if he was going to make a donation or maybe ask for patent rights to my hydration system. He looked me up and down carefully then told me that I was the wrong person; he had thought I was someone called Ray. I rode off trying to convince myself that his friend's full name was Raymina or Raymondette.

The days were getting hotter, and I was making sure I dampened my bottle socks regularly to keep my water cool. I also fell into a routine of having a nap in the middle of the day. I would find myself heating up slowly to the point that I was nearly dropping off to sleep on Bike, and then doggedly trying to stay awake long enough to find a rest area to have a snooze in some shady gravel. It was an odd type of lethargy. Maybe that's what happens to crabs when they are boiled alive. I was glad I got to have a sleep at the end instead of being eaten.

The time taken by my nap meant that I often ended up riding on through sunset, then dusk and then through the first part of the night. The moon would be out to light my way, and a warm wind blowing. It was a glorious way to spend an evening.

An evening at home in the tent in the Northern Territory.

An unexpected turn of physiological events was the development of a drool problem at night. I had been waking up in the mornings to find an embarrassing pool of saliva soaking into my sleeping mat. I had a few theories. One was that my electrolytes were slightly imbalanced, leading to a fluid transfer across the surfaces of my mouth. Another was that fatigue was causing a loss of muscle control in my mouth. Or, maybe since introducing powdered milk into my muesli at breakfast, I was consuming so much dairy that I had dreams at night about chewing cud, which somehow led to my nocturnal saliva-incontinence.

On this Sunday morning, after mopping up, I rode to the NT/WA border eating carrots all the way. I was trying to finish them before I got to the quarantine station, but had to hand over the last five, which I couldn't fit in on top of the morning's muesli. With the time difference, I managed to get into Western Australia before I had woken up, which made me wonder if I should hitch a lift back to my campsite to see if I could see what I looked like when I was drooling in my sleep.

In Kununurra, I stocked up on supplies, including a pair of white socks to add to the top of the blue socks on my water bottles. I hoped the white socks would absorb less heat than the blue ones, as well as add an extra layer of insulation.

Sunday 24 July
Great Northern Highway to Fitzroy Crossing, Western Australia
180 kilometres – 8 hours 27 minutes

The last section of road I was on took me through the Kimberley. I'm sure that off Highway 1, which I had been following for much of my ride, the landscape is even more amazing, but I was feeling a little overwhelmed even by the limited landscape that I saw as I rolled through on Bike. There were some occasional moments of jaw-dropping, picture postcard beauty; but the majority of what I saw was simply awesome – in the truest sense of the word. Each time I paused my busy mind and became re-conscious of my surroundings, I was amazed, with an almost physical loss of breath, at how hugely and completely beautiful this land is. Not pretty beautiful, but wise, and layered, and quietly beautiful. At first I wanted to get my camera out to try and capture each moment, but soon I realised it was pointless. For a start, a photo cannot communicate the feeling of a place; and as soon as the desire to hold on to the moment arose, I'd lost something of what made it so special. I heard the Buddhist monk on my shoulder telling me that if I spent my time trying to preserve this beauty for the future I wouldn't be able to experience it fully in the present. I promised to leave my camera in my bag and the monk gave me a one-handed round of applause before departing.

Interestingly, I found that the times of day I was most appreciative of my surroundings were during my toilet breaks. Earlier in the year I felt a bit guilty when I dawdled over toilet or food stops and felt like I should be rushing to get back on the road again. By this point of the year though, I let myself slow down and enjoy what was around me. To be more tasteful, I will explain the joys of a good toilet break in verse.

Call of Nature

Hours of mindful rehydration,
Some sugar, salt, to water add.
Grease the joints and please the rider
Cycling slow through hot outback.
Constant fluid sipped warmly
Makes its way to journey's end
Through the veins and finally lingers
In the bladder; time distends.
Minutes pass, surveilling cycling,
Looking for a place to stop.
Somewhere close with ample cover
So none will see the cyclist squat.
Apply the brakes when gladly found
A densely bushy patch of land;
Remove the gloves and helmet sweaty,
Find tissues for the task at hand.
Resting bike by side of road
Turn back on highway, face the scrub.
My sandals tread the sandy redness,
Arid soil still feeds the shrubs.
See the hollows, see the hillocks,
See the rocks, the termite mounds;
Revealed to me, the land's dimensions
When walking in this landscape found.
Metres from the roadside edges
Behind a bush I stand and pause,
Look left and right for watching traffic,

When coast is clear, I drop my shorts
Pale backside meets muscly thighs;
Halfway to my knees a line
Tanned by sun and dirty living
Tanned till sandals leave their sign.
Squat in red soil facing bushes,
Watch the tiny insects climb,
Find cobwebs adorning branches,
Busy bush with life sublime.
Wait till truck has passed me hiding,
Pull up shorts and stand up straight,
Shorts tattered with seams unwinding,
Shirt sweat-stained in faded state.
Take my time walking back,
Feel no rush to stand on road.
While red soil is under foot,
Nature calls its timeless ode.

It would have been nice if all this grace and beauty I was seeing had rubbed off on me a bit. Instead, my attractiveness levels were plunging. This was due to the brown dust that I was continuously coated in, the lack of showers, my permanent sunburn and the interference from flies.

The constant, visible posse of flies hanging out on my person, besides forcing me to wear an unflattering fly net, also sabotaged a potentially amorous moment at Turkey Creek last week.

I'd spent the afternoon with a nice fellow, and we were chatting at the picnic tables outside the roadhouse. During a pause in a deep and meaningful part of our conversation, I noted a concentrated gaze and a lean forward from my companion. As I prepared myself for a kiss, the gaze become even more concentrated on my mouth as the fellow awkwardly pointed out that I had a fly stuck between my

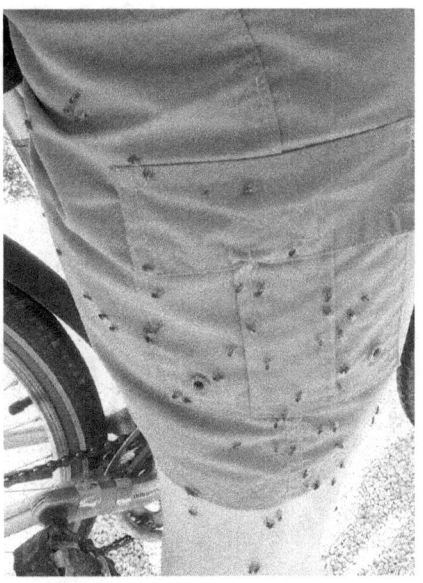

Some of the flies I met on the trip.

teeth. I removed it, made my excuses and executed a quick getaway towards Halls Creek. That is, as quickly as I could manage on a bike loaded down with 18 kilograms of equipment, nine more of water and a few extra kilos of smug flies hitching a lift.

Once I reached Halls Creek the next day, I tried to put my oral hygiene issues behind me by focusing on the water situation. Halls Creek to Fitzroy Crossing is nearly 300 kilometres, with no water available in between. I could probably have carried enough for the two-day ride, but I liked to know I'd have plenty of water in case I was delayed by a headwind or needed to refill a swimming pool along the way.

I bought a ten-litre cask of water from the Halls Creek supermarket and spent the afternoon carrying it around from caravan to caravan on the main street. I was hoping to find someone who would drop it off for me halfway to Fitzroy Crossing. I couldn't work out why it was taking so long to find someone to help until I realised that a dirty girl with nothing but a backpack and ten litres of water, asking people if they're going to Fitzroy Crossing, may give a bad first impression. They obviously thought I was

Heading to Turkey Creek, Western Australia.
Photographer: Mark Brenmuhl

a hitchhiker who would need lots of toilet stops and leave their car seat needing a shampoo. I finally found someone who listened long enough to agree to drop the cask off.

It eventuated that the ride to Fitzroy was wonderfully smooth and blessed with a tailwind. I reached my water cask before my bottles were empty, but still felt very smug with myself for coordinating the water drop. I stopped for the night at a rest area, with enough water on my bike for a long shower if I chose to take it, and then made good time to arrive in Fitzroy Crossing by noon yesterday, eager to make use of the last town before Broome, 430 kilometres away. During my chores around town, I had a number of interesting encounters.

In the library, I got chatting to a traveller at the computers who happened to live one street away from my usual address in Adelaide. I also spent some time with a book on boab trees, my favourite flora of the moment. I love how they are perfectly named and look so upside down.

After a stop at the supermarket, I was loaded up with milk, fruit and bread, but unable to carry my next cask of water. Luckily, I met a friendly couple that offered to drop it off at the caravan park for me. I also bumped into a motorcycling couple, Marlene and Steve. As with Lars and Ruth in the Northern Territory, I had been crossing paths with Marlene, Steve and their dog intermittently over the past few weeks and we had a chat each time. Compared with Lars and Ruth, they were seeing a much happier cyclist. Instead of coming across me every time I was collapsed somewhere – physically or emotionally – in a dehydrated, exhausted stupor, Marlene and Steve tended to find me eating reduced-price bakery products, wheeling happily into a caravan park, or riding down the highway with the wind at my back.

In the caravan park, I happened to set up next to a family of Fitzies. They were Fitzgibbonses and I am a Fitzpatrick, but since most people accidentally call all of us Fitzgeralds, we felt practically related. It was very appropriate that it was in Fitzroy Crossing that all our Fitz stars aligned. They had only limited success in plying me with stir-fry and alcohol, but then discovered that they could take charge of my water tomorrow and were finally satisfied that they were helping me enough. I repaid their kindness by almost stepping on their pet budgie.

Before I went to sleep, I was paid a visit by another caravanner who wanted to tell me he had passed me numerous times in the past few weeks and had always thought I was a man.

A consistent theme of the day was that everyone I met was perplexed by the socks on my water bottles. Maybe the new white pair was drawing more attention with their whiteness. After explaining the functionality of my dual-sock-water-refrigeration system so many times, I felt compelled to add a fourth item to Cycle of Learning's aims. Goal 4: to liberate socks into non-foot-related uses for the betterment of society.

Wednesday 27 July
Broome to Roebuck Plains, Western Australia
52 kilometres – 2 hours 55 minutes

The ride to Broome was notable for the range of cows in various states of life and death. The unfenced roads meant that they could wander wherever they like. At times, there were a few hanging around the side of the highway, not caring when cars drove past. They just stood, stared, and chewed their cud. I had no problem with that; it was the cows' prerogative. What was bothering me, though, was that this same herd of cattle, so unperturbed by cars, would get one glimpse of me on my bike, moo in fright, look terrified and run away, as if I was going to pedal after them, wring their necks and make cow and peanut butter sandwiches. I didn't necessarily expect them to know that I was vegetarian, but surely they should have realised that they could beat me in a street fight.

If I had been fast enough to catch one, I would have dragged it over to one of the bloated cow corpses on the side of the road. Then I would have sat it down, pointed out the skid marks from the road train, drawn some diagrams on a whiteboard and made it understand that trucks and cars are a lot more dangerous than bikes, even if the riders of those bikes have awesome leg muscles like mine.

I probably shouldn't have been criticising the cows for their social skills; mine left a lot to be desired at the time too. At Willare Bridge Roadhouse on Monday, I stopped to buy a litre of fresh milk. I drank the milk from the carton feeling a little out of place amid all the singlet tops, golden suntans and lithe legs of the hordes of Europeans who had disembarked from a convoy of tourist buses stopped at the roadhouse. I started feeling a bit embarrassed by my disintegrating clothes, weathered skin and generally dishevelled appearance. My scruffiness was amplified by the fact I'd been getting behind in my hair-brushing schedule. The "comb" I bought in

Chapter 10: Liberating the Sock   121

Darwin tended not to comb so much as to remove any strands of hair that offered resistance. This led me to lose motivation to attend to my hair, and left me a bit odd-looking.

I tried to compensate for my unkempt appearance and smelliness by showing off how hard-core I was. I used a number of water bottles full of bore water to hose down first my insulating sock system and then myself with a tough "showers and refrigerators are for sissies" attitude. Not surprisingly, I didn't make many friends at this stop.

My stop in Broome was a flurry of phone calls, emails, laundry, and some serious eating. My work in this last field made me realise what a large range of high-quality milks and yogurts Western Australia has. I did my best to sample them all, and the only disappointment I have to report is the spearmint-flavoured milk. It was one of those foods that I figured sounded so bad that it would have to be good, but I was wrong.

In my evening in Broome, I caught up with some new friends, Danielle and Craig. Maureen, my godmother, had passed through this part of the world earlier in the year and, being Maureen, had got to know the staff at the hotel she was staying at. One of them was Danielle, a young woman on a working holiday visa from the UK. Always the networker, Maureen arranged for us to catch up when I got to Broome.

Maureen has impeccable taste, and so it was a great evening with Danielle and her partner Craig. We swapped stories of our experiences in India, as they had spent time there helping to set up microfinance projects. They would normally have scored double points from me for arriving on bikes, but I was secretly disappointed. I had assumed they would be driving a big, strong, motorised vehicle, which I could ask them to use to drop the ten litres of water I'd just bought back to my caravan park. After they rode off into the night, I sat staring first at Bike, then at the water, then at Bike, then at the water, until I mustered sufficient energy to deal with the situation. I apologised to Bike, then forced the plastic container onto one of the handlebars and rode the seven kilometres back to the park using a level of balance and upper body strength that should probably have been reserved for wrangling the cows into my road safety classroom. Bike groaned and had a series of gear spasms throughout the journey, but was speaking to me again by the morning.

Before leaving town that afternoon I had recruited some water carriers at the caravan park gate, hung out at Cable Beach, chatted with passers-by, and was interviewed by the local paper. Afterwards, I took my time with some pre-departure chores since I had just a few kilometres to ride out of town before nightfall. I decided to make a premature departure, though, when I realised that I was consuming milk at such an exponential rate that I was in danger of triggering "The Great Broome Milk Shortage of 2005". I suddenly understood why cows had been running away from me. I finished off my last litre of 99-cent mocha milk and rode the 33 kilometres east to the Roebuck Plains Roadhouse, which is right where the highway heads south. From here, it is 290 kilometres to the next roadhouse, and over 600 kilometres to the next town. I thought the isolation was just what I needed to put myself on a milk detox program.

Monday 1 August
South Hedland, Western Australia
51 kilometres – 2 hours 37 minutes

Leaving Roebuck Plains Roadhouse on Thursday, I felt the excitement of riding in a new direction. In my mental map of Australia, I started going down instead of across. Once I checked a more accurate map, I realised that I was still riding in pretty much the same direction as before. Things felt different though. The scenery had become more open and there was a coastal feel to the area. I first noticed this with a damp tent, my first in four months (excluding the effects of my drooling problem).

On the ride down to Port Hedland, I regularly pulled over for chats with travellers along the way. Generally, whenever I was hailed down to talk to people, there were a few things I liked to do as they approached:

A. If singing, stop.

B. If listening to music, remove my earphones.

C. Take off as many of my head garments (sunglasses, fly net, helmet, hat, zinc cream) as possible. This was to make myself appear less scary, especially if young children were present.

D. Remove the hanky from the leg of my bike shorts and put it into my pocket. Although a handy place for hanky storage, the bulge brought unwanted attention to my mammoth legs.

E. Unclip my sandals from my pedals.

One afternoon, near Sandfire Roadhouse, a car slowed down next to me, as the occupants wanted a chat. They took me by surprise and consequently I managed only A through D of my socialising routine. My headgear was off and my hanky was safely in my pocket when they stopped. I stopped. They called "Hello" through the car window. I called "Hello" back. They asked where I was headed. Having still not completed step E yet, I fell over sideways. Very embarrassed, I jumped up and finished the conversation, pretending that I didn't have blood dripping down my leg.

Later I met someone who did not require a five-step process to become friends with: a small toy dog I found by the side of the road. I'd spotted an eclectic range of stuff by the side of the road thus far: shoes, hats, tables, mobile phones, toy cars, real cars, jewellery, clothes, CDs. I had a rule of not picking up any of the things that looked interesting, because I would have been stopping constantly and ended up becoming a travelling junk yard. However, I felt a strange affinity with this dog, so I picked him up and found a spot for him on the back of my seat, next to my bright orange spade. He was much lighter than ten litres of water so Bike didn't object and we all agreed to call him Ralf.

The next night I pulled in at Sandfire Roadhouse, where, on the way to the shower, I was approached by another guest who informed me that he'd heard of a girl riding from Broome to Perth. He'd also apparently passed a man cycling with a trailer earlier that evening, 40 kilometres out from Sandfire. He was hoping I had met these other cyclists, but I suspect they were both me.

From Sandfire, the winds picked up, the landscape became flat, and the vegetation low and prickly. All these factors made toilet breaks more challenging, but I continued to enjoy taking my time at stops, as well as being more leisurely in my morning and evening routines. Something about being so far from big cities, away from people

Ralf, bringing up the rear.

and immersed in the practicalities of riding these long stretches, made other issues fade into the background. Until a few weeks earlier, I'd been spending a large proportion of my time worrying about what more could be done to achieve Cycle of Learning's financial and educational goals. There, way out west, even though I was yet to speak to any school, church or service club in the state, it was obvious that there was not much I could do about it right then, so there was no point worrying.

With all this worrying headspace going vacant, I focused my concern on my hair. Something horrible had happened a few days ago and I couldn't figure out if it was because I was using that nasty comb too much or too little. I decided eventually to experiment with extending my hair combing intervals from two days to three. Additionally, until I got things sorted out, I made the decision to leave all my headgear in place whenever I met people.

Sunday's ride into Port Hedland grew increasingly gusty and the landscape changed at a rapid rate. The flat plains soon became hills dotted with trees. A few creeks and rivers appeared, and I saw things sticking up out of the ground in the distance. At times like that, I realised that this year's story would have had a much better scenic commentary if I'd chosen to pack my glasses.

The wind was slowly changing direction, and for the last 70 kilometres I had the mother of all tail winds. It was incredible to be a part of this force. As I picked up speed, I clicked through my gears until I entered a rhythm that matched the wind so perfectly that it felt as if I was completely still, but flying at the same time. I felt no breeze, my clothes didn't flap, flies crawled undisturbed over my fly net, sweat rolled down my face without cooling me down and there was no whoosh of wind passing my ears. I was part of a tremendous energy: the wind, the road, Bike, my body – we all worked together as we gradually sped up to 29, 30, 34, 36 km/h.

The winds became increasingly bossy as I got closer to Port Hedland, and I wasn't at all surprised to see a council sign announcing: *The current cyclone status is …* The section revealing the status was missing; I had suspicions it had been blown away.

I finally made it to a caravan park on the far side of town and nearly passed out when the manager informed me that unpowered sites cost $28. I told him I would have to think about it, and he suddenly became a lot friendlier and pulled out a map of the area to show me where I could find the other caravan parks. I may have been a little paranoid, but I got the feeling he took one look at me, my hair, and my BO (you know BO is bad when it's visible to the naked eye), and decided to set a fee that I would be unlikely to pay.

I retraced my route and stopped at a supermarket where a lovely woman whom I happened to have met while in Mackay, Queensland, served me. Chance meetings like this probably should have surprised me more, but at the time they just seemed to make sense. The supermarket also provided me with some chocolate to keep me moving along the final 20 kilometres I had to ride to reach an affordable caravan park. While going back past the huge salt hills, harvested by the local saltworks, I was overtaken by Andrew, Kate and their children Joanna and Matthew, who informed me that they, too, were headed for the caravan park that didn't mind what your hair looked or smelled like. We ended up at the same caravan park and spent the evening under the stars, looking at Joanna's rock collection, sharing stories and muffins and wondering what lay on the road ahead.

The next day, Monday, was a rest day in South Hedland. To be more accurate, it was a rest day for Trailer and the tent, but not for Bike or me. We two ended up riding more than 50 kilometres to travel between Port Hedland and South Hedland, but it was the first day since Darwin that I hadn't arrived or left somewhere. In the time saved in setting up and dismantling camp, I indulged in some personal grooming – I cut my fingernails and toenails, put my sleeping bag out in the sun, had two showers, let some soap loose on my clothes and on myself, and even combed my hair pre- and post-wash. These tasks took intense physical and mental preparation, though, so I spent the better part of the morning eating nearly a whole box of cereal and relaxing with Andrew and his family.

I saw Joanna and Matthew doing some of their schoolwork during the day. They were incredibly literate for four and six year olds, and could even write more neatly than I do. To be honest, possibly any one of the dead kangaroo carcasses I passed on my way into town could also do so. I thought I might draw up a work contract for these two to take care of my administration for the rest of the year, hoping to convince them to be paid in peanut butter sandwiches or pretty rocks that I might find on the side of the road.

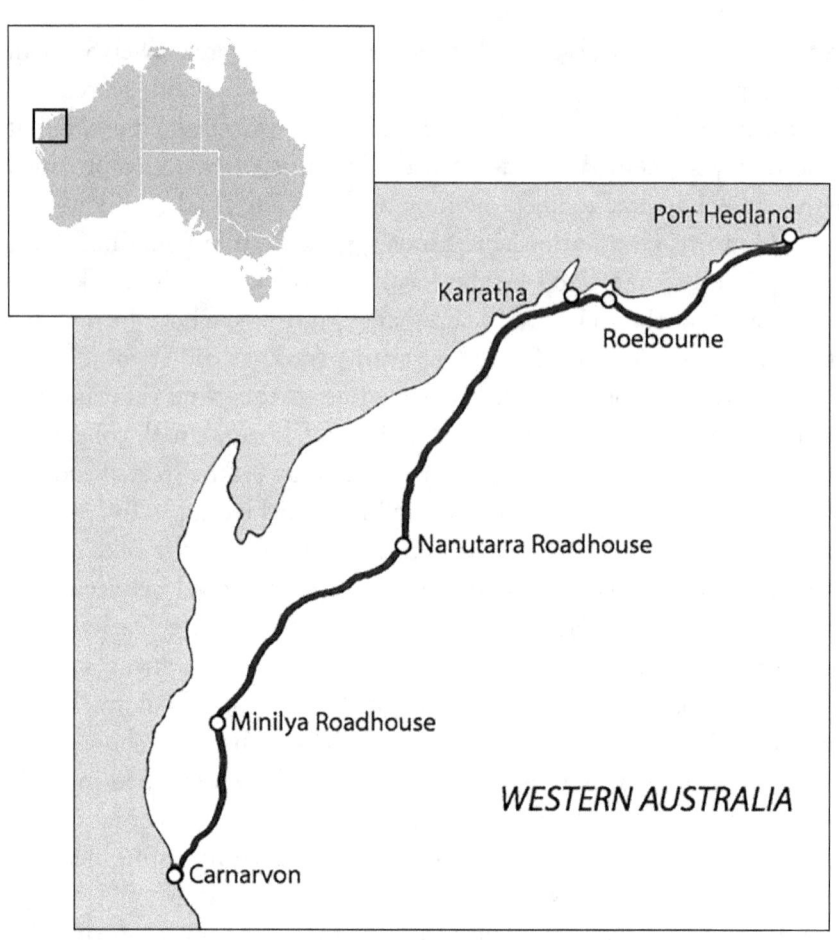

Chapter 11
The Fifth-Best Cycle Fundraiser in Town

Port Hedland – Roebourne – Karratha – Nanutarra Roadhouse – Minilya Roadhouse – Carnarvon

Totals: 15,076 kilometres – 810 hours 28 minutes – $14,275

Friday 5 August
Karratha to North Western Coastal Highway, Western Australia
115.39 kilometres – 5 hours 57 minutes

The ride from Port Hedland to Karratha felt different. On the Wednesday when I set out, it had been warm but overcast, and I'd felt a few drops of rain. This being the first precipitation I'd seen in months, I got a bit overexcited and completely waterproofed my gear – prematurely, I finally realised, since I was graced with no more than a dozen drops all afternoon.

The road also felt different. It seemed narrower – even though I knew it wasn't – and a bit claustrophobic, even though the landscape was bare in all directions. Eventually, I felt strange too, and started worrying that I was having a premonition of imminent doom for me or a loved one. In retrospect, it was probably the result of listening to a Moby album three times through in a row, combined with the fact I'd eaten a whole loaf of soy and linseed bread the day before.

Besides the rain, the other "first time in thousands of kilometres" event was seeing two towns in one day. I passed through Roebourne on Wednesday before I hit my final destination of Karratha in the late morning. I hadn't learnt my lesson from Port Hedland – that I should research accommodation options before riding aimlessly around town – and ended up covering 30 kilometres before I found a caravan park to stay in.

Once I'd found the caravan park and had tidied myself up, I presented myself for my first official engagement of Western Australia. I was a guest speaker for the local Soroptimist group and they absolutely made up for the 2000 appointmentless kilometres I'd ridden to get there. For a start, the work they were doing was impressive. They had a range of local and international projects on the go with foci on health, education, the environment, the status of women, and international goodwill and harmony. I shared the story of Karuppusamy with the Soroptimist Club.

Karuppusamy

My name is Karuppusamy, I am 13 years old and in Year 8. My father works as a coolie and I am an only child. My village only has 28 houses, which have been constructed by the government. There is no school or hospital but we do have a water tank and a community television.

When I go back to my village I work collecting beans. I work from 9 am till 5 pm and earn 35 rupees a day for my family. I don't like the work because I have to carry heavy loads. I also help my mother by fetching water for her. My father sometimes comes to the hostel to visit me, which makes me so happy.

Karuppusamy, age 13, 2004.

I enjoy the tuition I get by staying at the hostel. I do well in school and it feels really good when I can answer the questions I am asked. When I am older I would like to be a doctor. It would make me feel proud to be a doctor in my village.

Life at the PEAK hostels

The downside of the children attending the PEAK hostels is that they are away from their families. It is a difficult decision to make – send children away for the majority of the year and they can access education, or keep them home and they can't. Understandably, a lot of parents choose not to send their children to school. PEAK staff spend time every school holiday travelling village to village to meet families, reinforcing the importance that education has for their children, reassuring them of the care their children will receive in the hostels, and staying abreast of the social issues that the Dalit and Adhivasi families are dealing with.

Even being away from their families, weekends and afternoons at the Siruvar Ilum involved most of the same going-ons for the children as any rural Tamil household, just on a much larger scale. Between homework and play times, there were lots of jobs for the children to do. I never could figure out just how everyone organised themselves, but at chore time, suddenly small groups would form, older children calling the younger ones away from the end of their games.

One group would head for the forest to collect the firewood needed for cooking meals. The area close to the college and hostel is heavily wooded and safe for the children to be in. In other parts of the Kodai hills, women, whose job it is to collect wood and water as well as doing most of the other domestic tasks, aren't so lucky. Without trees and their useful fallen branches nearby, they walk, sometimes for hours, through the hills to land where they can find enough fuel for their cooking fires. Unfortunately much of this land belongs to plantation owners, and I heard stories of some landowners demanding sexual favours in exchange for firewood. To bring home enough wood they choose the longest branches, tie a shawl around them, balance the bundle on their head and walk home with a particular gait. The weight is extraordinary and I would see women heading downhill with their load extending out as far as three or four metres before and behind them. Their focus is intense as they trot downhill with the momentum and presence of a truck – other traffic knows to make way for these women.

The children luckily only had a short way to go, and didn't have to gather such large loads. The older children were already skilled at spotting the large, dry branches, while the smaller ones, and the inexperienced Australian, could only manage to pick up the odd damp stick from the forest floor.

Back at the hostel, some students would be sweeping, with the ubiquitous Indian handleless brooms that are made by tying a bundle of thin twigs together. A few older girls would be helping prepare for the next meal – sorting, washing and cutting vegetables with a blade mounted onto a heavy rectangle of wood which the girls would balance with a foot while they sat with it on the ground, using both hands to push the carrots or beans over the blade.

As they would in their family home, the older children would be called on by adults to do extra jobs – serving dinner, fetching water from the hand pump in the corner of the hostel yard – and in turn took it upon themselves to organise the younger ones, give them instructions for their chores and scold them for uncombed hair or being late into the dinner line.

Some afternoons a few boys and girls would fetch sacks of rice from the storeroom under the walkway that linked Sacred Heart College with the Grihini quarters. Two of them would help to hoist a sack onto the head of a third, as they got ready to balance their loads back to the hostel. Sometimes I'd grab a sack and put it on my own head, but inevitably the children would panic, visibly worried that I was about to damage my neck. Having a group of eight year olds worry about my foreign spine while they loaded the bags of rice onto their own heads was humbling and a sad reminder of the divisions that these children already recognised between me and them. As much as I got to know and appreciate these children and their ways of life, a huge gulf existed between us, unfair as it was, purely because of where we were born.

*

After my slot as guest speaker with the Soroptimists, we enjoyed an excellent meal, and by the time the meeting was coming to a close, I started thinking about the dark, hilly ride home ahead of me. But then someone from the hotel appeared in the suite we were using for the meeting, and gave me the key so I could use the room overnight. It seems the Soroptimists have another secret focus: providing accommodation to tent-dwelling guest speakers.

The next day I discovered the Soroptimist women had been working their Soroptimist magic all over town, organising everything I could want. First, they lined up a radio interview in the local ABC studios. Next, I was called by a school with Soroptimist connections that asked me to visit the same day, and then I discovered a $10-all-you-can-eat buffet. I never found out how the Soroptimists were involved in the last of these, but I was sure they must have been, somehow. Finally, I was invited along on a trip to some nearby gullies to see the exquisite local Aboriginal rock art with Stewart, the husband of a Soroptimist I had met the previous night. In true small town fashion, one of the others along on the excursion was Dave whom I had met earlier that day at the ABC studio.

My last day in town brought me even more respect for the good people of Karratha. In the morning, an internet cafe insisted on giving me internet access for free, having heard me on the radio the day before. Then, as I was sending off some emails, a police officer came in and, instead of arresting anyone, gave me a donation.

The school I spoke at obviously had high educational standards, since the students figured out for themselves what the socks on my water bottles were for. They also figured out the point of my bright orange spade at the back of my seat, wedged between two water-bottle holders. I overheard one lad daring his friend to touch it, and I don't think it was because they wanted to signal a search plane with it.

Friday 12 August
Carnarvon to North West Coastal Highway, Western Australia
89 kilometres – 3 hours 57 minutes

The 550 kilometres from Karratha to Carnarvon was broken up nicely by a few roadhouses, the Robe River and a regular parade of passers-by giving me encouragement, conversation and the odd donation. What I loved about these outback places was that you didn't need a reason to interact with other people. It was easy just to wander over to someone and have a pointless chat. For the truckies, travellers and roadhouse staff, it was such a small thing in their day to smile at someone and share a short conversation, or even a wave as they passed me on the road. For me, though, all these small gestures accumulated to a wonderful feeling of connectedness and acceptance.

I scheduled nearly a full rest day at Minilya Roadhouse to have access to a payphone for a follow-up interview with Pilbara ABC. I made it to the phone in time and then confused the roadhouse staff by asking for a campsite at 7:45 in the morning. I thought I had a good plan. While resting and rehydrating I would have lots of time to clean Bike, myself and my clothes, without the distractions of supermarkets, internet, fresh milk or mobile phone coverage. I would also have the time and energy to deal with my hair. The three-day plan wasn't working, neither for my hair nor for the comb. Prongs had broken off in the last few attempts at combing and I'd started noticing a lot of moths around my campsites at night. I wasn't sure how I would handle it if I found out they were coming out of my hair.

In theory, my rest day sounded like the perfect plan, but in practice, the "day" part of the concept mucked things up. First, there were too many flies outside, so I ended up sitting in my tent sweating more profusely than when I was riding. These were hardly ideal conditions in which to sleep or even simply relax comfortably on my inflatable mattress: I just left sweat patches on it. Second, my big plans for rehydration looked problematic. Around the caravan park there were numerous signs saying that if people needed to request drinking water, it would be given in small amounts only. I limited my initial requests (which were essential to replace what I was sweating out in my tent), and wasn't sure if the ten litres I would need for tomorrow would classify as a "small amount".

During my first water-sourcing venture I had an interesting lecture from the fellow manning the reception. He informed me that I had massive legs, was sunburnt, would never be able to wear normal leg-wear again, and would look like a prune by the time I reached home. I couldn't hold that conversation against him though, since later in the day, without hesitation, he handed over the better part of a 15-litre container of spring water, and provided some local tips for the road ahead.

After our chat, I decided to go find a mirror and see what stage of pruney sun damage I was in. I was pleasantly surprised: not by my hideous sunburn, but by the fact that my hair was looking great. Instead of passing some point of no return as I had feared, it had gone nice and curly in a way that it never had before.

That gift of water got me through the night and into Carnarvon. I reached town in the early afternoon and made my way to the supermarket. I came across some caravanners I'd met earlier, who had given me tinned peaches and ice cream, then a Japanese cyclist I'd met in Alice Springs, and, finally, a promisingly heavy loaf of banana bread on sale for $1.50. My rule of thumb is that any bakery product involving banana must be good; unfortunately, I was proven wrong with this one. Not only was it bad banana bread, its texture issues led to my thumb as well as four other fingers being required to give it my best shot and at least get my money's worth from it. The sight of a grotty girl in a fluoro vest gorging on a fistful of gooey brown mush did seem to scare a few passing pedestrians. It was times like those that I wished I had a sign to place next to me saying: *Please excuse me. I have ridden 150 kilometres today and haven't seen a supermarket in four days.* I would have a flip-over section to replace "supermarket" with "shower", "fresh milk", "hairbrush" or "all you can eat buffet" as the need arose.

I spent three nights in Carnarvon. After the first, I realised that I needed to invest in some tracksuit pants again. I'd left my old pair in Darwin, but now that I was riding further south, the nights were cold and the mornings damp. I found a replacement pair in an establishment clearly signed as a menswear shop. They were lovely and warm, but I felt a bit embarrassed, particularly when I realised that nearly all of my clothes were either made for men and/or had been worn by men before they reached the op-shop from which I bought them. No wonder I'd been having some gender identity issues on the road.

My second night in town I dined with Kate, Andrew, Joanna and Matthew at a pizza place proclaiming itself as having "The fifth best pizza in the world – voted by our customers". We hoped that their customers were very well travelled, since we had not seen any, let alone four other, pizza establishments in the region. Kate added to my cross-dressing regrets by informing me that there was a small department store in Carnarvon's back streets where I almost definitely would have found some warm pants in the women's section. To make it worse, the next day when I was back in the supermarket, avoiding banana bread, I noticed tracksuit pants that were $8 cheaper than the ones I'd bought yesterday, and in no way advertised as being for men. Since when did supermarkets sell clothes?

Half an hour later, while drowning my sorrows in a carton of unisex chocolate milk on the street outside, I was surprised to spot two bikes with BOB trailers attached. I staked out the shop front and discovered they belonged to a duo also from Adelaide. Sean and Tim were riding around Australia, unsupported and self-funded, to raise money for leukaemia research. I was starting to think that someone should set up a support group or maybe a credit union for all of us round-Australia fundraising cyclists. By the time I left their company, I was extremely impressed with them for the following reasons:

- They had an up-pace schedule to get them back to Adelaide in a month's time for the annual pedal-prix.
- They had rigged up a system to attach huge bottles of water to the back of their trailers. I closely inspected these and would have taken pictures with a miniature spy camera, if I'd had one, for future reference.
- They had found an impressive edible bargain, not in the bakery section where I usually found mine, but in a supermarket area where I had never yet ventured: the patisserie section. The cake they bought involved cream, food colouring, decorations and icing sugar. It gave an air of sophistication to its consumption on the footpath that I had never attained with my un-decorated banana breads.
- I couldn't say for sure, but the bandanas on their heads led me to suspect they had broken my hair-washing record.
- They were drinking one-litre cartons of flavoured milk.

I concluded my time in Carnarvon with visits to the local high school and the School of the Air. It was interesting to talk with the students who lived out on stations, and to compare the sort of work that they do on their families' stations with the work that kids around Kodaikanal often have to do to help their families. We thought the differences came down to the fact that whereas the School of the Air students are still able to learn a lot with the help of the teachers and technology here in Australia, many of the young people in Kodaikanal don't have the chance to get an education at all. Through the wonders of School of the Air radio and computer link-ups, we looked together on the Cycle of Learning website at the profile of Murugalakshmi.

Murugalakshmi

My name is Murugalakshmi. I am 16 years old and in Year 9 at school. The people in my village work in agriculture in vegetable gardens: men might earn 50 rupees a day, while women earn 40 rupees a day. They leave for work at 6 o'clock in the morning, and return anywhere between 2 o'clock and 6 o'clock in the afternoon. When I go back to my village, I work as a coolie, and also wash cooking pots and get water for my family.

The Dalit community I am from are not happy, because they are slaves to the caste people. They do jobs such as sweeping in front of the caste houses and washing caste people's things, so that the caste people will give them their leftover food to eat. If we don't listen to what the higher-caste people tell us, they won't give us any work or pay us our wages. The caste people tell one another if a Dalit has done anything against them, so there will be no work for any of us. People's homes and teashops have separate cups for the Dalits to use.

I enjoy studying. At home, I don't talk to people outside my family, but at school, I talk with a lot of different people, and learn how to get along with them and how to have respect for people. In the future, I want to be a teacher to teach people who haven't gone to school.

*

I gave a final "over and out" to the School of the Air kids, and headed towards Geraldton in the early afternoon, with the wind at my back. Although the wind was in my favour, the flies weren't. I was almost slowed down by the drag created as I rode through swarms of them. Often, when wearing my fly net, I would smirk at the flies outside it, in a taunting "you can't get me" kind of way, but today I didn't dare. There were so many I was terrified they'd decide to prove me wrong.

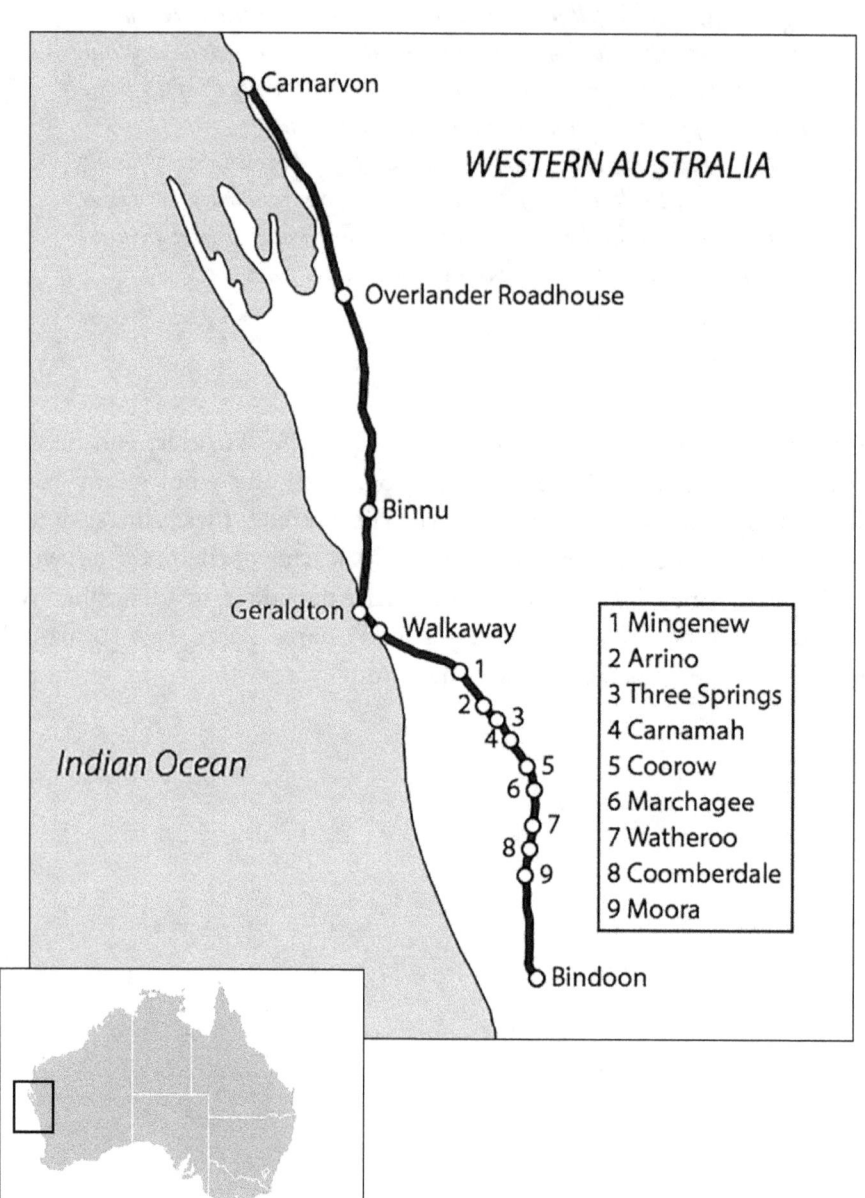

Chapter 12
Escaping the Outback

Overlander Roadhouse – Binnu – Geraldton – Walkaway –
Mingenew – Arrino – Three Springs – Carnamah – Coorow –
Marchagee – Watheroo – Coomberdale – Moora – Bindoon

Totals: 15,917 kilometres – 862 hours 22 minutes – $15,247

Saturday 13 August
North West Coastal Highway to Overlander Roadhouse, Western Australia
123 kilometres – 7 hours 24 minutes

Today was the day Trailer broke.

Over the past few weeks, I had been experiencing vague feelings of something being not quite right with the mechanical state of Bike and Trailer. It started a few weeks ago when I discovered some bolts were missing from my water-bottle holders. Then a steady assault of punctures began. Then my flagpole fell off. The latest symptom was a persistent rattliness and wobbliness that told me there was some sort of disunity between Trailer and Bike.

This morning, the sounds and wobbling had cranked up a notch, leading me to stop and investigate occasionally. All the possibilities – loose wheel, puncture, unevenly packed Trailer, drunkenness – were eliminated one by one, leaving one very confused rider and two very rattly metal entities. My frustration grew, as the world dumped increasingly annoying things onto my plate.

It started with flies and headwind, which led into a drizzle that left me feeling sweaty, slimy, shivery and sniffly all at once. Later in the day, at a roadhouse, I was accosted by a man who, when I responded to his questions about what I was doing, felt the need to tell me – in a round-about way – that I was a bad fundraiser because I didn't have any signs on Bike or Trailer promoting my cause. Then he made me feel more of a failure because I was using my legs and hadn't broken a world record – yes, he'd run into Handcycle Oz up the road. Even in my normal life I don't take criticism well, and with this year's chronic fundraising neuroses

I'd become even more sensitive. Obviously the procedure the dentist performed in Darwin had not worked.

I hit the highway trying to think of as many reasons as possible to justify my lack of advertising. I couldn't come up with many, so turned my attention back to Trailer and his vocals. I pulled out my Allen key and twisted something on Bike's axle near where Trailer hooks on. Instead of tightening the thing, I broke it. It was an important part too, given that it kept Trailer and Bike connected. Actually, "important" doesn't do this part justice; I would go so far as to classify it as "essential".

I did my best to remain calm, and used a hose clamp, some gaffer tape, and a piece of string in such a combination that it should all get me a bit further down the road. And if it didn't, I still had a garbage bag, band-aids, and half a bottle of golden syrup up my sleeve.

My repairs to Bike and Trailer held for a few more days, all the way to the bike shop in Geraldton, although I did start suspecting the incident was part of a larger plot to prevent me from leaving "the Outback". The Outback officially finishes at the Murchison River, and it threw everything it could at me to stop me crossing the boundary.

On Tuesday, packing up to leave the Overlander Roadhouse, I found that the morning damp had penetrated my clothes and merged with the residual sweat of two days' riding. I never knew getting dressed could be such a revolting experience, and I was nearly dry retching as I pulled my cold, clammy, smelly gear on. If the Outback thought a trick like that would make me turn around and ride back up to warmer, drier places, it was wrong. I soldiered on in my slimy clothes, trying to reassure myself with the fact that there was a roadhouse just 45 kilometres away. Every kilometre felt like ten, as a huge headwind screamed into me and the road rose and fell in endless hills. They were the useless sort that were the wrong gradient, not letting me build up any momentum coming down, and making me expend too much energy riding up. The surface of the road was rough too, slowing me down even more because of the extra resistance.

Physically and emotionally exhausted, I finally crept into Billabong Roadhouse and collapsed over iced coffee and hot chips. The sugar, salt and fat revived me only enough to conclude that I really didn't want to go back out there again. The Outback almost had me beaten. Once an hour had passed, though, I grudgingly gave up the idea of living in Billabong Roadhouse for the rest of my life and decided to try the "ignore it and it will go away" technique on the riding conditions.

I donned hat and sunglasses to block out all but a metre of road in front of me, cranked up Crowded House on my MP3 player, and pedalled as slowly as possible in a very low gear, so as not to disturb myself too much. It worked a treat: the wind died down, the road flattened out and, before I knew it, I was knocking off the kilometres at a reasonable rate.

The next morning was hideously cold. The process of packing up the wet tent left my fingers so numb that I had to squash them under my armpits and scrunch up my face. By the time I opened my eyes again, the sun was up, and I could feel three of my fingers. That was all I needed to get the rest of my gear into Trailer and ride over the Murchison River Bridge – the official end of the Outback.

I knew the Outback had finally let me go when it spat me out into an unexpected world of rolling green pastures with fluffy white sheep dotted on them. I wondered if I'd actually ridden through a wormhole in the space-time continuum, and ended up in rural English countryside. I took careful note of the passing WA numberplates and the fact that spearmint-flavoured milk was still being sold in the petrol stations, and had to abandon this theory.

Another indication that I'd left the Outback was the recreational lycra-wearing cyclist who, when I encountered him back at Bike where he was standing on the side of the road looking around for me, seemed a little horrified that I had just been on a toilet break. That sort of thing is not acceptable in non-Outback zones.

Thursday 18 August
Geraldton to Allanooka Springs Road, Western Australia
44 kilometres – 2 hours 50 minutes

I rode into Geraldton covered in dead bugs as I'd ridden through a swarm of alive ones on my way into town and collected a sizeable number in my sweat. I eventually found a bike shop for all my non-insect-removal needs. The shop had the part I needed to fix Trailer, a new flag and flagpole, and directions for a scenic route to Perth. They also had the recreational lycra-wearing cyclist I'd met earlier who, from the look on his face when I walked in, had been telling his friends about me going to the toilet in the bushes.

My other shopping priority while I was in a reasonably-sized town was a rainproof garment. It was raining on and off for my whole time in town and I was sure I would be meeting more rain as I headed south. In a fishing shop, I found a poncho that I thought would give me a good range of movement to ride in whilst staying dry. It had a special feature that I discovered as I used it around town. When it started raining, I'd pull the poncho over my head, do up the plastic press-studs, pull on the hood, and tighten the strings. By the time all of these steps were complete I realised that people were looking at me strangely because it had stopped raining. As promised, it kept me dry.

I had some Rotary and Soroptimist visits and a radio interview in town, so ended up staying in Geraldton for four nights. I camped in a caravan park right next to the beach with a little three-sided tin shed to set up my tent in. My stay coincided with massive storms, which did weird things to my tent. The first morning I woke up with a small truckload of sand on top of everything inside the tent, including me. My plan to market the experience as an exfoliation-while-you-sleep service was ruined by the evening, when I came home to find the tent in a completely new orientation. The roof was a wall, a wall was the floor and all of my stuff was not just sandy but also wet. I adjusted my business proposal, and thought I could rent the wreckage out as a home for crabs or a safe place for turtles to lay their eggs. I could leave my gear behind, and use my new poncho for all tent, sleeping bag and clothing needs.

By the next afternoon, the storm had become even stronger, and I made it back from a Rotary visit to huddle in the camp kitchen with the rest of the campers, gazing upon the caravan park fence that had been blown over. Most of the other people there were in campervans or had a car or ute to sleep in or block the wind from their tent. The one other person with nothing but a tent had been there for over a week and was stationed in the far corner of the yard. He had spent the afternoon moving his possessions in and out of his drenched tent, refusing offers of help or dry clothes. He had nothing else with him except a sturdy axe and shovel, both of which were leaning against the fence next to his tent.

One camper eventually ventured outside and returned to inform me that my tent was in a dire situation. I found it straining on its remaining peg, contorting in a very un-tent like shape. Everyone helped me bring my gear into the TV room, which we soon realised had been so easy to walk into because the door had been blown off. This held our attention for a while until someone pointed out that the ceiling was moving. Given my options, I thought I would still try my luck in the TV room that night, but under the pool table.

The rest of the evening was a bonding one for us all, as times of extreme weather tend to be. We spent hours chatting and I learnt a lot: how to escape South American revolutions; how reusable green shopping bags may actually be a sinister plot to take over the world; what truckies really think of cyclists; and what a "future" is in the stock market. Actually, to be honest, I didn't really understand that last one – I just pretended to.

At dinnertime, I shared my reduced-price tin of barbeque soy sausages with some other vegetarian campers. I was a bit worried, though, when one of them was especially excited because those were his favourite brand and he told me he hadn't had any since they'd stopped making them a few years ago. That might explain why the tin cost only $1.

One of the bittersweet aspects of life on the road is how quickly acquaintances can gain the intimacy of firm friendships and then just as quickly you part ways, likely to never meet again. The Tamil language and culture has a nice way of avoiding the finality of farewells. You have two choices for saying goodbye in Tamil. When you are the one departing, you say "Poytu Varen" – "I'll go and come back", and when someone is taking leave of you, you tell them "Poytu Vanga" – "Go and return". It is a wonderful way to leave, and captures the essence of Tamil hospitality. Every place I've visited and family I've stayed with in Tamil Nadu, I have left only after being cajoled into making promises to return.

Back in the camp kitchen at Geraldton, we weren't yet up to farewells, but the disquieting guy from the other tent finally came in out of the rain. However, he remained silent and just stared out the window as he ate his food. You never can know what anyone else's story is, but I hoped he was all right and had somewhere to go, where there were people who cared about him.

Sunday 21 August
Watheroo to Bindoon, Western Australia
135 kilometres – 7 hours 17 minutes

The road I took to Perth offered a new kind of riding experience for me. Instead of long stretches of unpopulated outback, I went through a few towns each day, with farmland lining the roads in between. It was also the first time since Queensland that I had a choice in the route I took. The guys in the bike shop back in Geraldton had suggested this back road and assured me that it had only one major hill, with a climb of just a few kilometres. It turns out that a "few" in Western Australian means 60. After the long hill out of Geraldton, most of my issues came from the weather.

I had icy headwinds and minor flooding across some roads, which required the removal of my socks so that I could walk Bike and Trailer through the water. I had also picked up a cold in Geraldton, which I suspected would show genetic links to tinned soy sausages if DNA analysis were to be carried out on it.

Damp and cold, I reached Three Springs by nightfall on my first night out of Geraldton. My legs, brain and nose all felt strangely disconnected from each other, but united in their desire to find a warm haven. I made the decision to spend some extra money for an on-site van or room, or at least some sort of accommodation that didn't involve a wet tent and cold fingers. Just like the other times I had tried to spend money on proper accommodation, when I arrived at the caravan park my plans were dashed, this time as I read a sign informing me that the place was manned only until 4:30 pm. It was already nearing seven.

There were spaces in the yard where I could pitch my tent, but then I found a deserted camp kitchen with a large patch of floor that would be quite possible to sleep on. I towed my gear indoors and started eating my cous cous in the dark, weighing up the moral implications of surreptitiously sleeping inside. I'd just about made that decision when a group of people burst in, turned on the lights, looked a little scared of me and started cooking dinner. The tables had turned. In less than a day, I had gone from wondering about the eccentric guy with his axe and shovel, to being the girl with the crazed look in her eye who smells, brings her stuff with her into the kitchen, and eats huge quantities of cous cous. Also, I had my spade on the back of my bike. A small, plastic, orange, relatively unthreateningly one, but a spade nonetheless. I slept outside in my tent that night.

The ride on the Sunday was punctuated with a town every 25 kilometres or so. It put my rhythm out a bit, because I was still expecting a town only every three or four days. I kept having urges to stock up on half a week's supplies at every shop I saw. It did give me the opportunity to use my Official Town Entry Scoring System more regularly. The rules are as follows: you have officially "arrived" in a town when you have fulfilled three of the following criteria:

- You pass the turn off for the rifle range.
- You find a sign stating which year they won the Tidy Town competition.
- Drivers stop waving at you.
- You can buy food.

- There are enough road options to get lost and confused.
- You feel embarrassed by the hat, shorts, socks, zinc cream, dirt or plastic bags you are wearing.

During the afternoon, a car driver pulled over for a chat because he had seen me leaving Geraldton a few days ago. His opening remark as I pulled up next to his window was something of a surprise: "Don't worry; I'm not a murderer or anything." I appreciated the reassurance, and thought I might try it myself as a greeting in the next few weeks – maybe when arriving at the front office of a school; when asking for the keys to the toilet at a petrol station; when sending official emails; or when people turn the lights on and illuminate me in caravan park kitchens.

The final town for the day was Watheroo. I spent a while trying to decide whether to stop there and make use of the shower facility that a caravan park could offer, or ride a bit further out of town so no one would hear me yelling obscenities at my wet tent as I set up camp. Either option would be nicely complemented by a litre of milk, so I stopped at a deli, followed by a man who told me to get back to the road works that were in progress down the street. Damn you, fluoro vest.

Doing my best to stop looking like a construction worker, I chanced upon Jess, the owner of Watheroo Station Tavern, which doubles as the caravan park. I asked her how much an unpowered site was. She told me that if the bike outside belonged to me then I could stay for free, and then uttered the best eight words I'd heard for a few hundred kilometres: "In fact, would you like to stay inside?" I gratefully took up the offer before she could get close enough to smell me. With a litre of milk in my hand, I was escorted over the road to a dry, warm, completely un-tent-like room.

I had a glorious night, occasionally waking up to grin to myself under my huge pile of blankets. Having no wet tent to deal with, I set off early and at a decent pace, thanks to the long straight roads and unobtrusive winds. I was out of carrots, but made sure I ate enough from the crunchy food group by eating ginger nut biscuits and rice crackers. I covered my orange food group needs with a big bag of mandarins from a roadside stall, and the food group that starts with C by having coffee-flavoured milk.

By the time I stopped thinking about food, I had reached Bindoon, just 85 kilometres from Perth. I wasn't sure how I would feel being in a big city again. Life had been nice and simple for the past few months: sleep, ride, eat, camp. I had better prepare myself for traffic lights, houses, and a social life once more.

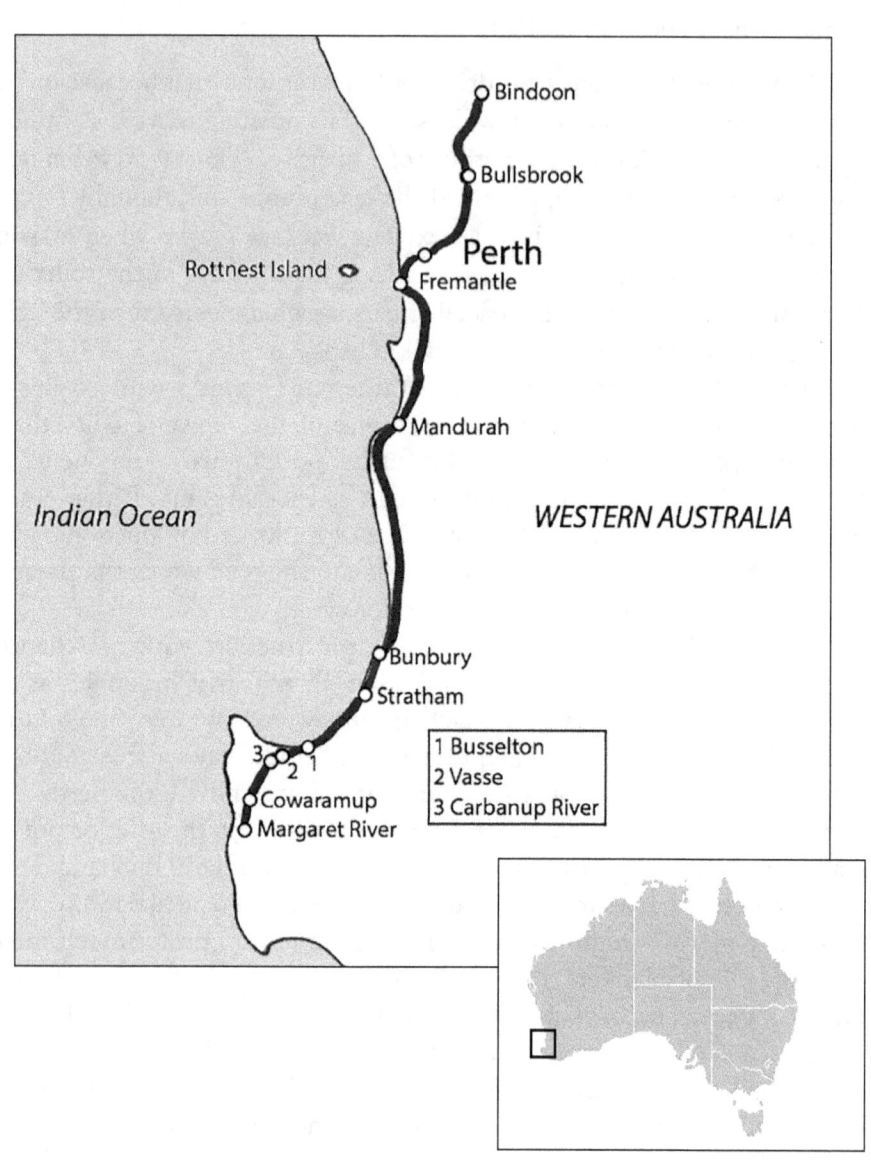

Chapter 13

Getting Muftied

Bindoon – Bullsbrook – Perth – Fremantle – Rottnest Island – Mandurah – Bunbury – Stratham – Busselton – Vasse – Carbunup River – Cowaramup – Margaret River

Totals: 16,524 kilometres – 896 hours 47 minutes – $17,812

Tuesday 30 August
Perth to Mandurah, Western Australia
70 kilometres – 4 hours 2 minutes

Before riding into Perth a week ago, I made all the appropriate preparations for entering a capital city. I let my tent dry out in the morning sun, washed my hair and located my one set of city-appropriate clothes in the bottom of Trailer.

During my time in town, I went to a range of Rotary and Soroptimist groups, at one of which I repeated my trick from Darwin and won a bottle of wine in a raffle.

When I wasn't winning their wine and enjoying the Rotary proceedings, I had a chance to present Cycle of Learning to the groups.

As part of my presentation I had a number of large laminated photos of the PEAK students. One of my favourite ones was a dinnertime shot at the primary hostel. Meals at the Siruvar Ilum are logistical and culinary triumphs.

Meals at the Siruvar Ilum

Huge pots of rice and curry are placed in one corner of the undercover area that the children eat in. Older students sit on low stools behind the pots with long spoons to ladle out the contents into the metal plates of their peers. Once their plate is full the children take their food and sit on the ground in lines, leaning forward over their meal to eat with their right hand, as is the norm in India. I soon learnt to eat this way too, using my fingers to test the temperature, mix just the right proportions of rice and curry, then gather a mouth-sized portion in the scooped ends of my fingers and deliver it neatly into my mouth with a push of the thumb.

Being made in bulk, the meals were not exactly gourmet, but provided the children with a diet of varied vegetables, legumes and, once a fortnight, meat – to the excitement of everyone involved, from those that went in the college jeep to pick it up from the butcher in town, to the staff and students who cut the large sinewy, bony hunks into smaller sinewy, bony ones, to each of the children who received a few of these prized morsels on their plate. The hospitality bred into them by their rural families meant that they would demonstrate their excitement at the meal by asking repeatedly for me, and any other mealtime visitors from the college, to taste some of their dinner with encouraging prompts of "nalaaku!" – delicious!

*

The half dozen or so schools I visited around Perth were tricky to get to, but well worth the effort. One required a 3 am start to get to the top of a mountain range, one was on Rottnest Island, and another involved a train trip. At all the schools I visited, I was impressed by how engaged and involved students were with their own learning and within their school communities. At one, a class had directed their own research about Cycle of Learning and India from the website and other resources online, introduced other classes to the project and instigated their own fundraising. At another, the school's student body had organised a mufti day recently to raise a spectacular amount of money for the Cycle of Learning trust fund. Initially I wasn't sure exactly how one "muftis", what a "mufti" is, or how dangerous it is to bring a "mufti" to school, but was later relieved to find out that "mufti" is what Western Australians call a casual or non-uniform day.

On Rottnest Island, I spent a whole day with its tiny, close-knit school. We rode our bikes to a beach, saw quokkas and prepared for an evening presentation about Cycle of Learning, which we put on together for parents and other island locals. Before lunch, we had a discussion about bike riding and safety, which inspired us to do some drawing. I did mine on the blackboard, and all was going well until I accidentally drew an emu with four legs. It took some observant students asking where I'd seen a dinosaur, and the intervention of their teacher, to rectify the situation.

In the evening, the students hosted a Cycle of Learning event for the community. There was chai and hot dogs and, thanks to an eloquent presentation from the students themselves, absolutely no need for me to say anything to the audience. Before my visit, the school had spent time on the Cycle of Learning website, read and discussed the student profiles and information available there, and done some of their own research. Perth gave me a taste of exactly what I had envisaged for Cycle of Learning: Australian students actively learning about their peers in Kodaikanal and the issues they face, responding in their own way to what they learnt, and sharing it with their community.

My education in Kodaikanal

My own education in Kodaikanal started off comfortably. At first, along with the regular reactions of pity, anger and concern about the different situations I saw or heard about, I also felt privileged to be learning first hand about the issues and hardships of oppressed communities: it felt like something to be valued. I was witnessing "the real world" and I can't deny that at the back of my mind, I was slightly self-righteously proud that I could add these people and their stories to my accumulation of experiences from my year of travelling.

A conversation with Father Prem brought my self-righteousness and accompanying detachment to a screeching halt. "So how do you feel being an oppressor of my country's people?" he asked me politely, during a morning stroll. In karate, there is a particular feeling that comes when your sparring partner beats your guard and sinks a perfectly placed punch into your solar plexus. You are winded and shocked, but full of appreciation for the technique and you feel a strange exaltation as you snap into the reality of the present moment. You may need to have lost a lot of karate fights to follow my analogy, but Prem's question was as perfectly placed as one of those punches, and shook up my world view in the few seconds it took for me to realise I couldn't answer him. I didn't feel anything about it, because I hadn't thought about it, because I had not considered myself an oppressor of anyone before.

Prem wasn't picking on me – we went on to discuss how he felt as a man, which placed him as an oppressor of women, and about the fact that being of a higher caste, he was positioned as an oppressor of the Dalits he worked with. And the fact that when we do realise that we are in the role of oppressors, and go on to sympathise with a cause, or work actively against an oppression, we still cannot change our position as oppressors until authentic liberation has taken place. And that this removal of both sides of oppression, both of oppressed and oppressor, was something that he, as a Christian, was working towards as part of his faith in the Kingdom of God.

Amongst other questions this conversation raised, it made me think about oppression and my position in the world in a different way. To ask myself where I am positioned – as an oppressor or amongst the oppressed – when it comes to things like gender, socio-economic status, age, physical ability, sexuality, ethnicity, citizenship, education, consumption, language and as one of the species on planet earth. And that this positioning means that it is impossible to be neutral in any issue of social justice. Apathy, or not wanting to be involved or sitting on the fence, is actually giving my support to the status quo that is part of the institutions of oppression.

That morning, it wasn't only how I felt about my role as oppressor that I couldn't answer, but the question that was left unspoken – "And what are you going to do about it?"

Father Prem was a good person to look to for tackling the role of oppressor head on. When it came to the oppression and inequality faced by women, he consistently refused to accept the status quo. He would debate and argue about female representation in activities. He would acknowledge and encourage women in all their roles in their villages. When I accompanied him on a trip to his family home, he took the bowls from his mother's and aunties' hands and served them first, when usually they would have waited for all the menfolk to finish eating before they took any themselves.

This was just one place to look for inspiration around me. Every day I saw transformative acts being carried out by the Fathers, students and PEAK staff to challenge and overcome the caste, gender, economic and political injustices around us. Even so, by the time I left Kodai, I still didn't have an answer. I still didn't know what I would do about it. My education in Kodaikanal ended up being a challenging and uncomfortable one, as any good education is.

*

During my week in Perth, I stayed with two families, both cousins of my mum. I managed to spend time with three generations of relatives over cups of tea and big family dinners. A relative of particular interest to me was John, a dentist. I took all opportunities to steer the conversation around to the issue of my Darwin-declared "sensitive teeth". He couldn't shed much light on my malady, but did make it clear that I could avoid most dental problems by flossing twice a day. In fact, he rated the importance of flossing on par with breathing, so I resolved to do both much more regularly.

John's wife, Beth, a physical education lecturer, was less concerned with my flossing and more worried about the nutritional message contained in my online trip diary. She voiced concerns that by blogging about all of my hot chip, flavoured milk and chocolate consumption, I might be glorifying unbalanced, unhygienic, sugary and fatty eating habits. I agreed to use my blog to promote fruit and vegetables, in particular two and five serves a day of each respectively. I briefly wondered if I could ask Bonnie (my IT support friend) to write some special software for my blog that would automatically change any references of "muffins" to "cabbages", "chocolate milk" to "water" and so on.

I left the home of Beth and John with a gift from their army-reservist son Jarrah, which neither of his parents would have approved of if they'd known about it. I was quite excited, though, to have my very own stash of khaki-packaged regulation army chocolate. I had visions of eating it huddled in a trench with Bike and Trailer, while snipers tried to take out our tyres. Or maybe I'd eat it just before smearing my face in axle grease, arming myself with my orange spade and launching an offensive against a swarm of flies. I would make sure I flossed and ate a capsicum straight after, though.

Sunday 4 September
Margaret River, Western Australia
4 kilometres – 20 minutes

Since leaving Perth on Tuesday, a nasty grey cloud of apathy settled over my head. A generous number of appointments in this area meant that I only had to ride short distances each day. The longest I had to travel this week was 60 kilometres between Bunbury and Busselton. I rode slowly, and stopped lots, yet still arrived in each town early, with nothing to do but wander around the main streets, and then wait for the sun to go down so I could go to bed. I missed the west coast, where I had been moving all day and by nightfall was content and nicely exhausted.

I didn't have anyone to talk to, except for a reporter from the local paper who interviewed me in Bunbury. He moved through his questions rather rapidly. I think I freaked him out with the outfit I arrived in. The morning was wet and cold, so I donned my rain poncho and went to the army surplus shop before the interview. I steered clear of the chocolate ration section, since I was still feeling a bit weird from eating the slab Jarrah had given me, and perused the sock and glove range. My second-hand socks had not been doing much to keep out the chilly mornings of this corner of the state, and my fingers were numb for a large proportion of the days. In the shop I found a pair of socks and gloves made from matching blue "scientific" material: a special fabric that has been tested at the International Sock and Glove Institute to ensure it properly does things such as "wick away moisture". I could have listed all the other quasi-scientific technical things this fabric claimed to do had I spent more time reading the packaging in detail, instead of ripping it off eagerly to gain access to the contents.

And so I rode up to my interview in shorts, shirt, gloves, socks and sandals, all covered with a bright yellow poncho. I think I could almost have made the outfit work for me if I had had a big smile on my face, and looked cheery and happily eccentric. From the glimpse I got of myself in the glass door on the way in, though, I had a sullen expression of gloom, and a red raw nose from the extended use of my starchy Alice Springs hankies. At least I could be grateful it wasn't a television interview.

Here in Margaret River, I felt marginally better, maybe because the town had a lively, bustling feel brought about by the number of tourists. During the ride in, there were many eye-catching signs advertising wineries, cheeseries, gourmet fooderies and aqua golf. These didn't excite me since I don't really like wine, cheese or small pieces of expensive food. Large and cheap is more my scene. And even though I don't know what it is, I didn't think I'd like aqua golf either. Either aspect of it.

I was too quick to judge, though, and spent the Sunday morning buying a small, expensive piece of mango fudge, eating fetta cheese, and taking Holy Communion at a local church. I still didn't try the aqua golf. Instead, I partook in some aqua clothes washing at the caravan park I was staying at. Since I'd been moving base each day, and the weather was wet and cold, I hadn't had the chance to launder anything since Perth. It had been so cold that I'd also been wearing every item of clothing I owned at least once each day, so this chore was well overdue.

That evening I took a significant material and psychological blow, in the loss of my MP3 player. As the unpowered sites I paid for at caravan parks were intrinsically without electricity, I had to recharge my phone, camera batteries, and MP3 player in communal areas such as laundries or kitchens. I always knew that it was risky, but there were not many other options. I just tried to be as discreet as possible about when and where I plugged my gear in. Tonight my gamble didn't pay off, and instead of returning to find a fully charged source of music, pleasure and distraction, I discovered an empty power socket next to the washing machine.

There were tears. I hadn't been getting on very well with myself lately, and listening to music had been a nice way of not having to spend as much time with Anne. On the road, or in my tent in the evenings, I'd been savouring the escape that music gave me.

I took myself to the payphone to call a friend who neither needed recharging nor was susceptible to theft. Besides these two key aspects of her character, Jean has an incredibly soothing way about her that always makes me feel more peaceful and ready to face the world. In person she'll greet and farewell you with a warm, patient hug; listen so deeply to what you have to say that you know she's heard more than just the words that come out of your mouth; gently tease out the uncomfortable and tangled edges of your thoughts and problems; and give advice from her unique position in the universe that seems to tap into the serenity and positivity that eludes most of the rest of us. Jean did her thing, minus the hugs that wouldn't fit through the phone, and suggested that maybe this was an opportunity to appreciate my own company again. I hung up feeling better.

The access to Jean and the rest of my family and friends by phone this year was invaluable. A lot of the time, I was out of mobile coverage, but there had usually been a pay phone available every couple of days. Being able to debrief with friends and family, and stay in touch with what was going on in other people's lives, kept me on a relatively even keel. I often thought of something Colin told me – that when he called his family he made it a rule never to complain or tell them anything negative about his situation. I was sure he never called his sister from Renner Springs and sobbed into the phone that he thought he might die. I was not even close to being that mentally tough. I had only wet a few phone receivers with my tears, but I had whinged, complained and moped into many more.

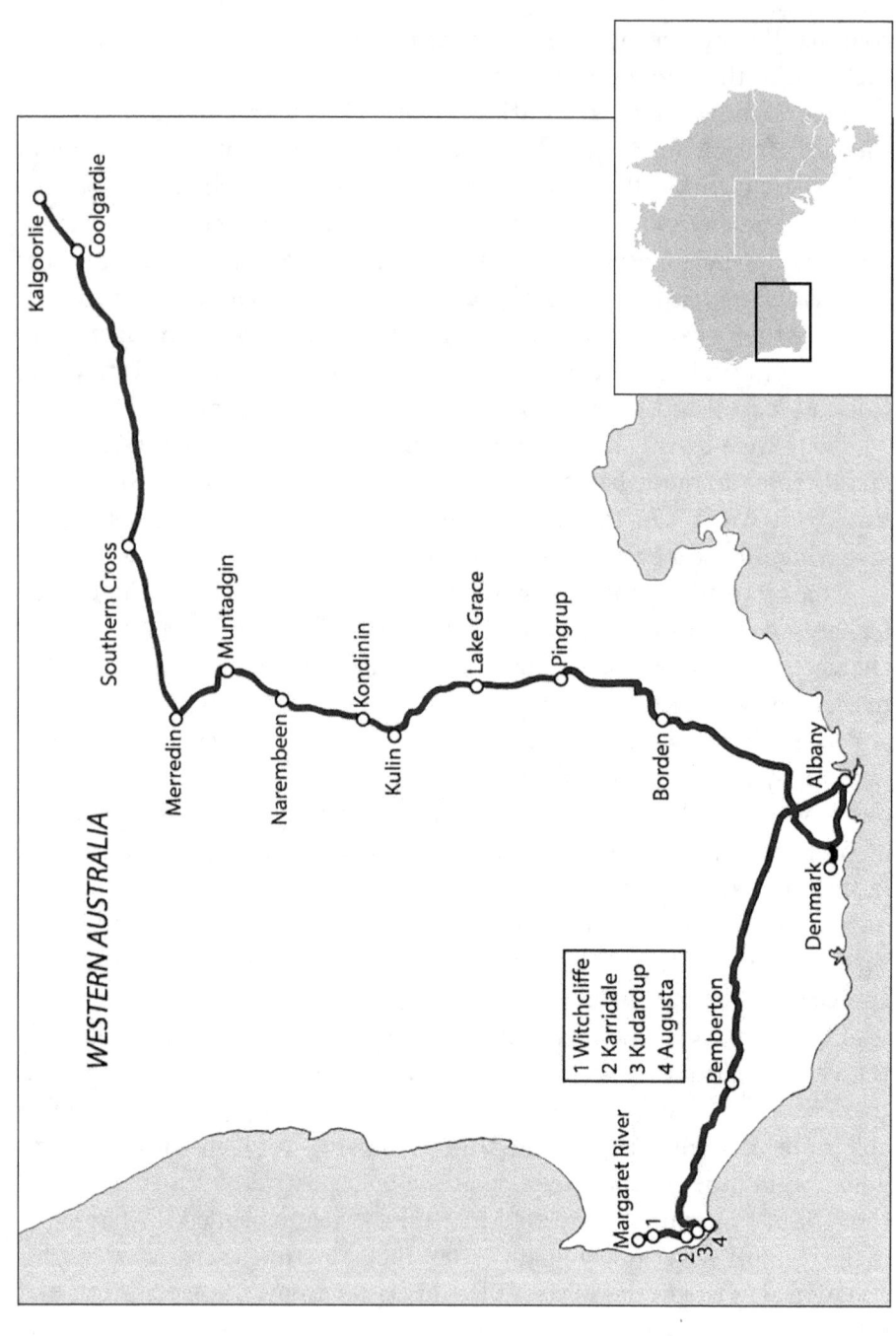

Chapter 14

The Demise of Poncho and the Rise of TYPHOON JACKET

Margaret River – Witchcliffe – Karridale – Kudardup –
Augusta – Pemberton – Albany – Denmark – Borden – Pingrup –
Lake Grace – Kulin – Kondinin – Narembeen – Muntadgin –
Merredin – Southern Cross – Coolgardie – Kalgoorlie

Totals: 17,987 kilometres – 974 hours 49 minutes – $19,653

Thursday 8 September
Pemberton to Albany, Western Australia
0 kilometres by bike – 213 kilometres by bus

A week ago I was complaining about boredom and the lack of riding adventure in my life. The world was listening and kindly organised some surprises for me along the road between Augusta and Pemberton.

The ride south from Margaret River was uneventful, but by the time I arrived in Augusta for some school visits, heavy rain had set in. Near the end of my last visit, some students asked what I was carrying in my handlebar bag. I pulled out soggy gloves, soggy sunscreen, soggy fly net, soggy hat, soggy carrots and, finally, soggy tissues. I'd never realised that carrots could get soggy, but living in a handlebar bag in southwest Australia seems to be able to do it. I don't think I made the cycling lifestyle look very attractive.

By the time the school's end-of-day siren sounded, it was still bucketing down, so I took refuge in the school until the downpour had eased off slightly. I finally made a break for it, waving goodbye to the students heading home to their nice warm, dry houses.

Jealous, I waded and sloshed around town, my poncho acting more as a fashion statement rather than a waterproofing device. I ended up at a caravan park late in the day and enquired after accommodation that didn't involve setting up a tent in the pouring rain. The only options offered were beyond my budget – which I knew they would be, as soon as I heard the words "deluxe" and "chalet" being used to describe them. I did my best to hold back tears of disappointment – which may have just been rainwater dripping out of my hair – and signed for an unpowered site to camp on.

I took my gear into the camp kitchen to wait for a pause in the rain so I could set up my tent. After a few minutes, however, the park owner found me and very kindly handed me the key to an onsite van that was in the process of being renovated. I may have been the happiest, and wettest, person he had seen all week. The rain didn't let up all night, and I got a thrill every time I woke up and remembered I was inside.

The next morning the rain came and went in showers, and a gusty tail wind pushed me to my next school and then down the road towards Pemberton.

At some stage during the afternoon, I became aware of a funny noise coming from Bike's back wheel. On closer inspection I found a small bulge where the metal rim had worn through and given way. I had been warned

Post-explosion wheel in Pemberton, Western Australia.

Chapter 14: The Demise of Poncho and the Rise of TYPHOON JACKET   155

at a bike shop in Bunbury that this might happen, but my adviser thought I would be all right to make it to a bigger town, where I could buy the correct-sized rim. I began to hope that it would get me to any town at all.

I unclipped the brake to stop the rubbing, though when I was descending hills this just added to my anxiety. I wasn't sure which would be worse: my tyre bursting mid-descent or the rest of Bike careening uncontrollably from lack of brakes.

At the bottom of a particularly heart-stopping hill, I dismounted and took another look at my misshapen wheel in the last light of day. I had picked my moment perfectly as I was just in time to witness the tyre exploding, causing an ear-shattering BANG to reverberate through the forest. Now my wheel didn't fit the geometric requirements of wheel-dom. I had a mangled collection of metal and rubber at the back of my bike instead. With a little force, and a loud screeching noise accompanying us, I kept Bike and Trailer moving as I walked us all towards Pemberton. There's nothing more disheartening than trudging through a dark, drizzling forest pushing a newly-crippled member of your fundraising team.

Seven kilometres later, after assuring a few passing motorists that I was fine and didn't need any assistance, I spotted the lights of Pemberton not too far off. I made it into town and found a caravan park with a shelter under which I could pitch my tent. I didn't have the heart to look at Bike's injury properly, so I propped him on the other side of the shelter, out of view. I crawled into my tent and tried to lose my troubles in a 1975 National Geographic magazine that I'd picked up for 20 cents a few days earlier. I ended up falling asleep only after reading a story about a man who tried to sail solo around Antarctica, and realising that my troubles were of a much lower order.

It was still raining yesterday morning when I emerged from my tent to face the world and its mechanical challenges. The Pemberton Caravan Park staff were incredibly kind when I told them about my situation. They drove me into town, found phone numbers for me, let me use their telephone, didn't allow to me pay any camping fees, and offered to fetch bicycle parts from neighbouring towns. What I appreciated the most, though, was the sympathy and concern they lavished on Bike and me, on what would have been a horrible day to face alone.

After I'd been around town, seen what the garage had to offer in the way of tools, phoned bike shops in other towns, and done some research online, I narrowed my options down to three:

1. Replace the wheel rim and a part of my bike known as "the cassette". This would involve getting the parts and special tools sent across from Albany. I wouldn't be able to guarantee that the rim would be the right size, and although I had seen the tools once before, I had never used them. Also, I didn't really know what a "cassette" was.

2. Buy a ticket for the next bus to Albany, get Bike fixed there and become the girl who is "riding around most of Australia".

3. Stay in this hilly, green town for the rest of my life.

Given that I had to be in Albany by Friday, I grudgingly decided on number two. I was upset that I would be missing part of the ride. I'd come a long way, and had never really doubted that I would ride it all. No matter how my pride and I were feeling, I had to try to keep the aims of Cycle of Learning in sight. I reminded myself that the goals of the project did not actually include riding a complete loop around Australia. This omission of a couple of hundred kilometres would not affect the fundraising, provision of education, awareness raising, or promotion of cycling. It was a turn of events that was disappointing to me but, ultimately, no real issue for Cycle of Learning.

Once I made all my bookings for the bus trip, I set about keeping myself entertained. The only cheap book I could find in town was a Mills and Boon, which I started reading in the fish and chip shop and accidentally left behind. I then had to retrieve it from the crowd of bemused teenagers who had taken over my table. Feeling rather distraught, I had to remind myself that there were no Cycle of Learning goals about not being publicly outed as the owner of something entitled *Seduced by a Sultan*.

The next morning I lugged Bike, Trailer and my gear into the town centre in four stages. This task made me realise a few important facts. First, Bike was much better at towing Trailer than I was; second, wheels that moved around were really quite handy; and finally, bikes weren't nearly as much fun when you had to carry them. I suspected Bike disagreed.

I farewelled the kind people of Pemberton Caravan Park, and made it onto the bus feeling thoroughly defeated. It was such a pleasant environment to be defeated in, though. It was warm, there was carpet on the floor, the radio played softly in the background, the rain hit the outside of the windows and not me, and the amazing Karri forest looked dark and mysterious from where I sat.

Chapter 14: The Demise of Poncho and the Rise of TYPHOON JACKET

I arrived in Albany, locked Bike and Trailer up to the nearest pole, and indulged in another novel experience: staying in a backpackers' hostel. It felt a bit strange being around so many people my own age. I hate to admit it, but I think I might fit in more with the grey nomad crowd than with the backpacking youth scene. Retirees are always friendly, and when it comes to the cleanliness of communal kitchens, far superior to young backpackers.

Monday 12 September
Denmark to Chester's Pass Road, Western Australia
93 kilometres – 4 hours 48 minutes

In the past few days, I travelled the 95 kilometres between Albany and Denmark three times, using bus, station wagon and fully functional Bike. The logistics were so complex I nearly had to purchase NASA software to figure them out, but they allowed me to visit relatives, schools, Soroptimists and churches, and to have Bike's rear wheel repaired. Sadly, I also needed to replace my rain poncho. It hadn't been travelling very well, and once it became more of a holey piece of plastic than an operational poncho, I retired it to a rubbish bin.

For the last two nights in Albany, I found a different backpackers' hostel, with a very exciting guest. In the kitchen, while toasting some crumpets, I found myself face to face with another … SOLO FEMALE CYCLIST! I had been sure that there must be some others of my species somewhere out there, but the year had not produced any until then. It was fabulous to meet Sally who had travelled over from New Zealand to cycle around the Southwest in her holidays. She immediately impressed me with her finesse in the areas of travel cooking and food storage. The meals she prepared amazed me. I continued eating crumpets all weekend, but she pulled all sorts of things out of her panniers to cook up gourmet dishes. I witnessed a bottle of balsamic vinegar, a chopping board, butter, tortillas, parsley and a bag of flour come out of her portable larder. Between eating copious amounts of food, we had some extremely bonding evenings: cleaning our chains, wondering why people were always so worried about our safety, and comparing knicks designs and the length of time we'd go without showers.

Sunday 18 September
Great Eastern Highway to Kalgoorlie, Western Australia
177 kilometres – 8 hours 40 minutes

From Albany, I made my way up to the Great Eastern Highway through the Stirling Ranges and small back roads in order to speak at a tiny primary school in Muntadgin on Friday. During the year, I had been intrigued by how different the atmosphere of schools and staffrooms could be. Some staffrooms were much happier than others, and occasionally I found myself in one so happy that it felt as if they were throwing a party.

Muntadgin Primary was one such school, and it felt increasingly party-like as I waited for the morning bell to ring. A steady stream of teachers, students, bus drivers, parents and community members passed through the staffroom, all full of good cheer, plates of food, and news. I finally realised that the party-like atmosphere was because there actually *was* going to be a party the next day for the 75th anniversary of both the school and the town pub. I am not sure if, back in 1930, the teachers needed somewhere to drink, or if the drinkers needed somewhere to send their kids.

Once school began, I joined all six students for a chat. There would have been more present, but two-fifths of the student population were away at a regional sports day. I shared my interviews with Karnan and Packialakshmi with the group.

Karnan

My name is Karnan. I am 14 years old and in Year 7 at school. I am from a village that can be reached by bus. There are about 40 houses in my part of the village (the Dalit section), and over 200 from higher castes in the other part. My part of the village is located below the caste part. We live in that part of the village because we have no education – why my community misses out on education, I don't know.

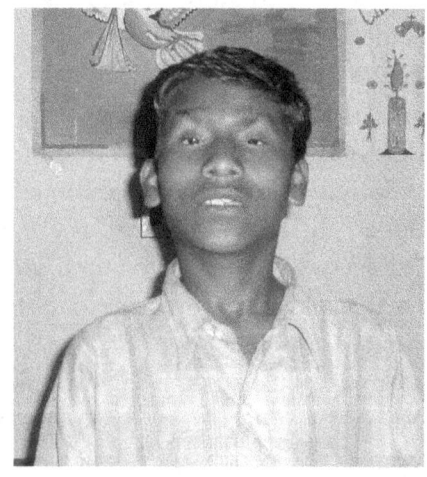

Karnan, aged 14 in 2004.

I have two younger sisters. However, they dropped out of school after Year 5 because my family didn't have enough money. My mother and father had no education; both work as coolies in bean and vegetable fields. I would like to be a doctor. Many of my people suffer because they have no money to pay for treatment. When I am a doctor, I plan to work in the fields for my income, so I can treat the people for free.

Packialakshmi

My name is Packialakshmi. I am 14 years old and in Year 6 at school. I have one brother and one sister. My village has no road and no hospital; many people get sick, but there is nowhere to go. The people in my village aren't educated, so they work as coolies.

I like reading stories, maths, dancing, and helping other people. In the future, I would like to be a teacher or doctor, since there are none in my village.

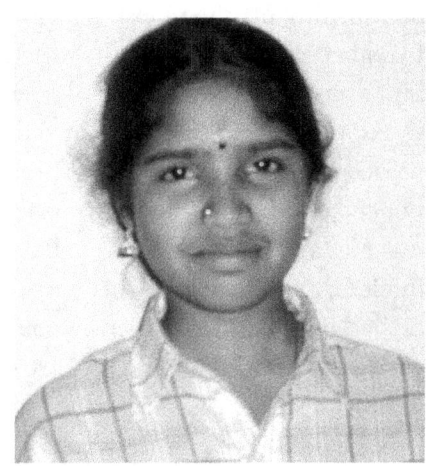

Packialakshmi, aged 14 in 2004.

*

After listening carefully to these stories, one lad in the group had a question for me. Obviously concerned about the lack of medical services in Karnan and Packialakshmi's villages, he asked if people in Kodaikanal ever get meningococcal meningitis. That threw me, since I wasn't sure of the correct answer, or how such a big medical word came out of such a small boy. We also had a good look at Bike, Trailer and the scab on my knee from the last time I'd fallen off. We decided that helmets are a good idea since scabby knees aren't too bad but massive head wounds are.

The landscape along the route I next took, through the Stirling Ranges, felt as though I was riding through an Escher painting: climbing neverending hills all day, only to find myself at the bottom of still larger ones.

Yesterday morning, on the Great Eastern Highway, I awoke to discover a strange, warm wind blowing. I was unsure of what this meant: maybe a hot day, maybe rain, maybe a tornado, maybe a good day to drink flavoured milk. Whatever it boded, I reaped the immediate benefits of a dry tent and warmer fingers while I was packing up. I made it 15 kilometres down the road to a tiny town before I found out the meaning. Rain. The town seemed to be deserted, but had a dilapidated park with a functioning tap from which I could fill up my bottles, and a shelter that I retreated to as the downpour began. I waited to see if the rain would go away, passing time by finishing off the muesli bars given to me by the teachers at Muntadgin. I soon cooled down though, which left the prospect of riding through the rain even less appealing. Until I remembered TYPHOON JACKET.

As mentioned, my time in Albany saw the demise of Poncho, once it proved too weak to be part of the Cycle of Learning team. As the era of Poncho ended, another dynasty began: that of TYPHOON JACKET. He was made of sturdy but soft yellow plastic, and had a multitude of buttons in clever places, helping his parts overlap in waterproof ways. Until then, he had been waiting patiently, folded in his own little yellow bag, labelled with his name in capital letters. (This was how I know he needs to be written in upper case.)

Excited at the chance to try out my new friend, I pulled him out, put him on, did up the buttons, and tilted my handlebar mirror so I could check myself out. TYPHOON JACKET and I looked very dapper as I pranced and posed, singing "na na na na na na na na – TYPHOON JACKET!!" to the tune of the Batman theme song. Then I realised that, while this town had seemed deserted because it was only 7:30 on a Saturday morning when I rode in, and everyone had been asleep, it was now 8 am and people were out and about.

I straightened TYPHOON JACKET and hightailed it out of town through the rain.

As I rode eastward, TYPHOON JACKET did such a superb job of keeping me dry, and was so much fun to wear, that I didn't want to take him off once the rain had stopped. For the first hour of rainless riding, I used the excuse that it might start raining again. I kept him on for the second hour in case he needed to be seasoned – like when you use a wok for the first time. I kept him on for the third hour just because I wanted to. Four hours later, I realised things were getting a bit silly so I took TYPHOON JACKET off and stashed him in his bag again.

Throughout all the TYPHOON JACKET wearing, I had an outstanding tailwind and an interesting afternoon as far as trucks were concerned. In addition to the usual road trains, I was warned by the driver of a front-running car that "two 20-foot loads" were approaching me from behind. Being a metric girl, I wasn't sure if I was meant to be impressed, but I followed his instructions and pulled over. The two trucks that passed were each carrying enormous pieces of metal that were parts for mining dump trucks, and they took up both lanes of the highway. At a roadhouse a little later, I chatted with a policeman who was part of the convoy, and found out they were going all the way to New South Wales. I also found out that 20 feet is about six metres.

My tailwind died down the next day, and there were a few more hills, so my pace slowed. I was running out of food, but luckily chanced upon the Billabulling Pub at about two in the afternoon. I suspected I brought the credibility of the place down by requesting a litre of milk, a glass, and a vegetarian pasty. The owner, who had been serving the bikies at the table outside, came back in, saw what I was consuming, and gave the bartender a look that said, "What have you done to our pub?"

Prepared for a typhoon to hit the Nullarbor in TYPHOON JACKET.
Photographer: "Dan"

I got back on the road once I'd dealt with my lunch, and charged onwards to Kalgoorlie. I found an inexpensive caravan park, which provided 24-hour light thanks to a nearby streetlamp. Even better than the night light was the fact that I ended up camping next door to the year's first solo, red-headed cyclist I'd come across. Dan had just come across the Nullarbor from Adelaide and had the same brands of trailer and tent as I had. I thought he might also have the same stomach as me, as he celebrated our meeting by shouting me a chocolate bar.

Tuesday 27 September
Kalgoorlie to Coolgardie–Esperance Highway, Western Australia
152 kilometres – 7 hours 39 minutes

I decided to have a good few rest days in Kalgoorlie in preparation for the daunting Nullarbor crossing. The first four days in town were spent in the caravan park, making plans with Dan for a joint crossing of the Nullarbor. I also had big plans to get a massive amount of publicity rolling for my entry into South Australia. However, thanks to a monopoly on internet access by the single (and very expensive) internet cafe in town, I could afford only a minor assault on South Australian school email inboxes. At least this did leave plenty of time for using the discount vouchers for the local pizzeria that our caravan park neighbours passed on to me and Dan.

The other people I met on the front lawn of the caravan park were another highlight of Kalgoorlie. I spent some wonderful mornings playing soccer and reading books with the kids from the caravan next door, and was given regular drawings from young Ada to keep monsters out of my tent. There were sunny afternoons tinkering with Bike in the company of the neighbours working on their own vehicles. I was plied with hot Milo when I came home soggy from the rain on the way back from Rotary meetings. There were family photo albums to be viewed and washing powder to be borrowed. Actually, now that I think about it, the friendliness started only after I'd borrowed the washing powder and was able to clean my clothes.

A few other old friends made appearances around town – of particular interest, the soy sausage eaters I had met in Geraldton. I forgot to ask them if they caught the weird soy sausage cold, and if they had, whether they'd analysed the virus.

Day by day, I added to my stockpile of supplies for crossing the Nullarbor. I reasoned that if I could accumulate enough food, gear, spare bike parts and sunscreen, my crossing would be guaranteed success.

On Thursday, I farewelled the community at the caravan park and found the home of Tristan and Karen. Tristan taught at one of the high schools in town and invited me to speak there as well as to stay with him and his wife Karen. Together they were taking a group of students to India later in the year to do some volunteer work in Mumbai. If this wasn't fantastic enough, Karen was a massage therapist and Tristan an exceptional cook. My muscles and stomach had never been quite so well looked after in the one home.

Friday morning, I rose early to find the headquarters of yet another Rotary club. As well as having the highest pub-to-population ratio, I think Kalgoorlie might also have the most service clubs per capita in Australia. After the breakfast meeting I made my way to the high school, where I spoke first to the whole school in an assembly, then later to the group preparing for their "Journey to India" trip. Tristan and Karen had been facilitating preparation sessions with the small and enthusiastic group over the previous few months, and I was delighted to hear that one session was dedicated to "How to use an Indian squat toilet". I personally think that the Department of Foreign Affairs should make such a workshop compulsory before any Australian citizen travels to a Squat Toilet Nation. In fact, maybe they should make it compulsory for every Australian, and then enforce Squat Toilet construction throughout the country. Those toilets make a lot of sense.

In the afternoon, I headed home to make use of Karen and Tristan's bookcase, and to watch an episode of *Dr Phil* on TV. I'd sorted out all my psychological problems by evening, when we packed their car to drive down to Esperance where they and some of their friends were having a holiday and running a marathon. We were joined by Joanne who scored double Kalgoorlie points for being both a Rotarian and a teacher from the high school I visited, and triple Adelaide points for knowing the man who has the same name as my father. Over the years, I have been mistaken for this other John Fitzpatrick's daughter a number of times, and I finally met him last September when he bought petrol from me. He had more hair than my dad. I love the intricate web of connections that you discover in the most unexpected places.

The trip to Esperance disconcerted me a little because we were travelling faster than 25 km/h; it was raining and I wasn't getting wet; and

I spotted my first sign pointing to Adelaide when we stopped at Norseman Roadhouse. I remained calm and managed to last the trip without trying to put on the handbrake, open all the windows, or insist on detouring thousands of kilometres east to visit home.

Once in Esperance I spoke at a church, held out cups of water for the marathon runners and generally enjoyed tagging along on other people's holiday. We drove back via Le Grande National Park. It was the sort of place I rarely got to on Bike, as it is off the highway and down dirt tracks. It had beaches with clear blue water, white sand, hills to climb and big open views. As stunning as Le Grande was, it was nice to get back to Kalgoorlie and be reunited with Bike and Trailer who had been having a holiday of their own in the shed.

After three days with Karen and Tristan, I had a new official declaration to make. While I had many gastronomic adventures during the year – some scary, some tasty, some downright unhygienic – I had discovered the finest chef of my trip. After a solid performance in various kitchens over the previous few days, Tristan pulled out all the stops on our final meals, to cement his place at the top of my rankings. While I was tapping away on the computer for what seemed like only a few minutes, he whipped up a green salad/baked taro/udon noodle nest/miso soup/sushi extravaganza. I was not sure how he managed it, but it left me a little emotional. Then the next morning, he created all of my South Indian favourites for breakfast: idli, dosa, sambar, accompanied by Karen's freshly squeezed vegetable juice. Had I regained my powers of speech properly, I might have

Road train, Western Australia.

Chapter 14: The Demise of Poncho and the Rise of TYPHOON JACKET

asked that they adopt me. Instead, I could only manage cries of delight and praise for the meal. I left this wonderful home laden with leftover sushi and dosa, plus a final parting gift of a ziplock bag full of powder to mix up rehydrating electrolytically balanced drinks.

Heading south towards Norseman, the wind was extreme, sometimes slowing me down to a crawl, sometimes tugging me across the road, and sometimes combining with the slipstream of a passing road train to take control of Bike for a few seconds of terror and exhilaration. None of the wind's antics bothered me much though, since I knew I had Japanese and Indian snacks waiting for me in Trailer.

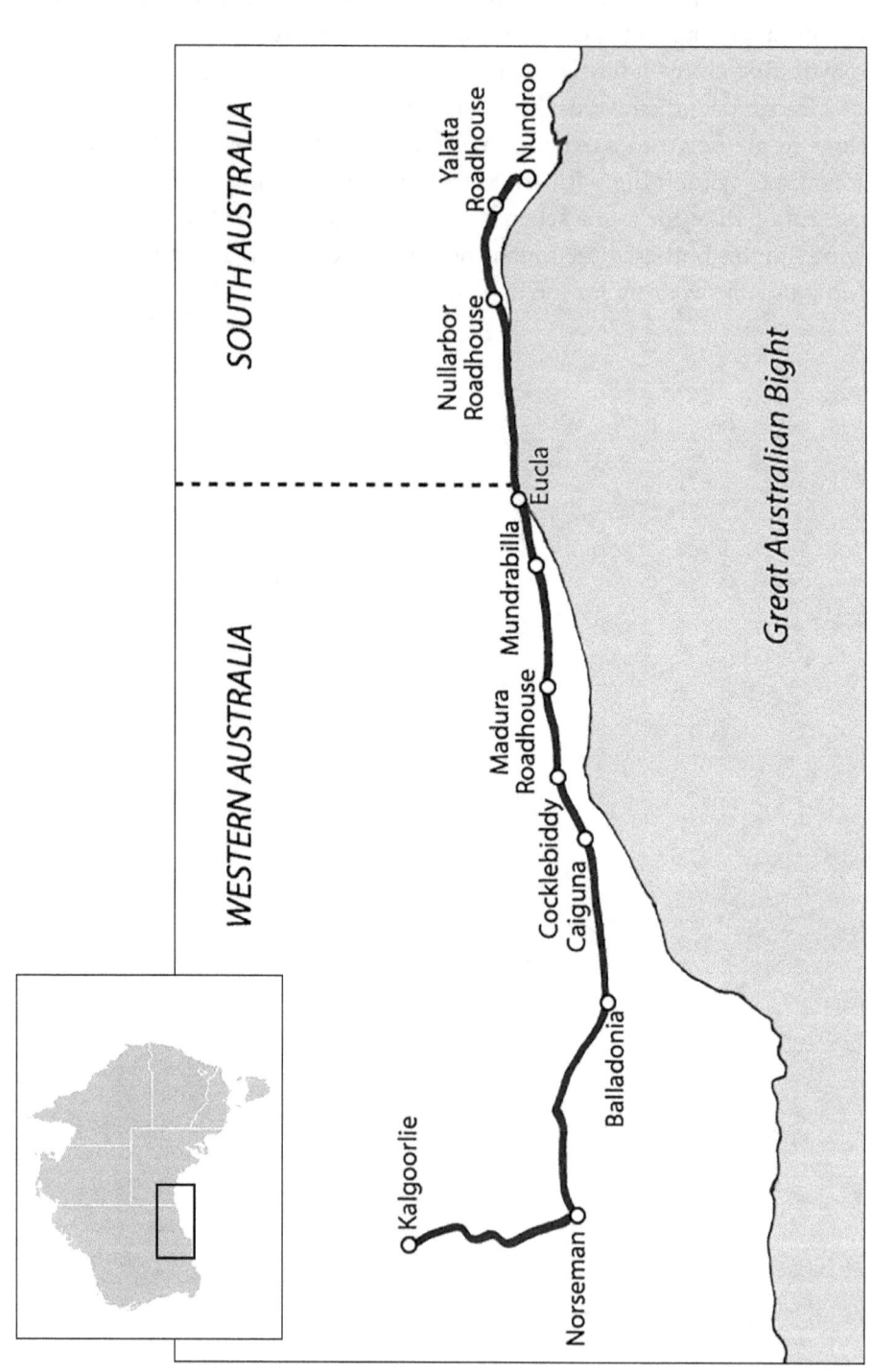

Chapter 15

The March Flies Made Me Do It

Norseman – Balladonia – Caiguna – Cocklebiddy –
Madura Roadhouse – Mundrabilla – Eucla –
Nullarbor Roadhouse – Yalata Roadhouse – Nundroo

Totals: 19,177 kilometres – 1038 hours 14 minutes – $20,583

Friday 30 September
Eyre Highway, Western Australia
136 kilometres – 6 hours 7 minutes

I got into Norseman on Wednesday and located my two new cycling companions. The first was at the post office: an MP3 player sent to me by my sister Claire. While appreciating her extreme generosity, I thought her motivation was probably that she wanted me to return to Adelaide sane enough so she could still tease me.

My sister's most recent teasing cleverly combined both my wrestling and my fundraising activities. Even though the wrestling I do is freestyle wrestling – a highly technical and strategic Olympic sport – Claire likes to confuse it with the completely non-real, TV entertainment wrestling. She'd been suggesting lately that when I go pro my name should be "The Do Gooder", with my catchcry – while looking threateningly at the camera – "This is for your own good" and my signature move be "The Charity Drive". It would be no fun making that kind of joke to someone who had gone crazy from lack of musical entertainment while crossing the Nullarbor.

The other travel companion was Dan from Kalgoorlie. Having only recently ridden the Nullarbor, east to west, he now needed to ride west to east to get back home. We decided to give cycling together a shot, until Ceduna or until we got sick of each other, whichever came first.

At first, I was a little apprehensive about riding with another person: not because I was worried that Dan might be a bike stealer or axe murderer, but because I'd become set in my solo-travelling ways. I was used to stopping when I wanted to stop, riding hard when I wanted to ride hard, dawdling when I wanted to dawdle, singing when I wanted to sing, and being grumpy when I wanted to be grumpy. Nevertheless, I thought it would be a good experience for me. Dan seemed a good choice to be the other person, since he was easy-going, very funny, and had a pantry that rivalled Sally's: spray-on olive oil, cayenne pepper, rosemary, sunflower seeds and dehydrated peas. On the surface, we made a good team too. We both had red hair, BOB trailers, overdeveloped sun smartness, the same style of legionnaire hat, and were both Aquarians.

On Thursday we began the Nullarbor Plain by making an early start from Norseman and tackling continuous hills all through the morning. It wasn't quite my geophysical idea of what a plain should feel like, but you can't really argue with the earth's upper crust. Dan and I only had a few grievances with each other after Day 1 together.

Dan's first issue was that Ralf, the dog on the back of my bike, was looking at him "funny". Dan informed me that Ralf might receive a piece of metal through his furry little heart by the time we reached Ceduna if he didn't change his expression.

Next was the fact that I had too much "pus" attached to Bike. "Pus", according to Dan, was anything that a) wasn't on Bike when I bought him and b) could have been removed with a screwdriver or methylated spirits. This included both of my handlebar bags (I had managed to attach two, something I was quite proud of until I met Dan), ockie straps, all four water-bottle cages, kick stand, reflective tape, reflectors, Trailer flag, orange spade, and, of course, Ralf.

My complaint was that every time Dan grumbled about something (eg sore back, sore knee, leaky tent), then it happened to me too. I didn't know if I could handle experiencing two people's problems the whole way across the Nullarbor Plain.

My only other issue with Dan was that he didn't have enough pus on his bike.

Criticisms aside, the day was enjoyable. Time passed a lot more quickly than usual, and it was a nice change to have to stop riding and pull over because I was laughing too much instead of because I was so hideously bored that I needed to throw a solitary roadside tantrum.

On Friday our ride took us past Balladonia Roadhouse and an abandoned telegraph station. We took a detour off the highway to check it out and found a building with a creepy vibe, smashed windows, old newspapers under the floorboards, a toilet sitting all alone outside, and a pit with snakes in it. As tempting as it was, we didn't camp there for the night but headed down the road for a patch of bush with a far superior atmosphere and no snake pits.

Saturday 8 October
Yalata Roadhouse to Eyre Highway, South Australia
92 kilometres – 5 hours 19 minutes

After a week and a half of travelling together, Dan and I parted ways. While he was a few dozen kilometres behind, at Nundroo Roadhouse, I was off the side of Eyre Highway, setting up camp for the night, back in the familiarity of my old, solitary routines: routines that I was able to view more critically now, thanks to having had a riding partner. The other thing I was in a better position to analyse was my old solitary self, and I was a bit worried about the conclusions I came to. Overall, Dan and I got on well, and things ultimately concluded amicably between us, but my personality gave me a rude shock. I had hoped that my riding adventures this year had added some positive aspects to my character. I had envisaged that my ride had somehow given me more equanimity, made me more flexible, patient and gracious in my dealings with people. The last ten days of social experimentation had shown instead that I had a volatile, self-righteous, know-it-all side of my personality I was not previously aware of. I seemed to have lost the power of constructive socialisation in interactions with a greater complexity than waving at drivers or buying milk.

Cycling differences between Dan and me arose early on in our time together. While we shared an appreciation for frequent eating stops and toilet breaks, Dan was much more of a "stop and smell the roses" kind of cyclist. Or "stop and admire the wedge-tailed eagle", "stop and pick up the dead snake", or "stop and check if the sick looking kangaroo is OK". With my terrible observation skills, minimal interest in wildlife and poor eyesight, I'd evolved a rather different riding style. While I was riding, I tended not to smell the roses and instead kept riding while I wondered what the big bird was that flew past, tried to figure out if that thing on the road was an old piece of tyre or an animal, or wondered why that kangaroo carcass didn't smell as bad as the rest of the roadkill.

The other main difference between our travelling styles was our contrasting approaches to visibility. Between Trailer's flag, Bike's reflective tape, my safety vest and various other fluorescent or flashing possessions, I had positioned myself on the "put on your sunglasses" end of the visibility spectrum. Across the Nullarbor, I even had a chance to be conspicuous fashionably, by modelling bright yellow TYPHOON JACKET whenever the sky got a bit overcast. By contrast, Dan's rain jacket was navy blue, in keeping with his Stealth Policy. He had no reflectors, flags or fluoro paraphernalia, and was committed to dressing in dark-coloured clothes. Dan liked to ride in a way that robbers, murderers or people trying to steal his identity couldn't track him down. He even made me promise that I would change his name if I ever wrote a book about the ride – hence the short, easy to type pseudonym. I would have changed the route we took as well, in order to protect his identity further, but I am a little limited when it comes to this part of the world.

I learnt a thing or two from Dan about stealthy camping. When we finished riding for the night, we would have to wait until there were no cars in sight. We would then rush to drag our rigs at least one hundred metres

Sometimes stealthy camping is difficult.

back into the bush to find the perfectly hidden campsite. Throughout the evening if we heard a car passing on the highway, Dan would give the signal and we would silently turn off our headlamps.

The only time Dan failed to execute a covert operation was when trying to fix a worn tube of his that had led to a slow-leaking puncture. I suspect he would have loved to drag his bike into the bushes to repair it, but he restrained himself and got to work on the side of the road. I tried my best to help, but that ended up requiring me to let go of whatever tool I was holding each time a vehicle went past, as Dan was worried that it would look as though he needed a girl to help him fix his bike. I suggested that it might instead appear that Dan was helping to fix my bike, thus looking gallant. However, the fact that this would mean that my bike (including Ralf and all my pus) was his made Dan even less happy.

Despite our differences, the kilometres passed quickly as we crossed the Nullarbor. It was a nice change to have someone to chat to and make plans with for the day's riding. We had lots to talk about and stories to share, and Dan would regularly have me in hysterics with his jokes or road train impressions or attempts to wipe his snot on my handlebars.

As we passed through the slowly and subtly changing landscape, we encountered a raft of different characters. At Cocklebiddy Roadhouse, we met a Canadian couple, Betsy and Jeff, who were cycling round Australia, having started from Perth. They had fascinating tales of living in the Arctic and using sled dogs for transport. I wish I had asked them to have a word to Ralf about putting more effort into the trip.

The next day we only had a short 90 kilometres to get to Madura Roadhouse. Probably because of the low target, we lost our motivation along the way and pulled over to sit in the shade for a mid-morning break. We were discovered by Marek, the most hard-core Czech cyclist you could ever want to meet. He used to race in Europe, carried next to nothing with him, drank just 750 millilitres for every 50 kilometres, and, in his youth, rode from Sydney to London. It wouldn't surprise me if he hadn't used any boats or planes either.

We spent nearly an hour enjoying his amazing cycling stories, and by the time he left, he was our new hero. We felt so ashamed of our own lazy riding ways that we jumped back on our bikes and rode off at a cracking pace. This lasted about half an hour until I got hungry and Dan needed a nap.

Just before the South Australian border, we caught up with some of our Kalgoorlie caravan park neighbours: Drew, Susan, Ada and Jasper, who were spending some time near the sea in Eucla. We chatted while young Jasper rode his tiny motorbike and Ada painted me another picture to go with the others she had created for me in Kalgoorlie. As promised, they had been doing an exceptional job of keeping monsters away from my tent.

I should have asked Ada if she could design a picture to have the same effect on the March flies that made regular appearances across the Nullarbor. Compared to normal flies, March flies (also known as horse flies) are stronger, smarter and about four times bigger. Even worse, they know how to bite. They make regular flies seem like fun friends you'd be happy to invite into your tent to share an open honey sandwich with. I hold March flies indirectly responsible for one of the most undignified, unhygienic incidents in my life that year.

After setting out from Madura Roadhouse last Monday, Dan and I stopped for a roadside lunch break. The March flies descended en masse,

Flouting the law on the Nullarbor.
Photographer: "Dan"

and to avoid them, we spent 20 minutes huddling under Dan's full-length fly net eating lunch and bickering.

We decided to make our own ways to Mundrabilla, with me setting off first, leaving Dan swearing at the flies from under his net – and probably at me, too. After just a few kilometres of riding, the headwind increased even more, to a point where it blew most of the March flies off my legs.

Soon after I left the rest area, I realised that the wind had slowed me down to such a pace that I had nearly finished the five litres of water I'd packed. I normally carry a lot more than that, but I had thought today would be an easy ride. Plus, according to Marek's calculations, a body should need only 1.8 litres for the 120 kilometres to Mundrabilla. No matter what my excuses were, I was in a less-than-ideal situation, and should have been a lot better prepared.

While there was always the option of flagging down passing motorists to ask for water, I didn't want to have to resort to doing so. I'd put myself out there in that situation, on the road, in the heat, and I should have been prepared enough to look after myself. I resolved to put my emergency hydration plan into action.

I had been working on a hypothesis all year that, if needed, it should be possible to survive off fluids scavenged from discarded bottles by the side of the road. There were so many bottles that often had a bit of liquid left in them, carelessly thrown from passing vehicles. My first few collections were unsuccessful. Left out in the sun, cola fades and starts looking like water, but tastes nothing like it. The chemicals in it turn it into an evil-tasting concoction that makes you reconsider drinking the fresh, unbaked version ever again. I stuck to clearly identifiable water bottles from then on, and managed to deal with my thirst sufficiently all the way to Mundrabilla. There was one exception to the water bottle rule: the half-full bottle of lemon squash looked totally inviting, it seemed relatively new, and did indeed taste like lemon squash should.

The last 30 kilometres took me three hours to complete, and by the time I arrived in Mundrabilla, it was getting dark. I was exhausted from battling the strong winds, as well as from the little voice inside my head that kept asking what my mother would think if she saw what I had been drinking.

If it hadn't been for the March flies that put Dan and me in a bad mood at lunch, I'm sure we would have stuck together for the rest of the day. Dan would have found a better solution to my water situation. He would have known how to dig a hole for ground water or coordinated a stealth mission to syphon off a few litres from a caravan, using his low visibility blue clothing and some snake carcasses as camouflage.

The next time Dan and I parted ways was over the border. At a break early on Wednesday afternoon, all the nasty parts of my personality came out and picked a fight with Dan. The long roads, strong winds and my inability to adjust to considering someone besides myself came to a head. I'm ashamed to admit it, but I think the final straw was a bizarre internal conflict that played out inside me over the first bottle of honey I'd owned since Newcastle, something I knew I should be offering to share with Dan, but that I really wanted to keep all to myself.

At this break, I shoved down my anti-sharing impulses, and covered them with a self-absorbed rant and then yelled at Dan for a bit. He quietly absorbed my outburst and told me to ride on without him. Frustrated that I wasn't getting the response I was after – an apology or a decent argument – I cried at Dan for a bit, and even found myself stamping my foot at him.

I finally rode off, feeling awful inside and shocked at how naturally foot stamping had come to me, the first time I'd revisited it as a mode of communication since I'd abandoned it at age three.

Within half an hour of riding alone, the emptiness of the Nullarbor was getting to be too much, so I turned into a rest area. I was hoping that I might find some company in one of the caravans I saw parked there. Sure enough, within a few minutes of pulling in, I was eating biscuits and drinking coffee with a lovely older couple. Having experienced their no-nonsense hospitality, I wasn't at all surprised when I found out they were from Culcairn in New South Wales and knew my godmother, Maureen. It was a lovely case of serendipity that reminded me of how the world looks after us when we need it most.

I saw Dan in the distance riding past, so said my goodbyes and rode after him, hoping to apologise and salvage something of our friendship. I pushed myself to the limit, catching glimpses of Dan just going over the next hill or around a bend ahead. My eyes were having a particularly bad day, and these sightings turned out time and again to be signposts or bushes, or nothing at all. My knees started whinging at the furious pace I was attempting against a nasty headwind, so I pulled into a rest area around 6 pm and battened down the hatches in preparation for a windy night. (If you want to be technical, I was actually pushing in the pegs and tightening the tent strings, but nautical imagery is always more exciting.)

I packed up the next morning and had only 45 kilometres to cover to get to Nullarbor Roadhouse. The headwind had gained momentum overnight though, and my knees began kicking up a stink. The wind howled past my ears, and my knees complained with every revolution of the pedals. I eventually had to choose between riding at eight kilometres an hour with pain shooting through my knees or walking at six with my pride sagging around my ankles. I went with the ankle problem, riding only when the wind calmed down a notch, or if I had a hill to roll down.

Hours went by before I finally hobbled into the Nullarbor Roadhouse feeling physically and emotionally spent. I had a look around, still unsure if Dan was behind or ahead of me, and spied his bike leaning against an old shed. I wandered over and found flies hovering around a sleeping-bag-encased, Dan-sized lump. Worrying how I would break it to the roadhouse staff that my riding partner had died next to their shed, I thought I should probably make sure first. I called out "Dan" in the direction of the red hair escaping from one end of the mound and started looking for a poking stick. Before I could find one, the lump sat up, revealing a rough-looking, but breathing, Dan. He told me he'd ridden on through last night's winds and collapsed by the shed just before midnight. Not having the apparatus

Bike, me, Dan's bike and the Nullarbor.
Photographer: "Dan"

to set up an IV line to rehydrate him, I left him with three litres of Tristan and Karen's electrolyte solution and headed to the roadhouse shop. I thoroughly enjoyed being able to buy hot chips from them without having to mention there was a corpse outside.

The winds kept blowing all day, so Dan and I declared an official rest day and spent the day chatting, eating, and meeting other travellers passing through. It turned out we had left our little conflict about 100 kilometres behind us. I was relieved to get the opportunity to make things up with Dan, who, despite his low visibility, was one of the kindest-hearted people I met this year.

The rest of our time together was harmonious and free of any foot stamping. The changing landscape gave every day a different mood. We camped for a night right on the edge of Australia with blue ocean stretching southwards, and the cliffs marking the perimeter of the country running east and west as far as we could see.

The treeless plains gave way to a more layered terrain as we crossed the border. The Eyre Highway on the South Australian side suddenly required more attention in order to ride safely, and left little room for error. The shoulder was very narrow, and the road wound around in such a way that trucks appeared with little or no warning. I found myself taking a few too many unplanned, wobbly detours into the gravel on the verge, as traffic took me by surprise from both directions.

Drizzle and overcast skies accompanied us through the Yalata Aboriginal Lands. This gave a refreshing vitality to the landscape that was greener and more wooded than I expected. The roadhouse was also more revitalising than the rest of the Nullarbor's stops. They made a mean meatless hamburger, cute kiddies ran around having a great time, and things were significantly friendlier and cheaper than some expensive, grumpy roadhouses west from here that shall remain nameless. Dan and I could even afford to invest in some fuel of the chocolatey kind.

We left Yalata and rode through windy land that became progressively more countryside-ish and less Nullarbor Plain-ish. We made it to Nundroo Roadhouse, where Dan discovered a television with car racing on it and I found a litre of milk, and then Rafael. Rafael was a Spanish cyclist heading west, with a bike and a trailer that, judging by its size, might have originally been made for a car. It was difficult to communicate in detail, given Rafael's limited English and my non-existent Spanish. However, Rafael got his point across about the debilitating winds loud and clear with a wonderfully Spanish, "MAMMA MIA!" It sounded so much better than an ocker "Gee, it's windy".

The afternoon was progressing, and from his couch in the roadhouse Dan was getting a glazed look of contentment on his face. I knew that he really wanted to stay there and enjoy the racing, and he knew that I wanted to keep moving, so we decided to part ways, this time amicably and without any of my tantrums.

I rode on, into some surprisingly favourable winds, and after just a few kilometres felt a huge lonely hole inside myself. I had gotten used to having company in just over a week. Even though I dealt poorly with the social interactions that came with having that companionship, I had it for long enough to highlight my loneliness now that I'd left Dan behind in Nundroo.

This dichotomy seems to be a recurring theme in my life. I am drawn to solitary endeavours, but then spend my time in them lonely or brooding over my isolation. Then when I'm back around people again, I crave the self-sufficiency of being far away and by myself. I'm not sure that a bike ride around Australia was a practical setting to resolve such psychological issues, but Bike, Trailer and Ralf all made good listeners, and tended to respond with appropriate creaks or rattles at just the right moments.

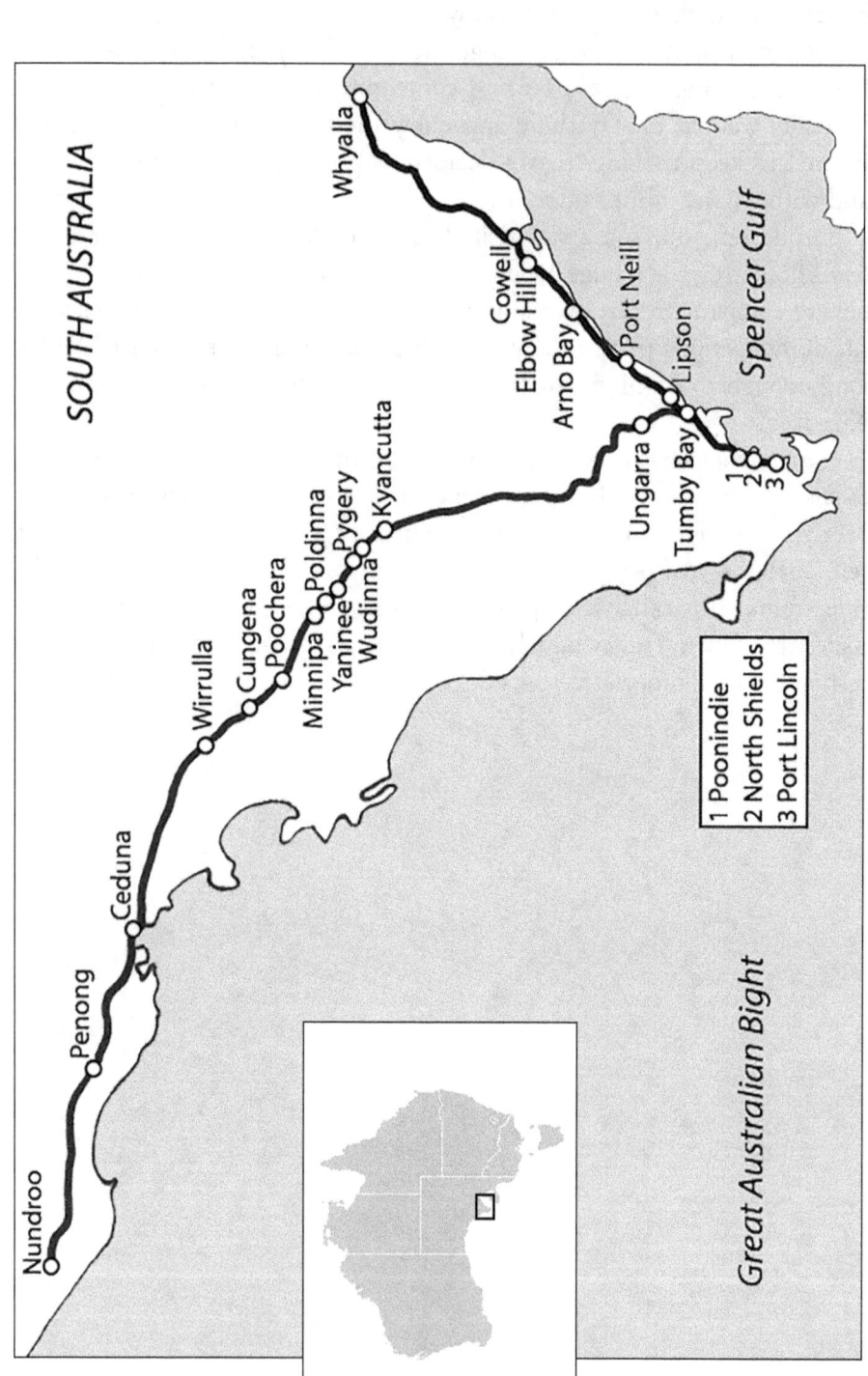

Chapter 16
Kindness Allergies

Penong – Ceduna – Wirrulla – Cungena – Poochera – Minnipa – Poldinna – Yaninee – Pygery – Wudinna – Kyancutta – Tumby Bay – Poonindie – North Shields – Port Lincoln – Lipson – Ungarra – Port Neill – Arno Bay – Elbow Hill – Cowell – Whyalla

Totals: 20,252 kilometres – 1097 hours 54 minutes – $24,756

Monday 17 October
Ceduna, South Australia
4 kilometres – 13 minutes

The wind mysteriously disappeared for my ride into Ceduna. This was a double-edged sword in that the riding was a lot easier, but the flies were able to come out and play. This made it nearly impossible to execute my plan to finish the bottle of honey before I reached the quarantine roadblock. Finally, I managed to find a way of eating my honey sandwiches while spinning in circles to lose the flies temporarily. It was no use running in straight lines while I ate, because the flies were too fast. Circles were trickier for them. I could have avoided the sprinting snack breaks entirely if I'd just shared the honey with Dan on the Nullarbor.

I rolled on, up and over beautiful hills, until I reached the quarantine roadblock that had been publicised ever since I left Kalgoorlie. I was really hoping they would confiscate my flies, but they didn't, so I took them along as I investigated all of Ceduna's caravan parks. I found an inexpensive one with grass and a rainwater tank, and a huge bath in the ablution block.

I held off on having a soak so I could dash to the supermarket before closing time to make an immediate start to my revegetation program. I hadn't had any fresh fruit or veg since I finished my carrots and apples back in Western Australia, so I stocked up on watermelon, carrots and a huge bag of oranges. After towing it all back to the caravan park and gorging myself on fruit, I ran myself a deep, hot bath and read the weekend paper. I couldn't imagine a better Sunday evening.

I spent over a week in Ceduna, preparing for the fourth term of school and my last state of mainland Australia. The novelty of being in a town kept me happy for the first few days. I made regular appearances at the bakery, joined the local library, found bike parts I needed, patronised a pub with a salad bar and spent long stretches of time in the caravan park bath in the company of books from the library.

Soon, though, I fell victim to a bout of stationary melancholy again. It wasn't just from being off the road: I was also getting anxious about my arrangements for South Australia. I'd worked myself into my usual new-state fluster and sent out emails, made phone calls, re-sent emails, posted letters and done everything I could to fill my schedule for the next few months. Even though things had worked out well so far, I always worried that each state would be the one where I had no one to visit and nowhere to ride, and that I would just have to hide in my tent for a few months. By this end of the year, though, I felt less frantic than I had before. I was down to

Being reflective at the Bight.
Photographer: "Dan"

one-quarter worry, one-quarter apathy, one-quarter faith it would turn out all right, and one-quarter relief that I had most of Australia behind me.

It was in this state of mind that I filled in my days trying to find the local radio station, glaring at the newspaper office that wasn't responding to my media releases, emailing the huge list of South Australian schools "just one more time", and kicking the phone box when the people on the other end just seemed annoyed that I was bothering them about this "Cycle of Earning?"

Halfway through the week, I took a new approach to my phone calls by calling schools in the middle of the night. This was cheaper because it took less time to leave a message than to talk to someone who just asked you to call back later; and it meant that I didn't have to listen to as many people politely refusing me. It mostly worked well, but occasionally backfired when a real person answered the phone and frightened me so much that I had to hang up on them.

My time in Ceduna took a turn for the better when I received a phone call from local family friends, Leigh and Tanya. I had been secretly hiding from them for the past few days since, if they'd known I was in town, I was sure they would ask me to stay, thus causing me to violate the Hospitality Policy that I'd recently developed. This policy was designed to ensure that I never out-stayed my welcome in anyone's home. The guidelines were as follows:

- A three night maximum stay if the hosts are blood relatives or personal friends of more than two years.

- Two nights maximum if they are close family friends or friends of less than two years.

- One night maximum if they are friends of relatives or relatives of friends or friends of friends.

- One meal if they are relatives of friends of relatives or friends of relatives of friends.

It turned out that my subterfuge had been unnecessary, as Leigh and Tanya had been out of town until that day. I went over to their house on Wednesday and had a cup of tea and a chat, and enjoyed having friendly company and good conversation again.

It turned out that Leigh and Tanya needed to leave town again for a few days and left me in charge of their home – providing a handy loophole in my Hospitality Policy. Initially I was worried that I would struggle with the fact that I couldn't clean the house by getting inside it, turning it upside down, and shaking it like I could a tent, but I resolved to rise to the challenge and take on the responsibility when I realised the gastronomic possibilities of having access to a kitchen. I'd been getting bored with the narrow range of foods I was limited to with no cooking facilities in my gear. Since arriving in Ceduna I had been experimenting with replacement cooking techniques in the caravan park by using a sink filled with hot water to sit a mug of noodles in. I just kept ending up with warm crunchy noodles instead of cold crunchy noodles and strange looks from the people coming into the ablution block for non-culinary purposes. In a real house, even baking a cake was possible. Food aside, Leigh and Tanya also had overflowing bookshelves of fiction, theology and back issues of *New Internationalist* magazines to read while cakes were in the oven.

One of my evenings was spent at a caravan park for a cycling convention. Congregated were Betsy and Jeff, the Canadians I'd met back at Cocklebiddy; another Canadian couple, Sandra and Laurence, who were on a tandem with a trailer and a roll of duct tape on their handlebars; and my adopted family, Andrew, Kate, Joanna and Matthew.

It was an epic night: masses of food for the combined appetite of half a dozen cyclists, a look at each other's photography, and gossip on the progress of other cyclists we'd met. We swapped tips on high performance nutrition and avoiding flies. We also discussed our preferred camping equipment, Jeff outdoing us all when he brought up "those ice picks you use to climb glaciers".

There was a collective air of achievement and pride at making it across the Nullarbor, and particularly for those with small children, at having survived Nullarboredom. Best of all was the communal understanding and support, which is what Andrew referred to as the Fellowship of the Road. This camaraderie linked our nomadic cycling community together by chance encounters, second- and third-hand stories and a sense of belonging to that breed of people who would rather do it by bike.

By my last day in town, I was getting worried about a visit from the South Australian Police threatening to issue me with a restraining order if I kept harassing the state's schools, inviting them to invite me to visit. Having access to Leigh and Tanya's internet had turned me into a Cycle of Learning spam virus.

When not on the internet, I spent the day trying to dispose of the debris from six kilograms of oranges and three of watermelon from my time in their house. Leigh and Tanya were coming home that night, so I was hoping to find a shovel in their shed to dig a hole and bury the evidence before they returned.

Friday 21 October
Tod Highway to Tumby Bay, South Australia
128 kilometres – 6 hours 31 minutes

I took the Eyre Highway as far as Wudinna and then headed south, right down the middle of the Eyre Peninsula. The riding was easy: moderate distances, tail winds that made me feel like a better cyclist than I was, and towns close enough together to provide ice cream on an as-needed basis.

The school visits I had en route had a distinct social justice flavour. At one school, students thought my bike ride sounded fun for me, but they were concerned about Ralf and how he coped when it rained. I was asked at a Wudinna primary school if Bike and Trailer fit in my tent with me. I tried my best to give an ambiguous response, but the way the girl looked at me afterwards made me worry that I was going to be reported for Neglect of An Inanimate Object.

After spending so many days in a house in Ceduna, it took me a few nights to readjust to camping again. My first evening on the road, I set up camp a little way off the road and held a short memorial service for all the flies that had perished in my tent since it had been up last. My camp spot was not very well hidden from passing cars since there was farmland on either side of the road and only a little scrub between my camp and the road. My reading material for the evening was poorly chosen: a newspaper with a report of the Falconio murder, and a review of the movie *Wolf Creek*. Sure enough, I was soon feeling spooked and then I heard a car pull up on the nearby dirt track. I held my breath and tried to remain calm as I heard what could only be the sound of footsteps approaching my tent. I wished I had followed Dan's protocols for campsite selection and tried to think of what I could use as a weapon: my cutlery set, my smelly shirt, or my headlamp that definitely weighed just as much as a candlestick from *Cluedo*.

By the time I'd settled on defending myself with an Allen key in one hand and my small orange spade in the other, I realised that it wasn't someone's footsteps after all. It was just my heart beating so heavily that it was making my sleeping bag rustle and sound like someone walking. A few moments later, I heard the car pull away. I left the spade near my mattress and did my best to think of raindrops on roses.

The flies maintained a constant presence down the Eyre Peninsula and my fly net attracted some strange looks from passing motorists. I think it had something to do with a technique I learnt from Dan that enabled me to eat food without participation from flies. All you have to do is put the food inside your fly net and then, using your hands on the outside of the net, manipulate the food into your mouth. It was incredibly effective, but looked a little odd.

I had finally settled back into camping again by the time I reached Lock on Thursday. I stopped at a deli and bought a chocolate bar to eat while I mulled over whether to camp in town or in the bush. I decided to check out the town caravan park, but didn't find it very appealing. There was not much there, just a rainwater tank and woman in a caravan who was determined that she would help me somehow. Among other proposals she made, she repeatedly offered to boil water for me. I wasn't sure what for, but hoped it wasn't because I looked to be in an advanced stage of pregnancy. I really didn't have the energy to be helped, so while she wasn't looking, I filtered a few bottles worth of rainwater through my hanky and quietly rode off and out of town. The hanky helped to remove the black floaty things, but may have added some germs of my own to the water. Maybe the water-boiling offer wasn't so silly after all.

I found a secluded spot that looked relatively free from insects, serial killers and serial helpers, and set up camp for the night. I reflected on the difference a good day's riding made. In Ceduna, a night by myself had seemed lonesome and tedious. On the road, an early evening was the epitome of contentment. I enjoyed a change into tracksuit pants, pottered around my tent making up peanut butter sandwiches for the next day, slowly ate a mugful of cous cous and baked beans, and listened to the night. When my body and mind felt like they'd accomplished something concrete for the day, solitude was a pleasure.

My ride today took me through Cummins and then east towards Tumby Bay. In the afternoon, I was passed by a number of buses taking students home from school. Knowing that I would be meeting many of these students the following week when I visited their schools, I made a real effort to stay on Bike even when riding up the most monstrous of hills. I kept my pride and didn't have to get off once, but paid the price by sweating horribly. It was the sort of sweat that releases all of the built-up smelliness you've accumulated since your last shower. My last shower had been on Monday, ie five days ago, hence an impressive odour was liberated by the time I got to the top of the range.

From the top of the hills, I could see 20 kilometres or so of farmland stretching out around me, with the town of Tumby Bay in the distance and the sparkling blue ocean behind it. The ride down the range added to the exhilaration of the moment, as did the breathtaking expanse of clear blue sky above me.

In Tumby Bay, I found the home of Olga, whom I'd first met the year before when I was in town on a teaching practicum. She probably remembered me being a little cleaner and a lot less smelly. Regardless, she – along with her son Darren and cat Jeffy – welcomed me into their home for a few nights. Actually, I didn't see that much of Jeffy after I arrived, but I guess that, being a cat, he had the most discriminating nose of the family.

Tuesday 25 October
Port Lincoln to Lincoln Highway, South Australia
43 kilometres – 2 hours 43 minutes

My time in Tumby Bay coincided with the Eyre Peninsula Lutheran Women's Camp, which Olga took me along to on Saturday. I had a guest speaker spot in the evening and was duly rewarded with an Eyre Peninsula Lutheran Women's dinner. I'd been hearing rumours all day about the desserts that appear at these functions, so took a gamble and had just modest servings of the main course. Sure enough, once the dessert table was unveiled, ripples of excitement went through the crowd and a dignified stampede began. By using advanced engineering principles to load my plate, and by seating myself in a strategic position for access to seconds and thirds, I managed to sample over half a dozen different dishes. The memory of these delights completely ruined my usual enjoyment of my tent dessert of a cup of instant custard powder mixed with some lukewarm water and a handful of sultanas.

The next morning I headed south to Port Lincoln after speaking at a local church. The ride was through heavy rain and a terrible headwind, making it a long and traumatic 50 kilometres to my destination. The trauma from the trip was soon fixed on arrival by a cup of tea and a chat with Betsy and Jeff who'd arrived in town earlier in the day and had already set up camp, *sans* ice picks.

Monday was spent on chores around town, and getting in and out of TYPHOON JACKET as the showers came and went. By the time we'd finished our chores, TYPHOON JACKET was looking a bit out of sorts as he was starting to tear and perish at the seams. As much as I loved TYPHOON JACKET's company, I was starting to wonder if he could really handle a typhoon as he bragged he could. On a brighter note, I found finger buns and oranges on special at the supermarket, and made friends with a neighbour in the caravan park. Dean was into boats and revealed himself to have special talents at repairing bike helmets with gaffer tape.

The next morning I set to work on the last of the finger buns and discovered just why they were on special. It seemed that at seven buns for $1.50, customers were expected to perform their own mould removal. Asking Dean, "Would you lose respect for me if I still ate these?" I got the response, "No ...", but I think he may have just been being polite.

Whatever I ingested with the finger buns gave me the energy I needed for a full day at one of Port Lincoln's high schools. I gave talks to seven different groups and was chuffed to learn that some girls from one class had been selling lemons over the weekend to raise money for Cycle of Learning. I still had quite a few oranges left and one finger bun, so I wondered about setting up my own stall for a few hours before I left town.

It was lucky I didn't, and I made a quick getaway instead; a strange wind had picked up as I rode back north up the Lincoln Highway. It got progressively stronger throughout the evening, prompting me to use my tent pegs for just the third time that year. Without them, I was worried that I'd wake up in the morning on the other side of the gulf on the Yorke Peninsula.

Monday 31 October
Cowell to Lincoln Highway, South Australia
121 kilometres – 6 hours 18 minutes

I spent a busy three days making my way up the east coast of the Eyre Peninsula, stopping in to visit schools at Tumby Bay, Port Neill and Ungarra. Many of the kids in these schools were from farming families, and I made the most of their practical knowledge. They gave me tips on how to ride down hills faster, what sorts of bike tools I should be using, and a peninsula-wide consensus that Bike required some stunt pegs. I knew what Dan's response would have been to the idea of adding more pus to my bike, but I promised them I'd think about it.

On Friday afternoon I found myself sweating through a hot headwind as I continued to make my way north. I finally took a rest stop at the turnoff to Arno Bay, and sat there for a while figuring out a plan of attack, greatly assisted by a jar of quandong jam I'd been given at the Port Neill school.

I was trying to figure out how to stop myself going completely crazy over the weekend. It was Friday and my next engagement was only on Monday, in Cowell, just a short ride away. Given that my mental state suffered when I was in a town too long with nothing to do, I hatched a cunning alternative plan, based on the comprehensive knowledge I had of Dean, the helmet fixer's movements. In Port Lincoln's caravan park, I had tried to distract him from the mouldy finger buns I was eating by asking him detailed questions about his travel plans. I knew that he was heading back to Adelaide that afternoon, and I reasoned that he would definitely stop to say hello as he passed me – at which point I could beg a lift, get back into Adelaide for the weekend movie fundraiser being organised by my friends and family, and then get a bus back to Cowell on Sunday. Fool proof.

I kept a sharp eye out all the way to Cowell. This required limiting my fluid intake to minimise my toilet breaks, as I didn't want to be off the road when Dean drove past. Once I reached Cowell, I sat it out by the roadside until I decided that Dean must be saving the drive for the following morning. I selected what I figured had to be the cheapest caravan park in town since it had the most flies and was furthest away from the town centre.

The next morning, I followed my assumption that Dean would be passing and decided to stake out the highway, determined to find him for a lift home. I could already picture the look on my parents' faces when I knocked on their door in the afternoon.

I rose at 5 am, packed a bag of essentials, secured my tent, locked up Trailer, and rode down to the highway. It was an hour before any vehicles passed me, and four more before I finally gave up. There is nothing quite so depressing as sitting through a grey, drizzly morning in a TYPHOON JACKET that is slowly decomposing, waiting for someone who never comes, who could have taken you home.

After I came to terms with the fact that I was stuck in Cowell for the entirety of the weekend, I directed my efforts to finding myself some entertainment before all the shops shut at midday. Weekend paper and a three-kilogram bag of oranges in hand, I returned through the rain to my tent to while away the hours. Things started looking up when I found a huge stack of back issues of tabloid magazines in the camp laundry, but quickly went downhill again when my tent started leaking. I fled back into town where I discovered a bakery/takeaway shop that was still open, and wallowed in a toasted sandwich and milkshake.

On Sunday, I continued with more expert loitering to avoid the flies of the caravan park and the sauna-like qualities of my tent. I bought a newspaper, took it to a deli and purchased a muffin. I sat at a table, reading the paper and taking uncharacteristically small bites of the muffin for a few hours. By the time I felt that I had outstayed my welcome, I moved on to the next deli and repeated the process, this time with an apricot slice. Since there are only two delis in town, I had to change my tactics when it was time to leave again.

I found a community art gallery next. I was enjoying both the art and the fly-free environment when the lady at the front desk started chatting to me. When she found out what I was doing in town (the Cycle of Learning, not the loitering, aspect of it) she insisted on giving me a donation. As I took her two-dollar coin and thanked her, a strange combination of social discomfort, melancholy and nausea swept over me. I left the gallery immediately to avoid anyone else giving me money and found a bench near the jetty to reflect on what had just happened. I seemed to have become allergic to fundraising.

All year, I'd known that I didn't enjoy asking for or receiving donations. In fact, I wasn't completely comfortable with any of the kindness I'd been given this year. Through Cycle of Learning, I wanted to repay the generosity and kind-heartedness I received in Kodaikanal. I had an idea that after this year I would feel the score had been settled and I could cast off the feelings of indebtedness I had been harbouring since 2001. It turned out that instead, I had a new country full of people to feel beholden to. I knew my perspective was upside down. I didn't really want people not to be nice to me or not donate to Cycle of Learning. I just needed to work on accepting what was given with grace and gratitude, and being happy to give people an opportunity to support the people of Kodaikanal. I once read a wonderful inversion of the first of Buddhism's Great Vows for All. The original vow is: "The many beings are numberless, I vow to save them." A Zen teacher called Ross Bolleter wrote: "The many beings are numberless, I vow to open myself to be saved by them."

In Cowell, though, I didn't have much energy left for numberless beings wanting to save me, so headed back to the caravan park and dealt with my nausea by eating numberless oranges while waiting for the weekend to end. When eventually it did, I sprang into action on Monday and visited the local school.

With the visit over, I left the town, glad to be on the road again. It was a hot ride to Whyalla, and March flies were lying in wait for me on the road. Thankfully, they were slightly smaller and more stupid than their cousins in the west. Accordingly, I dubbed them February flies, which then made me worry that I was leaving things open for April or even December flies to track me down before I got back to Adelaide.

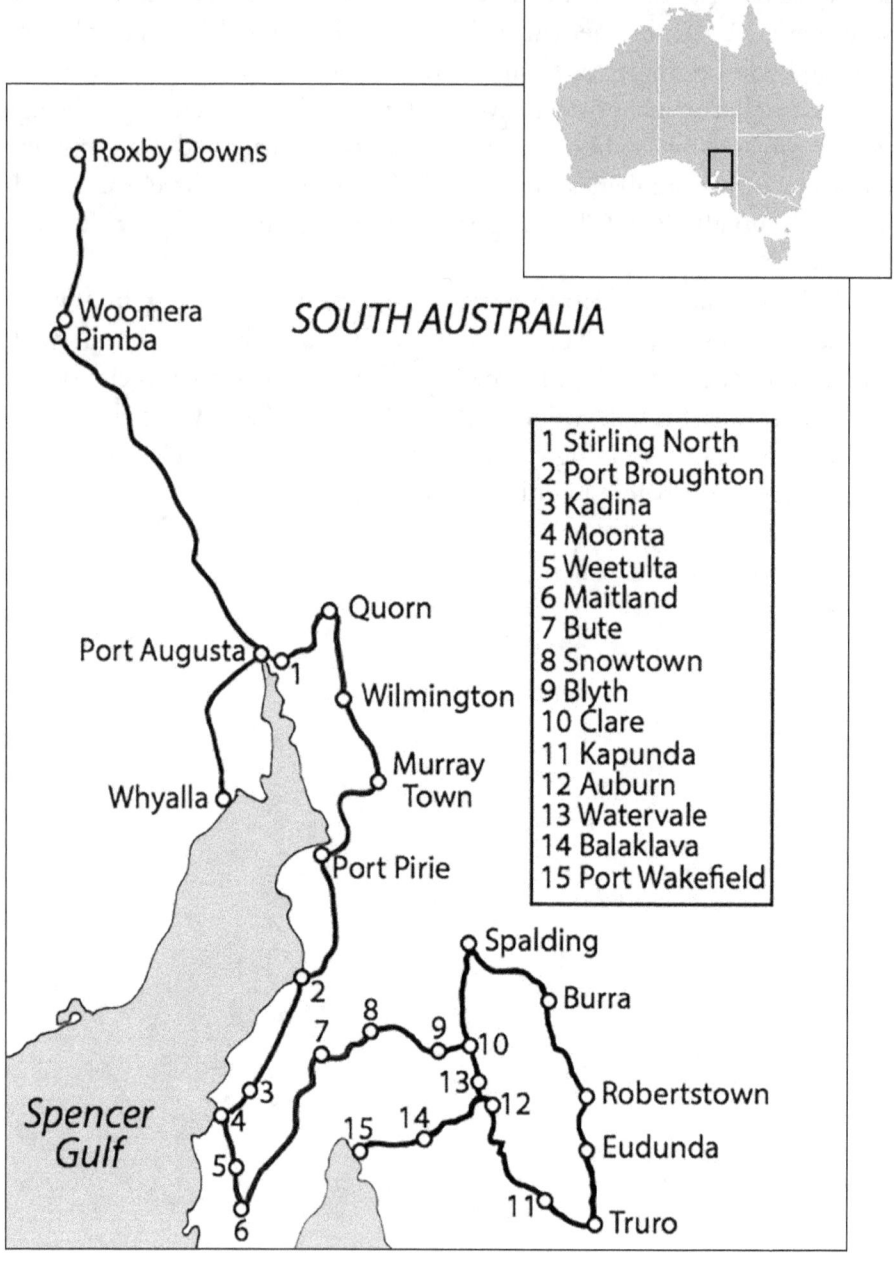

Chapter 17
Headwinds, Hayfever, Huge Heads and Hankies

Port Augusta – Pimba – Woomera – Roxby Downs – Port Augusta –
Stirling North – Quorn – Wilmington – Murray Town –
Port Pirie – Port Broughton – Kadina – Moonta – Weetulta –
Maitland – Bute – Snowtown – Blyth – Clare – Spalding –
Burra – Robertstown – Eudunda – Truro – Kapunda – Auburn –
Watervale – Clare – Balaklava – Port Wakefield

Totals: 21,804 kilometres – 1183 hours 47 minutes – $26,310

Thursday 3 November
Woomera to Roxby Downs, South Australia
86 kilometres – 3 hours 52 minutes

The heat increased as I continued north to Port Augusta and on to the bottom end of the Stuart Highway. As soon as I made my return to this road that runs right up the centre of Australia, the headwinds sprang into action.

Given the slow pace I was travelling through the wind, I was glad I had packed some extra water. It was 170 kilometres to Woomera with an overnight stop, so I had spent my time in Port Augusta arranging my rig in order to fit 16 litres on board Bike and Trailer. I knew it might be a bit overcautious, but I hadn't been able to find out any information about water availability for the roads ahead.

When I pulled over on Tuesday evening and set up camp, I wandered over to investigate the huge pipe that had been running parallel to the highway since I left Port Augusta. It turned out to be a water pipe, and where I camped there was a tap directly attached to it. The 16 litres I had brought with me was indeed rather excessive, given I had access to the water supply for the entire northern region of South Australia at my fingertips. It was nice tasting and cool, too.

I reached Woomera the next afternoon, after a slow ride through the hot, northerly headwind. Being a military town, there was a lot of replica – or maybe retired – missile-launching equipment decorating the roadsides. I also saw a lot of people in army fatigues. There were probably even more; they were just too well camouflaged for me to spot.

I found my way to the caravan park and headed straight for the camp kitchen, where some guests accused me of being a construction worker. Explaining my opinions about the importance of visibility, I settled down at the communal table to impress my accusers with my special skills in consuming Weetbix. Any credibility I accrued in the kitchen went totally down the drain later in the evening when various other campers had to rescue first my tent, which kept flying away in the wind, and later Bike, which while it couldn't quite fly, fell over a few times from its spot next to a bench. I felt a bit embarrassed but, more importantly, my helmet was now broken in even more places, as it was on Bike's handlebars at the time. I doubt if even Dean and his gaffer tape could fix this amount of damage.

Even the students at Woomera Area School were concerned about my head safety. They insisted that I find a new helmet at my next stop in Roxby Downs, rather than wait for my return to Port Augusta as I'd planned. Once the helmet issues were decided on, we moved on to the nature of the hostels the children stay at in Kodaikanal. It took some time to explain that these hostels are not in fact facilities where really naughty children are sent, but instead places for children to live, play and study at, close enough to schools so they can attend regularly, unlike in their home villages.

By the time I'd restored the reputations of the Kodaikanal students, it was time to hit the road to Roxby Downs. I got to Roxby in record time and headed for the sports shop to buy a replacement helmet. The staff there informed me that they didn't sell helmets – the newsagency did. Silly me! The newsagency did indeed have a wide range of helmets, all with a special feature that the newsagent demonstrated to me on the blue helmet I chose. It had a knob on the back that could be turned to adjust the helmet size, as your head gets bigger or smaller. This would be very convenient for me – I received a lot of both insults and compliments out on the road.

I found the caravan park where I set up in the company of two lads who were cruising the park on their BMXs. They were from the school I would be visiting the next day. The boys were intrigued with Trailer and wanted to know whether I carried a baby inside it. Inspired for my next fundraising venture, I watched the boys perform a few stunts on their own baby-free bikes, before they had to ride off to get home in time for tea.

Monday 7 November
Port Augusta to Quorn Road, South Australia
34.63 kilometres – 2 hours 16 minutes

After a short memorial service on Friday morning, I placed my old, gaffer-taped helmet in the bin, and headed to the local school. I was kept on my feet all day, with a number of groups to speak to and an onslaught of complex questions. The students thoroughly interrogated me and found out all sorts of details, from what people eat in Kodaikanal (and whether or not that involves tarantulas), to the names of the people who took the photos I showed them, and to the nature of the orange drink in my water bottles. I was disappointed that I didn't get any dinosaur questions though. Apparently, during a recent visit by the Premier of South Australia, he was asked if he had ever seen a dinosaur. I guess if the Premier hasn't seen one, it is hardly likely that I would have.

I made my way back south and was approaching Port Augusta again by Saturday afternoon. I was 30 kilometres out of town when I was met by a car coming in the opposite direction, headlights flashing. It was my parents, come to meet me for a weekend reunion.

We stowed Trailer in the boot of the car and my dad said that if he were in better shape, he would ride Bike into town for me. I nearly had a fit at just the thought of such an idea. A flood of arguments came to my lips. What about the road trains? Do you realise how hot it is? You're a Fitzpatrick; we have the same genetic sense of direction; you'd get lost! Over my dead body would I let you ride to Port Augusta!

It was in that moment that I realised what I had been doing to my parents for the past ten months. If *I* got that horrible, scared feeling just at the notion of my father spending a few hours on the highway, what must it have been like to have a daughter riding for a year?

My parents are quite wonderful. For as long as I can remember, they have never tried to change my mind about anything. When I deliver pronouncements on new plans I have, however unconventional or out of the blue, I can count on each of my parent's responses. My mum will begin brainstorming ways of making things happen, thinking of opportunities I could take and generally getting enthused. She is not a worrier; once I told her my bike riding plans she spent a day or two concerned about my safety, but then read a book by an adventurer, Dervla Murphy, who cycled from France to India in the 1960s, and decided what I was doing was infinitely safer since I didn't have to pack a pistol like Dervla. Being a social worker who is always busy on various boards, community groups and church activities, my mother doesn't waste her time worrying. She'd taken a pragmatic approach to my year's project, offering every ounce of her support by paying the bill for all the calls I made from my mobile or payphones, assuring me I could phone her any time of the day or night, and when I did, wholeheartedly agreeing with whatever I was doing or thinking, even if it completely contradicted yesterday's conversation. And then she would tell me how much she'd been bragging about me to whoever she'd been talking to lately. I remember once, a conversation came up about whether parents have favourites or not. Mum rubbished the notion and told us that children each need different things and to be loved in different ways. This was a lovely moment of realisation for me, that Mum has that perfected for each of her two daughters. This year she'd given me exactly what I needed – a supportive ear and pride in what I was doing.

My dad definitely invests in worrying. This year I thought it mostly stemmed from the fact that he did not see what it was that I might find enjoyable about riding my bike around the country. He's never camped, or been that interested in travel or the outdoors. He is not particularly interested in "big" projects either. Instead my father has a gift for taking pleasure and satisfaction in the mundane and the low-key. A few years ago Dad took up snorkelling with his brother. They meet at one of the beaches at Port Adelaide – the industrial part of town where they grew up that has nice enough beaches, but is not in the vicinity of any reefs or special fish. My uncle brings along a spear-gun, a relic from their coastal childhood, which is ostensibly to fight off sharks, but I think really because, like when they were kids, it's fun to carry around weapons. Dad's reports from snorkelling expeditions centre on how calm or rough the water was, and if they saw any crabs or not. When friends suggest he should go on a holiday to a place with reefs and actual things to see while snorkelling, Dad just shakes his head and expounds the virtues of the calm waters and crabs of Largs Bay and Semaphore. Dad also manages to draw those around him into his pleasure of pedestrian pursuits. When I'm home he'll decide on a whim that we should drive across town to look at an interesting fence he's seen recently. Or he'll call me into the backyard to have a go at a new test of reflexes he's invented, requiring you to throw a tennis ball off a particular spot of the garage wall and catch the rebound before it bounces.

Dad's great love – fences, crab-sightings and tennis balls aside – is music. As long as I can remember he's always been working on his own albums – writing, recording and mixing songs and designing the artwork for the covers. Some songs take months to mould into what he wants, as Dad chips away, making notes in an exercise book, strumming the same riff over and over trying out minor variations, or squashed into the bathroom with his recording equipment for the good acoustics. When each album is finally completed, with a few dozen copies ready, Dad will quietly give them away to family and friends with their Christmas card, and start planning the next album. A lot of the world seems to glorify ambition and big results. My father is a constant reminder to try to fully engage in a process and cherish the minutiae that everyday life provides.

Luckily, back on the Stuart Highway, my father didn't take his offer to ride my bike any further, so I rode it back, feeling rather naked without Trailer. I blitzed into town at glorious high speeds, found my folks at their motel, and enjoyed a wonderful family weekend. They drove home Monday morning, leaving me with a supply of cashews, red bean cakes, hankies, and a little bit of homesickness. The best of these gifts were the hankies, since my Alice Springs range were still failing miserably at performing proper hanky functions. They were more like pieces of cellophane. The ones my mum brought were from a second-hand shop, and thus had already been worn in over a few decades. I had a lovely clean nose for my visit to a kindergarten on the outskirts of town, before heading up the road towards Quorn and camping near the Pichi Richi Railway for the night.

For dinner I investigated a packet of allegedly "long life houmous" which my mother also brought up for me from Adelaide. She'd originally bought it for me back in January before I left Adelaide, but I didn't have room in Trailer for it at that stage. I had used up the room with masses of slightly useless stuff that only lasted a few weeks in Trailer – such as a tea towel and an astronomy almanac. Mum found the houmous recently while cleaning the house, so brought it up for me. Any food that can be found "while cleaning the house" should make you wonder if it's edible or not. I discovered that it *was* edible, but in the way that a tea towel or astronomy almanac would be, too.

Saturday 12 November
Bute to Blyth, South Australia
65 kilometres – 3 hours 32 minutes

I spent this week travelling down to Moonta on the Yorke Peninsula, and then east through Bute and Snowtown to Blyth. My movements were now dictated by my speaking engagements and, though not far from Adelaide, I would be criss-crossing this part of South Australia for the next month. I had been feeling worried that, now the Nullarbor was behind me, the dearth of cycling challenges would leave me bored with the riding, and susceptible to some regional, less arid, cousin of Desert Craziness.

While the riding was easier and I felt closer to civilisation, I was pleasantly surprised by the new relationship that my riding and I were forging. Instead of being driven by the motivation to cover great distances and get to the next place, this new, less-demanding meandering was allowing me to get to know my home state better. Most towns in South Australia had previously been just names to me, and it was wonderful to have their geography and character revealed as I visited them, and the misplaced assumptions I had about them dispelled.

Riding through Moonta held a particular thrill for me. When I was in primary school, Moonta was one of those exotic places that other kids went to on their school holidays, along with the Gold Coast and Goolwa. My family didn't really "do" exotic holiday locations. A big holiday trip for my sister and me was being taken to town on the bus by Dad. First, we'd have a toasted sandwich in a snack bar, and then we'd look in a pet shop, and maybe the toy section of a department store. Or, if we weren't up for such a long trip, Dad would declare an orange feast. This consisted of sitting in the backyard and eating a whole lot of oranges from the orange tree. At the end of the feast, Dad would wipe the pocketknife he'd been cutting the oranges with on his hanky (there is a close bond between Fitzpatricks and their hankies) and throw the knife into the lawn to make it stick in the ground. If this was the sort of fun we had staying in Adelaide, I couldn't even imagine what sort of excitement Moonta had to offer. It turned out to be less thrilling and exotic, and more a pretty, coastal town with cheap carrot cake in their supermarket.

Germein Gorge was pretty to ride through, but wasn't lined with the geraniums I'd been expecting, and Murray Town wasn't on the banks of the Murray River. Melrose had none of the actors from Melrose Place walking around in high heels, and Port Pirie wasn't covered in a layer of lead-covered ash, as I was worried it would be.

Port Pirie was so clean, in fact, that I took a critical look at the hygiene of my water bottles while I was there. A modest ecosystem of algae in the necks and lids of most of my bottles had been developing lately, but one of my more senior 1.25 litre bottles revealed itself to be even more fertile. I had been using it to store my supplies of the weak cordial and salt solution I used to rehydrate. In Port Pirie, I realised that the sides of this bottle were looking like a well-colonised petri dish and there was a strange, smoked-fish smell emanating from it.

This was no time for sentimentality or loyalty, no matter how far the bottle had travelled with me. I threw Old Mate into the bin and bought a bottle of soda water to use as a replacement. I did keep the lid, though, as it was a pop up one and good for drinking from while riding. As a precautionary measure, I spent a good 15 minutes removing the algae from the rim of the lid with a pen cap and my hanky. I realised only after the operation that the combination of those two cleaning devices might result in something even more exciting being grown, especially since I'd been using the same pen cap to clean out my ears every now and then.

Finally, yesterday I found a town that did meet my word-association expectations. I had anticipated Bute to be full of stocky farmers driving utes, giving each other cheerful claps on the back and thumbs-up signs. In the afternoon, riding into town, I was indeed overtaken by a steady stream of utes, driven by sturdy farmers, slowly towing silos or carrying massive bundles of hay. My self-congratulations on finally making an accurate generalisation about a town quickly evaporated as the hay blew off the utes into my nose and eyes, giving me terrible hay fever. My nose started running like a tap and my sneezes put me in danger of either dislocating my sternum or falling off Bike.

When I finally made it, undislocated but sniffing and spluttering, into the town centre, I faced a catch-22 situation. Bute was the cause of my debilitating hay fever, but I didn't have the energy to ride out of its allergenic clutches. I ended up camping in the council caravan park where they had a laundry and running water to deal with my overflowing hankies.

During the night, I admitted defeat and dosed myself up with antihistamines. I woke up in the morning enveloped in a groggy, medicated haze, but at least my nose wasn't running. I stumbled down the street for my other over-the-counter substance of choice: Weetbix. I discovered a

750-gram packet on sale for $2.55, which I couldn't pass up, so had to reorganise Trailer to fit the box in. It took up more room than my bedding, clothing and housing combined, but none of these tasted as good when I mixed them up in my mug with powdered milk and water.

Monday 21 November
Balaklava to Port Wakefield, South Australia
70 kilometres – 3 hours 42 minutes

The huge box of Weetbix fuelled my rides around the Clare Valley through Spalding and Auburn, south to Truro, and as far east as Eudunda. The headwinds and hay fever (which incidentally are my two least-favourite riding conditions that begin with H, just in front of hallucinations and hamstring injuries) that had followed me the past eight days were overshadowed by the high quality of schools, congregations and public toilets I visited.

The school in Eudunda bore the distinction of being my only visit that was entirely arranged by a student. James, a Student Council representative, contacted me the year before, and did an impressive job of organising things for the day. I was even more impressed on meeting James in person on my arrival when, by way of introduction, he apologised if he smelled, as he had been feeding cows before school. It was normally me who was apologising for being smelly, so I felt at home in the school straight away.

At an internationally-themed school assembly, I spoke about Cycle of Learning, and was given some practical advice from the students as to how to construct solar wells and bush dunnies. After the assembly, it was lunch time, so there was plenty of time to chat with any of them who wanted to have a closer look at Bike or to share their own cycling adventures. I was then escorted by a helpful band of students over to the staffroom where a lunch order was waiting for me. I must have had a cosmic link with the school because the lunch they gave me was vegetarian and included a finger bun. Double points!

Spalding was home to both a friendly school and fabulous public toilets. The 44 students at the primary school were a wonderful audience and had lots of fascinating bike stories of their own. There were stories about saving up money to buy bikes, tales of high-speed crashes into fences, and proud exhibitions of scraped knees and elbows. I hadn't realised how much I would have in common with kids in Spalding. They also asked me if I'd ever been so cold that I'd fallen off Bike. I almost wish I had had this experience as it would make a good story – but I had to answer in the negative.

A question that popped up all year, and once again on this day, was "What animals are there in Kodaikanal?" I should really have made some enquiries back in Kodai about that one, because the only animals I remembered were leeches and cows. I'm sure there were lots more; I just couldn't remember them because they never tried to attack me.

Once my visit was over, I rode off under the supervision of the entire school, feeling glad that it wasn't cold enough for a fall. Departure successfully executed, I spent the rest of my time in town admiring the public conveniences. Even with my newfound knowledge of bush dunny construction, I had been frequenting more public toilets, as going to the toilet in the bush was not really OK when towns were as close together as they had been lately. Throughout my life, I have done extensive surveys of public toilets both domestically and overseas. My favourite public toilets anywhere are in a park near the Adelaide foothills, in an old brick building with a roof that is partially open to the sky. You can hear birds singing and watch the treetops while enjoying the facilities.

The toilets in Spalding were not quite as nice, but I have declared them the Cleanest and Best Resourced. Their range of soap and hand drying options made me want to drink a whole lot of water so I would have to go again.

I visited Clare for a second time later in the week, on Friday. I came in on the road from Auburn this time, so avoided the hills, but instead had to ride through swarms of tiny biting insects that got under my clothes and into my mouth and tasted horrible. They also got much too close to my eyeballs, which probably also tasted horrible to them, although it felt as though they kept biting them just to make sure.

After a visit to the high school, I spent time in the Clare library, using the internet, reading newspapers, and nibbling dried fruit when the librarians weren't looking. I soon realised that I really didn't want to ride anywhere else that afternoon. It was humid, and I was sleepy and full of fruit. Adding to the sudden dip in my mood was the realisation that the weekend had hit and there was only a short ride to Balaklava to keep me busy until Sunday afternoon.

I decided to go just a few kilometres down the road to the caravan park. My big plans for an early night were sabotaged by a couple camped down the hill playing a noisy board game. From the sound of it, the game was one of those 1980s "popomatic" types, with the hard plastic bubble that you press down on to shake the dice inside. I complained to myself that even if this couple were 1980s fanatics who wore hypercolour T-shirts and snap bracelets and collected Care Bears and Transformers, couldn't they have had some '80s concern for their tired neighbours and chosen something a little less noisy to play: maybe *Guess Who* or *Twister*? I suppose I should have just been grateful that it wasn't *Hungry Hungry Hippos*.

As tempting as it was to get up ridiculously early the next morning and crunch my muesli loudly outside my neighbours' tent, I was feeling so gloomy that I could only muster slow, quiet chewing, with just the occasional sigh thrown in. With my mood swings creeping up on me so suddenly these days, I was glad to be nearing the end of my mainland ride. I had almost reached my limit of hanging around in tents, waiting for speaking engagements.

The ride to Balaklava was accompanied by a headwind that luckily had a bit more bark than bite, unlike Ralf who had neither. The wind was loud and blustery but didn't have much effect on my riding. Once I got into town, I added some bananas and a tin of spinach and ricotta ravioli to my supplies, and then found the caravan park. The tin of ravioli was the big disappointment of the afternoon. I had bought it on a whim, thinking it would be so incredibly bad that it would give me something to write about in my blog. Unfortunately, it was quite tasty, despite being cold and straight from the tin.

The wind was still going strong, now blowing bucket-loads of red sand into my tent. I realised that trying to continuously brush it out would be futile, so I left it all inside. I figured it wouldn't be a problem as long as water didn't get involved, and therefore resolved to abstain from indoor crying and drooling.

I kept my emotions and saliva under control over the weekend and occasionally emptied out my tent to prevent a serious erosion issue for nearby plants. Finally, it was time for me to visit the local church to give a talk and enjoy some human contact. Thanks to an offer of lunch with the pastor's family, I had to turn down my date with Weetbix, powdered milk and all the red dirt that would have been blown into my mug as well. Lunch consisted of quiche and salad, which made me even happier, since my life didn't have enough egg or leafy vegetables in it at the time.

After the slow weekend, I felt much cheerier with a school visit and a decent amount of riding on my plate for the day. The day's smile dropped off my face, though, when I discovered that I had lost my fly net somewhere in Owen. I first wondered if stealthy Dan had had something to do with it. He had admired it many times and even tried to negotiate a complex trade involving headlamps, instant noodles and the sacrifice of Ralf to secure possession of it. If anyone I had met this year was capable of secretly following me for a month, it was Dan.

However, the additional fact that, of all the people I met this year, Dan was also the least likely to ever steal anything, turned my suspicions away from him and onto the flies. I had been bragging a lot lately about the fly-stopping prowess of my fly net, not only to people I met, but also to the flies on the other side of the mesh. I was getting a bit smug, and I think the flies might have decided to teach me a lesson. If stealing my fly net was the first part of the plan, I was scared about what part B might be. I was also concerned that the student at the school in Owen who asked if the fly net was a dress would be the first person to find it.

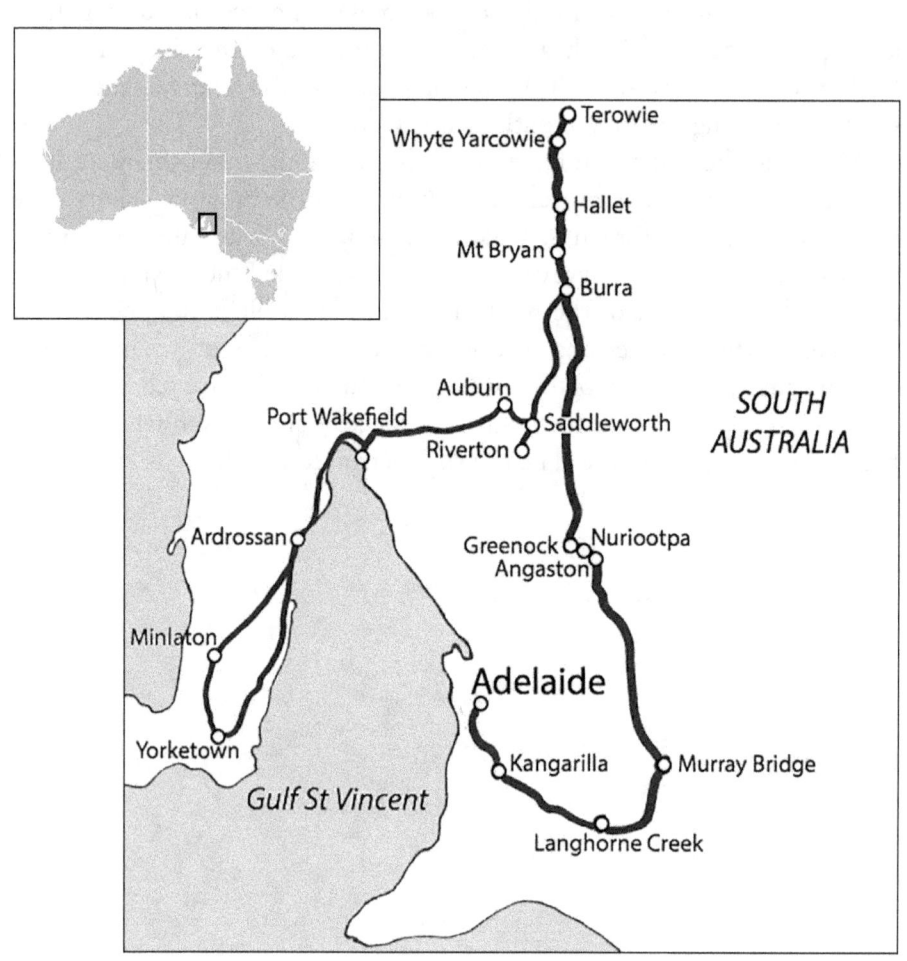

Chapter 18

Home

Port Wakefield – Ardrossan – Minlaton – Yorketown – Auburn – Saddleworth – Riverton – Mount Bryan – Hallet – Whyte Yarcowie – Terowie – Burra – Greenock – Nuriootpa – Angaston – Murray Bridge – Langhorne Creek – Kangarilla – Adelaide

Totals: 22,808 kilometres – 1238 hours 42 min – $29,616

Sunday 27 November
(Adelaide to Auburn, South Australia)
6 kilometres – 18 minutes

Had Dan or anyone else been following me, I would have well and truly shaken them from my trail last week. My first step to confuse them was doubling back and revisiting the Yorke Peninsula. I visited schools in Port Wakefield and Yorketown this time around, and found many bike enthusiasts at both schools. In fact, down in Yorketown, the students took bike riding very seriously, and I felt out of my depth. I faced a barrage of technical questions, including what makes a bike expensive, why I hadn't opted for a road bike instead of a hybrid, whether bicycles are more expensive than motorcycles, and whether I wore "professional" riding gloves. I said yes to the last question, but I think I was lying. Part way through my question answering I managed to swallow a fly, but I was sure that just added to the air of professionalism I was trying hard to maintain.

The suicide mission down my throat may have been a statement from the fly community about the replacement fly net I'd purchased in Ardrossan. I took the message as: "You may have a new fly net, but if you're not respectful to us, you'll pay the price by us flying into your orifices."

After riding a few laps of the tennis courts with some of the students on their bikes, and then accepting a generous donation raised by the students for Cycle of Learning, I headed out of town. I'd originally been planning just to ride as far as Ardrossan, but after phoning home in the morning for my mother's birthday, I thought maybe I should aim for Adelaide instead.

A sudden sprint across the countryside would lose any pursuers once and for all. I calculated that I could make it to Auburn that night ready for the first bus the next morning. One hundred and eighty kilometres was not too far for someone who claimed to own professional riding gloves.

By the time I got to the top of the Peninsula, I had changed angles and was riding into a nasty headwind for the last leg into Port Wakefield. Also, my phone was beeping to warn me that the battery was about to run out. I decided to scout around Port Wakefield's petrol stations for a power point from which I could borrow a bit of electricity. I may have been amateur in the bicycle department, but I was expert at appropriating water, power, campsites, and untouched second-hand food that would otherwise be thrown out.

I discovered a bank of power points around the side of one service station, and furtively plugged in my charger. Moments later, I thought I'd been found out when a caravan pulled up next to me with a grumpy-looking man. I was sure he was either a holidaying policeman or the president of the Citizens Against Electricity Theft Council. However, the fact that I was wearing my fluoro vest and messing with the petrol station's infrastructure worked in my favour. He merely asked me where we kept the air hose. With the authority that comes with many years working in the petrol station industry, I pointed him in the right direction and, once I had just enough charge in my phone, headed off down the road that runs through Balaklava and onward to Auburn, riding through the beautiful cool evening stillness.

By nine o'clock, it was completely dark, so I ploughed on at a good pace with my lights flashing and headlamp in place until I hit the range that I had forgotten stood between Auburn and me. I slowed right down and took my time, reminding myself that I had until 8.40 the next morning to get there. I was inching my way up a particularly steep section when my gears went all funny and refused to stay in their lowest, easiest settings. I tried what I could to fix the problem, but to no avail, and realised that Bike might be asking for a trip to Adelaide too.

Finally, midway between the middle of the night and the early morning, I got into Auburn, found my way to the caravan park and threw my mattress down next to a building. I plugged my phone in for some extra charge in the laundry, devoured a cucumber and the last of my Weetbix, and hoped the bugs wouldn't take advantage of my tent-less sleeping arrangements.

A few hours later, I rose with the sun, packed up my gear, and set about solving a few logistical problems. Specifically, I needed to get my phone out of the now-locked laundry, procure a bus ticket for myself, find somewhere to stow Trailer and negotiate Bike's passage on the bus with me. With the kindness of many strangers, I took care of everything, with a few minutes to spare. At 8.40 sharp, Bike, my phone and I were safely on the bus to Adelaide.

Between visiting grandmothers during my time back home, I tackled a small mountain of Cycle of Learning administrative work. My official return was less than two weeks away, and I was doing my best to muster whatever radio, newspaper and TV coverage I could for the event. I secretly wished I could hire a stand-in to smile and wave and be interviewed in my place on that last day while the real me just snuck back home, threw my clothes in the washing machine, and went to bed for a few days. I loved to ride. I loved the road. I loved speaking to young people and members of the community about Kodaikanal and the people there. I just was not a big fan of fanfare and ceremony.

As much as I was not looking forward to my finale, I was also stressing out at the possibility that there might not be a finale to endure. I had a high school enlisted to host my return, but I desperately needed some sort of media coverage: television, radio or newspaper.

More superficially, I spent a lot of the weekend coming to terms with people's reaction to my skin. By this end of the year, my face had entered a whole new realm of sun damage. In Adelaide, everyone seemed to think I was sunburnt, and while I was sure what had happened to my skin was just as much a precursor to skin cancer as sunburn, it was *not* sunburn. The state of my skin was the result of living outside for the majority of the year and probably similar to what you find on an old farmer or a weather-beaten sailor. I had done my best to cover up from the sun, but the sun is a difficult thing to hide from 100 per cent of the time.

There was a consensus that I would require some serious exfoliation on my final return home. I wouldn't have been too worried about that if it was being advocated only by people who worked in beauty salons, but as it was suggested by people who had worked as dairy farmers and pig hunters, I felt a little concerned.

By Sunday night, I was back on the bus, rolling through the streets of Adelaide to head back to Auburn. I made the most of a quiet, comfortable bus trip to reflect on the two worlds I was moving between. Watching the city and its people through the window, I remembered how much I enjoy the energy and diversity of city life: being in a crowd; meeting up with friends; watching passers-by in Rundle Mall; riding from home to the market, to a friend's house, to a bookshop, to my grandmother's, and home again in one day along the flat roads of Adelaide. It's such a nice lifestyle.

But then, as the bus headed further north, we were rolling through fields with gracious hills in the distance and the changing colours of the setting sun washing over the calm, open spaces. At the beginning of the year, I'd felt a bit overwhelmed and out of place in the countryside and outback. After spending some quality time with nature, I now felt that Australia and I had an understanding of each other, a familiarity, respect, and appreciation. I would like to think that it was a two-way, mutual thing, but Australia may just have been being polite.

Thursday 1 December
Burra to Greenock, South Australia
110 kilometres – 6 hours 32 minutes

I based myself in Auburn for a few days while I visited schools in nearby towns. I was relieved to pack up and leave on Tuesday, due to the overwhelming attention from my local fan club. Auburn's large community of earwigs camped outside my tent the entire time I was in town, looking for any opportunity to sneak inside and go berserk, wriggling around on the floor of the tent.

Once I was packed up, I visited a local school that presented me with a huge poster of a bike and the words "Cycle of Learning" covered in coins they'd brought in from home. Since the support crew who normally carried these large works of art for me was about ten months behind schedule, I took a photo instead and arranged for the coins to be swapped for a cheque.

The school I visited in Riverton gave me much more than just a donation. After finding out I didn't have a safety plan for riding through a lightning storm, I received a wide range of suggestions as to how to stay alive if I found myself in that situation. Some students thought I should find a wheat field to lie in; others wanted me to wait it out under trees; and a few were convinced I would be fine staying on Bike since he had rubber tyres. I thanked them for their advice and we all hoped that I experienced some electrical activity soon, to find out who was right.

The next evening, while setting up my tent in Burra, I noticed some lightning in the distance that should have warned me that my wish was soon to become a reality. Unfortunately, I was distracted from finalising my lightning-survival plans by a strange feeling in my nose. I had been inflating my sleeping mat, which requires energetic nasal inhalation and strong cheek muscles, when I suddenly had a feeling similar to the one I get when I eat carrot, laugh and get a chunk stuck somewhere in my head. I hadn't eaten carrot for three hours, so blew my nose carefully. Eventually, a fly came out, slowly waving its legs in a post-traumatic stressed kind of way. I wasn't too happy either, especially since I'd been keeping up my end of the bargain, and giving deference to flies both to their faces and behind their backs.

In the morning, after tracking down more Weetbix and using the internet in the library, it was somehow nearly midday. I thought I must have lost a few hours at some point – probably while I was clasping the huge, newly purchased box of cereal in a euphoric reverie. Since I finally started out for Nuriootpa a lot later than planned, I managed to forget to eat lunch.

Early afternoon I stopped at a roadhouse and asked for a small bag of chips, which usually should have enough fat to keep me going for at least a few hours. The lady disappeared out the back and returned with a bag so full that I let out an audible gasp of shock. She must have run out of small bags and instead used an extra, extra large one. I knew she wasn't trying to feed me up on the basis that I was a cyclist, because as she handed me the bag she asked if I'd just knocked off work, nodding in the direction of the road works down the street. Mumbling something about bike riding and the importance of visibility, I accepted the chips, sat down at a table

Auburn's bicycle-shaped fundraising, South Australia.

outside, removed my fluoro vest, and set to work. The chips seemed to be just one more challenge I had to get through before I reached the day's destination. It took me an hour to deal with the mountain of fat and potato.

As it turned out, though, the hot chip lady had some foresight, since the rain began soon after I left her roadhouse. The thing about rain is that it isn't very conducive to stopping to get food out of your bag. If you stop to buy food, people don't like it when you drip on their shop floor; on top of that, you tend to get cold, and don't want to start riding again. So a belly full of chips was just what I needed to carry me through the rest of the day without any food breaks.

I passed through Riverton and collected some cheers and greetings from students as I rode through the town. I should have asked them if they'd come to a consensus yet about the lightning because, half an hour later, thunder and lightning joined the rain. I couldn't see any wheat fields or particularly hospitable trees, so stayed on Bike and hoped for the best.

The storm continued and the temperature dropped as I tackled the range between Tarlee and Kapunda. The hills went on and on, even past Kapunda, and my fingers and toes got more and more like prunes as the rain kept soaking into me. By the time I reached Greenock, I had some decisions to make. I was expecting a phone call in 20 minutes time, but Nuriootpa was at least half an hour away. I knew that if I stopped in Greenock for any more than a few minutes my core body temperature would drop past the point at which I could get back on Bike and into the rain. I looked around me at the street signs for ideas as to where I might spend the night. Bed and breakfast: way too expensive. Museum: maybe another day. Public toilets: could be useful. Church: definite potential.

I scouted around the public toilets and decided they would be good, but only for their stated use. Neither interior nor exterior offered much in the way of hygienic shelter for the night. I made my way to the church and discovered a lovely, long veranda at the back that was spacious, dry, out of sight of the road, and had plenty of room in which to drape my wet clothes and self on to dry out. If I didn't stay there, the only other option in town was the cemetery, and I was not up for that.

I dried off as best I could, and managed only a banana and carrot for dinner. That bag of chips from 80 kilometres back and six hours ago was still sustaining me. I settled in for the night in the corner of the veranda, a bit worried that someone might find me and be angry enough to call the police, or feel sorry for me – and, whatever their reaction, stop me from falling asleep.

Tuesday 6 December
Langhorne Creek to Kangarilla, South Australia
59 kilometres – 3 hours 40 minutes

I awoke on Friday morning undisturbed, unarrested, and unconfronted. I quickly packed up and rode on to Nuriootpa, where I visited the supermarket and was faced with one of my toughest decisions all year: the reduced-price shelf in the bakery section had four of my favourite bakery products. I spent 20 minutes deliberating, and finally settled on spinach and cheese scrolls going at four for $1.50. I hoped the raisin bread, chocolate and sultana loaves, and Boston buns would all find good homes, and headed on out of town.

In Angaston, I visited one of the primary schools, with which I had been in touch since the beginning of the year, getting regular updates on their activities. The students were following my ride around Australia and, by running around their school, adding up all of their distances and multiplying that number by three, were keeping up with my cycling.

I had prepared myself for students with outstanding fitness and mathematical abilities, but I hadn't expected them to be so friendly as well. Before and after my talk I had multitudes of students come up, have a look at Bike, ask questions, and request my autograph on a piece of paper, hat or arm. As I am not the neatest of writers, I was a bit concerned that there would be many parents confused about why their children came home with scribbles on their arms. I was also a bit worried that my enemies might get hold of one of the students and, above my signature, add something along the lines of "I, Anne Fitzpatrick, confess to stealing electricity, fly murder by inhalation, trespassing on church property, and having illegible handwriting. Signed…" Luckily for me, most of my enemies can't write, because they are bugs or headwinds.

I left the school with a card signed by all the students (which would be useful if I needed to forge any counter confessions), a cheque for the money the school had raised for Cycle of Learning through recycling and chapel collections, waves, and the cheers of the students ringing in my ears. I rode on, discovering some huge hills, impressive views, powerful winds and intriguing gastrointestinal sensations along the way. I suspected the latter were due to my digestive system still dealing with the previous day's hot chip saga, and the fact that my spinach and cheese scrolls seemed to have had cement as one of their main ingredients.

The hills and wind didn't let up as I inched towards Murray Bridge through the afternoon. The rain also returned, and by the time I finally made it into town, evening had arrived. I felt a sense of *déjà vu* and realised that it all felt suspiciously like my last entry into Murray Bridge, exactly ten months ago to the day. The weather, quality of the light, and the feel of the town hadn't changed much, but the girl riding in was completely different. Was that really me who'd arrived at the caravan park with a naked Bike, only half a dozen speaking engagements in her diary, significantly smaller leg muscles, and full of excitement, fear, and uncertainty at what lay ahead? I felt a bit embarrassed for that girl who, as amateur as she still was 10 months later, had been infinitely more amateur back then in all aspects of the project she'd undertaken.

I returned to the same caravan park as last time, since I remembered it had an outdoor camp kitchen with couches, communal saucepans, and – back in February – a friendly lad from Western Australia called Jason. I thought there was a good chance that Jason might not still be there, but was surprised to find the saucepans gone too – although that did confirm a theory I had at the time that I'd unwittingly borrowed someone's pot that night and they'd been too polite to say anything. This time I asked first, and borrowed some backpackers' saucepan to cook up some packet pasta I'd bought weeks ago but hadn't had the equipment to eat yet. The owners of the pot weren't really up for conversation, although I tried my best to be friendly by reprimanding them for being from Wales but not speaking Welsh.

After nearly destroying their saucepan with my out-of-practice culinary efforts, I summoned all the arm strength I possessed, and managed to clean the pasta sauce off the sides. I gave it a final rinse and handed it back to the Welshmen who were ready to sprint back to their campervan as soon as I passed it over.

The next morning, as I pottered around the caravan park, I smiled awkwardly at the Welsh travellers each time I passed them, but they resolutely avoided eye contact. It seemed that I might have found some enemies that were more literate (although not in Welsh) than bugs and headwinds. And there was a good chance that the kids from yesterday's school hadn't washed their arms yet. I wondered whether I should hire a lawyer.

On Monday, I stopped back at the first school I had visited back in February. I was drier but a lot scruffier than the last time, and the kids were all four terms taller and wiser than in February. The only low point of the visit was when a boy asked, "Do you carry insect repellent?" I calmly replied, "No, that would have been a good idea." However, I really felt like grabbing him by the shoulders, shaking him and shouting, "Why didn't you ask me that last time I was here?!" I was so upset that I had to track down some fried ice cream before I left town.

The next day, I made a leisurely exit from Langhorne Creek and cycled to Strathalbyn to get some chores done. I thought I had kept a low profile in the town centre, until a woman walked past me while I was finishing off my grapes and asked me if I was having a progressive lunch. I couldn't quite remember her. Was she the lady who'd sold me the roast vegetable wrap, the one I'd bought my iced coffee from, or the one in the supermarket where I'd bought my vegetarian faux-deli slices, or the owner of the fruit and veg shop? Her remark was an epiphany for me, as I realised that the whole year had actually been one massive progressive lunch for me.

Content once I had a full stomach, I headed to the visitor centre to make enquiries about caravan parks in or around my next destination: Clarendon. The main reason I needed to find a proper place to stay was that my mobile phone desperately needed charging before an interview I had lined up for the next morning. The thorough women in the visitor centre spent over half an hour poring over maps and street directories, making phone calls, and rushing between brochure stands to try to help me. They finally admitted defeat and informed me that there were no caravan parks where I was heading. They offered me their phone to call either Clarendon Primary School or the Clarendon Bakery to find somewhere to stay. I'm still not sure why they suggested this last one as an option. Maybe the bakery rents out gingerbread houses.

I politely declined calling either place, and tried my best to reassure them I could find somewhere to sleep by myself. This was a bit difficult, since by nature, visitor centre staff don't consider roadside scrub to be accommodation. I deflected their concern by asking if I could recharge my phone in their power point, which they obligingly let me do.

Charged up, I finally left town mid-afternoon unaware that the beautiful flat riding would finish at Strathalbyn, and begin being incredibly hilly and thus sweaty for me. I had to walk up a lot of the hills and, while doing so, I reflected on something a cyclist I met the day before had told me. Apparently, if you have to push your bike up an incline, there is nothing wrong with you. It's a problem with your bike and its gear ratio. I felt a bit upset when I heard this, and wished I'd been given some warning so that

I could have covered Bike's ears. However, today I used the information to make myself feel better about my slow progress.

I eventually got to Kangarilla and looked for somewhere to sleep for the night. After some searching, I found a nice spot a kilometre or so out of town, at the graveyard, where I would be out of view from passers-by. It was a bit early to retire there yet, and it was still light so I back-tracked to the town centre where I ate Weetbix and read the last few pages of a newspaper I had saved from a fortnight ago for cases of emergency boredom. Around eight o'clock I headed back to the cemetery and spent a while wandering around gravestones, reading epitaphs and paying my respects to those buried here. I settled down for the night on a bench under a shelter at the top of the hill overlooking the dark rows of graves. It didn't feel scary at all, just peaceful with the lingering residue of memories, tears, and love laid down in the cemetery's earth.

Friday 9 December
Adelaide, South Australia
14 kilometres – 50 minutes

I rose on Friday morning with butterflies in my belly for the final day of the mainland leg of Cycle of Learning. Little did the high school and news crew preparing to welcome me know that I'd actually rolled into Adelaide on Wednesday and been skulking around my home since then.

After visiting a school in Clarendon on Wednesday morning, I realised I was less than fifty kilometres from Adelaide and had nowhere else to be before my official homecoming, two days away. I made an executive decision to just go home.

I found my way to Main South Road, looked out across the city, rolled down the hills, rode past Flinders University, and followed the familiar route home from there. Up Cross Road, down side streets and over the train tracks, along Greenhill Road, through the suburbs and down Osmond Terrace. I perfectly timed the turnoff into my parents' street, not needing to pause for the traffic or lose any downhill momentum, and cruised the last few hundred metres into our driveway. I dumped Bike and Trailer by the back door and found the spare key from its hidden spot in the backyard. I checked the letterbox, walked inside, made a toasted sandwich, and sat down on the couch to do my tax return. It was exactly the home-coming I wanted.

The majority of this year's most precious memories were – just like my ride into Adelaide – mundane and low key. I didn't often write about them because there was nothing to tell. Eating an apple as I was riding, tossing the remains into the bush and seeing them bounce along before disappearing into the scrub. Riding away from a school, especially the smaller ones, with the kids waving me off. Being asked where I would stop for the night and not having an answer. Eating a hunk of watermelon with a knife outside the shop that I bought it at. Nodding to the hitchhiker waiting with his swag in the rain. Turning at a highway intersection. Pushing my bike away from a campsite, looking over my shoulder and seeing no sign that I'd been there. Filling up my water bottles. Standing by the side of the road as a road train blasted past. Riding down a hill through the wind, feeling half exhilarated and half terrified. Chatting with people at rest areas. My grubby, tanned, incredibly useful body. The birds. The road. The setting sun.

That Friday morning I did my best to make it look as though I'd been doing some serious riding to get into town, instead of hanging around home with the blinds down so that nobody would see me. I filled Trailer's bag with some books and towels and got back into my cycling clothes, but decided against rubbing dirt all over myself to further authenticate things. Looking the part, I hooked up Bike and Trailer and headed towards my old high school. I waited down the road from it as I'd been instructed, and was soon joined by a TV news crew and some students and teachers on their bikes. My favourite cyclist was the one with a bin strapped to the side of his bike to carry a trumpet.

Once we were all assembled, we rode in convoy down the road and into the school. What an amazing reception it was! Cheering students were lining the driveway, and there was even a ribbon at the end of the drive for me to ride through. The magnitude of the occasion left me a bit speechless, which made my interview for the night's news a lot less articulate than I'd have liked it to be.

Luckily, a celebratory drinks reception coincided with the evening news, so I didn't have to watch the embarrassing ordeal on TV. Instead, dressed in a skirt – since the prophesy from Minilya Roadhouse had come true, and I couldn't fit my thighs into any of my trousers – I stationed myself at a nearby pub and spent the evening catching up with friends.

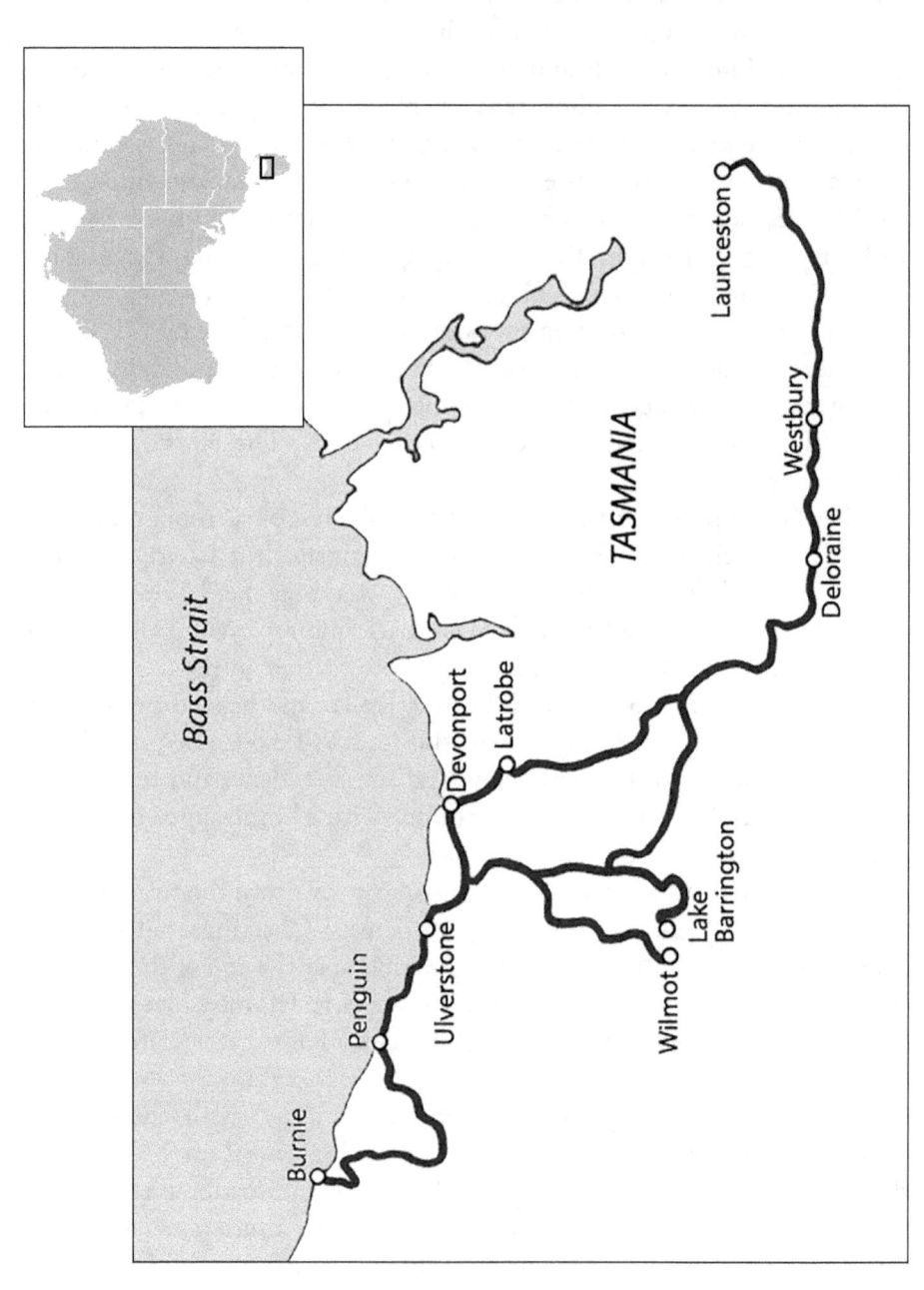

Chapter 19

Zip-Lock Bags Can't Solve Everything

Launceston – Westbury – Deloraine – Latrobe – Devonport – Ulverstone – Penguin – Burnie – Lake Barrington – Wilmot – Launceston

Totals: 23,316 kilometres – 1272 hours 49 minutes – $34,943

Wednesday 15 March 2006
Adelaide, South Australia, to Launceston, Tasmania
35 kilometres – 2 hours 15 minutes

My decision to extend Cycle of Learning from mainland Australia and ride around the island state of Tasmania was made in April last year. I'd just met the walking fundraiser, Colin, in northern New South Wales and made a teary phone call to Christine: "... and he is going to have a parade thrown for him when he arrives in Brisbane ... and people have given him huge donations by the side of the road ... but I've decided that I'm going to ride around Tasmania." A few days later, I found out that Colin had already walked around Tassie, so it didn't really prove anything, but I have a problem in that once I say I'll do something I have to do it.

It looked like it would be a good decision, however misplaced the motivation was. I'd had four months to get organised, and there had been a fantastic response already from the Apple Isle. In fact, I was just a few appointments away from crossing the line from fantastic response to logistically impossible response. I wasn't complaining at all. After the speaking I'd been doing in the past few months in Adelaide, on the morning of my departure there was $34,000 in the Cycle of Learning account, and I hoped Tasmania would play a significant role in raising the last $16,000 to reach the target.

Since my return to Adelaide in December, I'd been in touch with various friends from the road. I caught up in person with Colin the walker at one of his homecoming events. We agreed that it hadn't been at all difficult getting used to things like beds and houses. Andrew, Kate and their brood, after stopping in on my parents on their way through Adelaide, were settling back into life in Bendigo. Andreas the Handcycler was currently on his home stretch, just above Sydney, focused on his finish line in Brisbane.

The two grubby trailer-towing boys I met in Darwin, Jack and Simon, were still having adventures, though somewhat different from each other. Simon was riding through Asia and, when last I heard from him, was concerned about how he could have started off with one book and a trumpet in his trailer, and ended up with ten books and a bass guitar. Jack had surprised me more recently when I was in Adelaide's Rundle Mall watching a street performer juggle fire while simultaneously tightrope walking. I didn't recognise him until midway through his act, when he paused during a trick and asked me if we'd met in Darwin.

Besides riding to get to work and around Adelaide, the only preparation I had undertaken to get ready for my final leg was to acquire some exciting new gear to help me deal with Tasmania's lower temperatures. I had new thick socks, balaclava and a very fluorescent rain jacket that looked as though it should last longer than my old friends Poncho and TYPHOON JACKET (RIP) did. Lastly, my most talented beanie-knitting auntie had put together a purple replacement for the green and white one that provided a woolly safe haven all around the mainland.

I enlisted Paul, the cyclist I met in Brisbane and its surrounding unisex toilets, to help me out the morning I left for Tasmania. Even with a slightly broken collarbone, he was good enough to ride with me to the airport and dismantle Bike while I dashed about inside procuring a bike box and tape. I was hoping that there would be room in the box for Paul as well so that he could help me reassemble Bike and Trailer upon arrival in Tasmania. However, after I'd thrown my tent, spare tyres, handlebar bag, and other miscellaneous items into the bike box, I felt a bit bad about asking him to travel in such a small space, so let it pass.

After an uneventful flight, I landed in Launceston and dragged my bike box out of the airport terminal. I successfully put Bike and Trailer back together, except for the odometer, which now served merely aesthetic purposes. I rode the 16 kilometres into town from the airport and can confirm from first-hand observations that Tasmania has all of the trees and unusual marsupials and hills that people say it has. The marsupials might have looked less unusual when they were alive and not squashed by cars, but I still couldn't recognise them.

I diligently followed all the signs pointing to the visitors centre in the middle of town so that I could get information on caravan parks and supermarkets. Once I found the centre, I realised I had been too focused on riding there, and had obliviously ridden right past the caravan park and shops I was riding to the centre to locate. I retraced my route, but had a much more dangerous and illegal time than during my ride into town, due to Launceston's penchant for one-way streets.

I settled down in the caravan park and found my camping routines coming straight back to me. Bike, Trailer and I were also enjoying being back together again; it felt like the past three months out of the saddle might have been just a dream. However, as I pottered around my camp, I was hit by a swell of loneliness. I tried to remind myself that it is always a shock going from having a bustling life, surrounded by people in Adelaide, to suddenly being by myself in a state where I don't know anybody. Being alone, like any skill, needs practice to perform it gracefully. And I felt out of practice.

A good distraction was the new implement to replace my old enamel mug: a saucepan. I now had the superpower of cooking. I got a lot of joy from constructing a lentil, onion, cheese and mushroom risotto: a real, cooked risotto that didn't involve sitting anything in a sink of warm water.

Tuesday 21 March
Burnie, Tasmania
12 kilometres – 55 minutes

In the past few days, I had rediscovered the things I love about long-distance cycling. I had made the most of the empty roads to sing loudly at the countryside, and snacked on apples and carrots as I steered one-handed. I'd savoured the process of solving simple and practical problems such as waterproofing my gear and calculating routes and distances, and recalculating them each time I got lost.

I'd had a few hours of this sort of problem-solving in Latrobe as I looked for its caravan park. I'd asked directions at a deli and was told clearly, "It's less than one kilometre away. Just turn right down Axeman's Drive before you go over the river." I have very selective hearing when it comes to directions, and only latched onto the phrase "over the river". I ended up with a 14-kilometre detour, but passed enough tourist information boards to be sure that I was in the platypus capital of Australia, and the hometown of my favourite woodchopper.

As much as I enjoyed those first days of riding through Tasmania, Tasmania didn't seem keen to have me on its roads. If anything, I got the impression that the state was testing out my resolve to see if I really deserved to be there.

On my first day, I was eating a leisurely – and, may I add, cooked – breakfast at 8:30 in the morning, in the caravan park in Launceston. A fellow guest found out that I was planning to ride the 110 kilometres to Latrobe that day and became quite agitated that I hadn't left hours ago. He insinuated that I wasn't taking my riding seriously, so I tried to placate him by explaining that I had ridden that distance many times before, and I knew I would have plenty of time to reach my destination. This just made things worse, as he changed his tack and started interrogating me as to how I, a solo cyclist of the fairer sex (yes, my tan faded a few days after my return to Adelaide), had survived all of the thieves, rapists, murderers and other generally bad people I must have met on my travels. I wasn't sure if he had a skewed, scary view of life on the mainland, or if I had a skewed, naïve view of what lay ahead of me here in Tasmania.

While I hadn't been outright murdered so far, there had been a few attempts on my life. The first time was when a car that was parked on the side of the highway, just out of Railton, suddenly had a door opened by the driver. I gave them something to think about by shrieking maniacally for at least 20 seconds, as I passed and rode into the distance. I completed the screech with a dirty look over my shoulder.

The next assault to test my mettle was from a large hairy spider that ambushed me at a snack break. He waited until I was busy with my sultanas and then crept up my leg, probably with the intention of biting me on the calf or tampering with my brakes to make my death look like an accident. I spotted him at ankle level, flicked him off, and sped off, checking my brakes in case he was the decoy spider.

I must have passed Tasmania's test, because the scares let up by the time I got to the coastal road between Devonport and Burnie. These winding roads that are tucked in between the green mountains and blue-grey water were empty of scary stories, car doors and spiders. Instead, I was passed by happy motorcyclists who waved as they overtook me, and local residents on their own bikes, who slowed down to ride and chat with me for a while before turning off into properties down side roads.

While life on Bike was finally under control, I struggled to keep my spirits up during the times that I was dismounted. My evening in Latrobe was so lonesome I would have even welcomed a chat with the paranoid man from Launceston, and I felt even worse by morning. It had rained through the night, and stopped by the time I got up. Unfortunately, it had left my tent and everything in it somewhere on the spectrum between damp and drenched. Along with the moisture, it had been a cold night, requiring the wearing of every one of my new, cold-beating clothes. I was worried that I wouldn't have any more layers to add as I rode further south. Besides the worry about the wet and cold, I felt generally downhearted for no particular reason.

I loitered around the caravan park to let the sun dry my gear out, spent a small fortune in town on zip-lock waterproof plastic bags, and made a teary phone call to Christine. The tears were mostly because I didn't have many words to explain why I was feeling so upset. I managed to verbalise a few concepts – "It's cold here … and I feel lonely … and all my stuff got wet" – and then let the tears slide down my cheeks while I waited for Christine to find some way to cheer me up.

From a project point of view, I should have been jubilant. I had the majority of the ride and a large amount of the fundraising successfully behind me, a full calendar for Tasmania and only a few weeks to make it through, no matter how cold or lonely I was. I had put some distance between me and my old friend Melancholy for the past few months. Routines, family, friends, TV, socialising, movies, music and books had served as barricades between us while I was back in Adelaide. Back on the road, my defences were down and Melancholy had rushed in to deliver an almost crippling blow to my morale.

Christine did her best to raise my spirits and helped me brainstorm on-the-road gloom-avoidance strategies. A lot were not viable. It was now too hot to wear my beanie. I wasn't hungry enough for watermelon or finger buns. Singing wasn't socially acceptable on the main street of Latrobe. I could purchase a trashy magazine and drown my sorrows in brain-numbing crosswords and Hollywood gossip, but this move would be more an admission of defeat than a mood-enhancer. My mainland methods provided no answers.

I had to come up with a new scheme, so decided on buying a nice new pen and empty notebook. I hoped to channel enough of my pensive emotions into bad poetry or philosophical treatises to leave me free to operate in my daily life without crying. The purchases were extremely effective. Just knowing the notebook and smooth-writing black pen with the nice grip were in my backpack, waiting to be used in the creation of literary masterpieces, was enough to lift my mood.

I made it to the local high school to give a talk, completely tear-free, and I managed to smile at the people in Devonport who booked my place on the ferry back to the mainland for next month. I parked myself in a pub with a $3 salad bar for the evening, and jotted down very important ideas in my new notebook.

I kept myself busy before bed by putting my smaller possessions into zip-lock bags and bigger ones into rubbish bags in an attempt to stop them from getting damp overnight. In the morning, it was just like Christmas, as I unwrapped dozens of packages and found everything completely dry. I now had control of moisture as well as my mood.

It was a short-lived victory, since after Devonport I stayed in Burnie for the next four nights with a family that looked after me and let me sleep in a bedroom where I didn't have to zip-lock-bag all my things before I went to sleep.

My hosts were Danny, Michelle and their daughters, Mollie and Ella, and I couldn't have asked for a friendlier family to stay with. Danny, a police officer, didn't hold it against me when I confessed to getting a fine for riding without my helmet in Mount Isa. Michelle spent the evenings driving me along the routes I had to ride the next day so I wouldn't get lost. Ella let me watch Care Bears DVDs with her, and Mollie let me use her special spider mug to drink tea out of.

During my stay, I visited nearby schools, Rotary clubs and church congregations. A common theme between all these visits was people's interest in my plans to ride the west coast of Tasmania. I had been told that it rains 300 days a year in that part of the state. I was wondering if I would need to buy a giant zip-lock bag with just a few holes in the bottom for the wheels of Bike and Trailer to poke through.

On my last afternoon in Burnie, I caught up with some local cyclists that I had been introduced to through mutual friends. One of them, Matt, had cycled the length of North and South America, and had some amazing tales to tell. I resolved to remember that if I ever felt sorry for myself in the

Tasmanian weather again, I should just be grateful that I was not riding through Alaska where it actually gets warmer when it snows.

I finally rode back home for one last evening with Michelle, Danny, Mollie and Ella. On arrival, I discovered my place in the family, at least at the dinner table, had already been replaced by a large, oversized, home-grown zucchini.

Thursday 23 March
Lake Barrington to Launceston, Tasmania
172 kilometres – 12 hours 8 minutes

The household rose the next morning to discover that both Ella and I had been struck down by a mysterious sore-throat causing lurgy. I personally would like to blame the zucchini. Ella got to stay home from school, and I thought about having the day off too, but I wasn't sure who I would get to write a note for me or, for that matter, to whom the note would be addressed. Instead, I sadly farewelled the family and rolled down the street for a Rotary meeting, then as far east as Ulverstone, before turning inland for the small town of Wilmot.

I encountered my first serious get-off-and-walk Tasmanian hills that day. They were beautiful hills to be walking through, though. I had majestic mountains surrounding the area, the Forth River running next to me for most of the ride, and multi-coloured parrots in the sky above. The effort of the hills gave me the feeling that I was sweating all of my sore-throat germs out of my body.

From Wilmot, I exchanged all my altitude for a spot at a camping ground down near Lake Barrington. The campground overlooking the lake was nothing short of breathtakingly beautiful – and not just because I had cold-induced respiratory issues either. The lake was huge, still, deep and ringed by forested hills of stately trees. The only other thing in the campground was a large, mysterious tent that required a poem in my Tasmania notebook.

Tent on the Mountain

Tent, a tent on the mountain
Surprised me when I trudged into this place
Waiting here overlooking the lake
Lake circled by forest, full of grace.

Tent, waiting tent on the mountain
Must be waiting for campers' return
Campers that hike through majestic trees
Or glide over lake, paddling in turn.

Evening covers the tent on the mountain
Covers the lake and the trees.
The tent must have travelling owners
Work in town, then sleep here for free.

Night comes to the tent on the mountain;
Torchlight reveals it's been here a while –
Left up for a family with children,
Weekends fishing, the toys left outside.

Morning breaks on the tent on the mountain
Breaks too on the cold silent lake;
A cold morning for those who are tentless –
This tent seems wrong, it seems out of place.

Weathered tent, large cheap tent on the mountain,
Zips broken, door kept closed with pins;
Spare tyre, embedded in the foliage outside
Next to toys, empty bottle of gin.

Call out to the tent on the mountain
"Are you there?" through the faded nylon
Wait ten seconds more then unpin the door
Slowly gaze at what's left by those gone.

Used plates, plastic mugs, instant coffee.
Grey quilt, but no mattress to sleep.
Powdered milk, tinned food, an assortment of clothes,
Colouring books, pencils, broken toy jeep.

Tent, vacant tent on the mountain,
Vacant of people but not of their things.
It seems they meant to come back to this place,
Eat the food, wear the clothes, colour in.

Tent, waiting tent on the mountain,
I hope they're somewhere kinder than here.
I hope it was a happy choice that was made,
I hope that there's nothing to fear.

Chapter 19: Zip-Lock Bags Can't Solve Everything   **223**

I walked Bike and Trailer back up into Wilmot this morning and spent some time enjoying the newspaper in the sunshine before I visited Wilmot Primary School. I'd noticed a number of Wilmot students riding around town yesterday afternoon and made enquiries at the end of my talk. Sure enough, the school boasted a large proportion of bike riders, who were keen to give me some Tasmanian riding tips on how to properly descend and ascend a hill. The former involves taking your feet off the pedals, with your legs sticking out, and the latter requires not getting off and walking.

I tried the trick with my feet a few times on the road back to Ulverstone, before my respiratory system took up all of my attention. The cold that the zucchini gave me had progressed and, combined with the steep hills, was leaving me quite out of breath. I took regular breaks to cough up interesting substances and made it down to the plains by afternoon.

In Ulverstone, I followed instructions given to me by Matt, the Arctic cyclist that I'd met in Burnie earlier in the week. I rode to the designated location, opened the letterbox I found there and, sure enough, there was

The get-off-and-walk hill into Wilmot, Tasmania.

a pair of wetsuit booties waiting for me. Apparently, these are the best things to keep your feet warm in wet conditions, and Matt was kind enough to lend me his pair for my time in Tassie. I just hoped I got the right letterbox; it wouldn't have surprised me if a lot of Tasmanians keep wetsuit booties in their letterboxes, just in case.

I decided not to model my new footwear for the Rotary meeting that night. It was a combined meeting for two clubs, and so was very well attended. The night had a positive feel to it, although I was a little concerned that my guest speaking performance wasn't quite up to par. The combination of the germs coursing through my system, the over-the-counter medication I'd been dosing up on, the cosy effects of the heating system in the dining room, and the wonderful three-course meal left me a bit dozy and slow to function. There was one point in my speech when I realised I was slurring my words, but a lot of Rotarians made very generous donations afterwards, so I must have got the message across. In fact, the donations were so generous that I wondered if I should make a habit of speaking under the influence more often.

I also received many offers for a spare bed to sleep in for a few hours before setting off back to Launceston, but I was keen to get started on the ride straight away. One hundred and twenty kilometres stood between me and an 11 o'clock school visit the next morning. I was prepared for the night's ride, being stocked up on oranges, fruit tingles, raisin bread and fruit juice to consume along the way. I changed out of my speaking clothes and into my riding gear, adding tracksuit pants, jacket and socks. The extra clothes were not so much for warmth, but more to put a layer between me and the night. I sometimes felt a bit strange when I rode in the dark, as if I were not meant to be out on the road. Even though too many clothes would make me a bit sweaty, they also made me feel slightly more detached from the middle-of-nowhere night air.

It was a relatively mild night, with a strong headwind and occasional drizzle. The ride was tough because of my fatigue from the day's activities, my cold and the kilometres I'd covered, but by talking to myself in a very patronising but encouraging way, I kept myself moving.

By early morning, I was getting closer to Launceston, but losing my motivation. Through the moonlight I started looking out for goat houses in the paddocks I was passing. Someone had told me that there is a law in Tasmania that every goat must have its own goat house, and it did seem that whenever I saw a goat there was always a small triangular shelter nearby. I kept a sharp lookout for one, which I could quite easily have curled up in, and maybe made the goat ride into town for me.

However, goats were not popular in this area, so I persevered and rolled into town at about 5:30 am. I cleaned my teeth in a park and got into my sleeping bag for a nap on a bench.

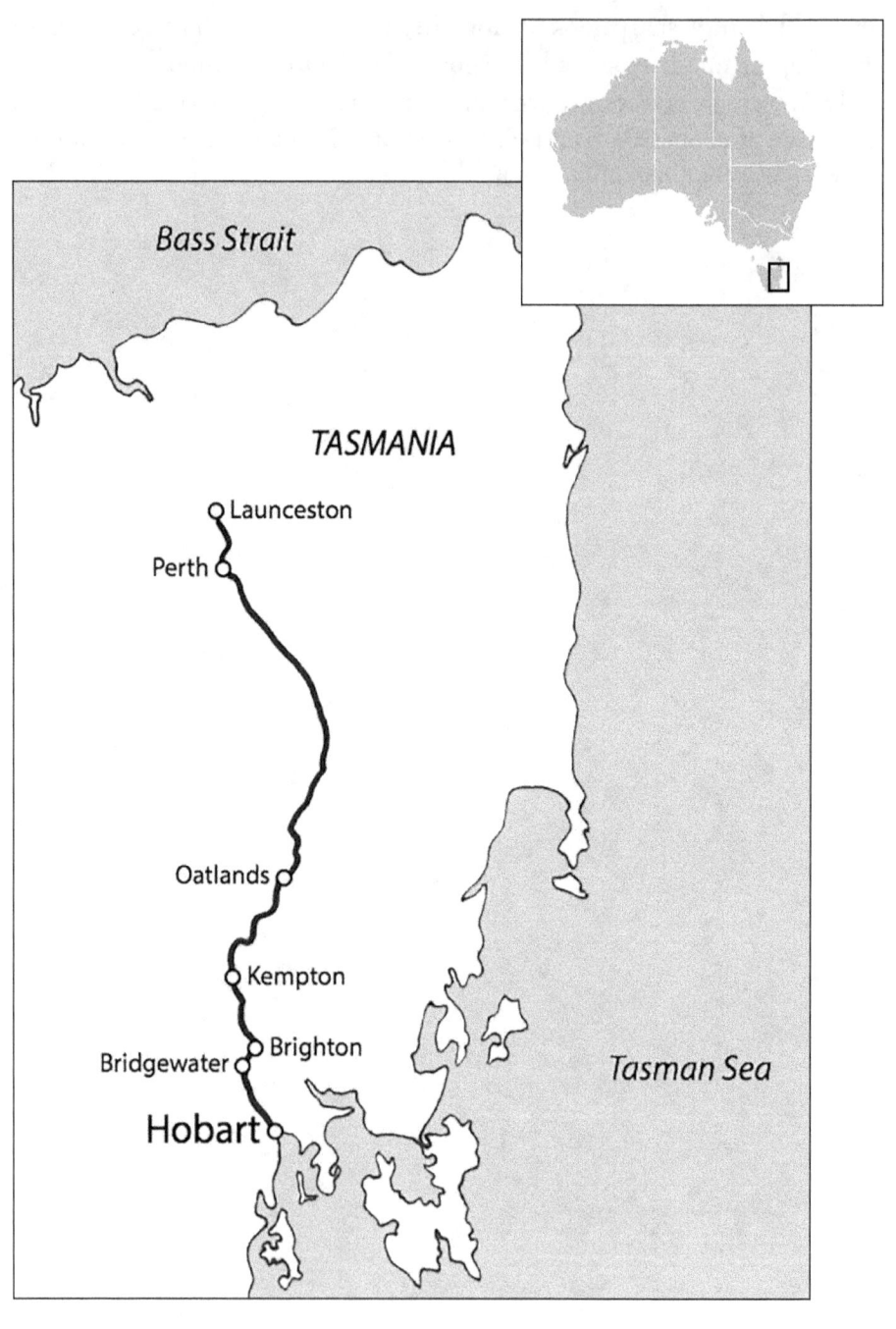

Chapter 20

Cycles

Launceston – Perth – Oatlands – Hobart –
Bridgewater – Brighton – Oatlands – Kempton

Totals: 23,776 kilometres – 1304 hours 33 minutes – $42,000

Tuesday 28 March
St Peter's Pass Rest Area to Oatlands (to Hobart), Tasmania
34 kilometres – 2 hours 18 minutes

After a few hours' sleep on Friday morning, I unfolded myself from my park bench in time to get to my school speaking engagement. After that, the rest of my time in Launceston was a snotty, drowsy blur, filled with piles of used tissues. I treated myself to three days in a backpackers' hostel and left only to search out soup, oranges or fresh tissue supplies. I have some recollection of a church full of people praying for my health, so I must have had either another speaking engagement or fever-induced hallucinations.

By Monday, it was time to face the world again. I awoke to discover a grey sky and a whole lot of rain. I tried to ignore the weather, instead concentrating on cleaning the gunk out of Bike's chain and my lungs. Noticeably lighter, I waterproofed up and headed into town. I rode to the bus station to see what options I had for the next few days. The original plan was to ride the 200 kilometres from Launceston to Hobart between the hours of 3 pm and midday the following day. The idea of doing another all-night ride in the rain while I was still feverish, snotty and coughing wasn't appealing. I threw up a few possibilities involving buses and riding sections of the route on another day. After making multiple enquiries into bus schedules, I finally had a plan. I could ride just as far as Oatlands, catch a bus the next morning into Hobart, and ride the missed stretch of road the next week when I would be coming that way again from the other direction.

Feeling quite relieved, I stepped outside and into the rain. Ah yes, the rain. Any sort of riding in this weather was not going to be happy. If only

I knew what the forecast for the day ahead was going to be, I thought. At that moment, I looked up to find myself standing outside the Tasmanian Weather Bureau. I went in and discovered not only huge video screens with meteorological information, but also a helpful man who could tell me that the rain would be gone by 1 pm. We had a short chat and I discovered that he had recently been looking at the Cycle of Learning website. I had a strange feeling of the world not quite making sense. Or perhaps making too much sense.

I had an enthusiastic reception at my school visit in the afternoon and eventually pedalled off to the heartening cheers of the primary students, heading south for Oatlands. The rain had stopped as the weatherman told me it would, but I'd forgotten about the southerly wind that he mentioned. It was a strong headwind, and it slowed me down all the way to Campbelltown. I made my conversion to night-time riding kit there: trackies, jacket, lights, socks, headlamp, gloves, and some more swigs of cough syrup straight from the bottle. I also called home to boost my spirits. I cannot describe just how comforting it is to be able to talk to family when you're in a cold, dark, windy, unfamiliar place with a colder, darker, windier 50 kilometres ahead of you.

Buoyed by motherly sympathy, I managed the remaining distance in good time. I found St Peter's Pass rest area by about 11 pm, donned every piece of clothing I had, and set up my mat and sleeping bag on a table in the barbeque area.

When you sleep on a tabletop, the price for saving on set-up time is that:

- it's rather cold (especially when the table you choose is it at the top of a mountain pass),
- you sleep very lightly because you're worried you'll roll off, and
- you wake up in the morning to find people walking past you to get to the public toilets.

I made a quick getaway, avoiding the stares of the public toilet patrons, and rode the final ten kilometres to Oatlands. There I found a deli-cafe and thawed out over a hot chocolate and the remains of last weekend's paper while I waited for my bus. It was right on schedule and got Bike, Trailer and me into Hobart with just enough time to ride to a lunchtime Rotary meeting.

After the meeting, I headed into town and was thrilled to discover, amongst Hobart's many hills, the existence of a flat bike path. It runs the length of the city alongside the Derwent River and is populated with smiling, happy cyclists.

I found a cheap and friendly caravan park to set up camp in, the only downfall being its lack of a camp kitchen. I sadly had to revert to my pre-cooking days and for dinner made do with uncooked watermelon, cucumber and chocolate.

Monday 3 April
Hobart, Tasmania
68 kilometres – 4 hours 32 minutes

I was in Hobart nearly a week and had started to feel like a local. I had membership for the city library and had lost count of the number of times I retraced the bike path into town. My caravan park was a long way from everything and I suspected I was their only guest. The constant rain – varying in strength from drizzle to downpour – throughout the week left me in a tricky situation. I would have been happy to pay a bit extra to move into the dry comfort of a backpackers' hostel, but it never stopped raining long enough to be able to pack up my tent.

I averaged one visit a day, to schools and Rotary clubs, in the time I was there. One of the most exciting rides to a school was when I'd arranged to meet a teacher and troop of students from a nearby primary school at the Cenotaph. They arrived on bikes, and led me back along the river path towards their school. There was a small crisis as one member of the group had a pedal malfunction that rendered her bike useless. Alternative transport was arranged for her and the teacher, and the rest of the students escorted me to their school where an assembly was convened and awaiting our arrival. With the fleet of cyclists behind me, I felt my talk carried more weight than usual, as if I were some kind of cycling superstar with an escort of bodyguards or maybe backup singers.

Before leaving, I had the pleasure of meeting a small Year 1 student, who sought me out to offer two "platypus coins" for the children in Kodaikanal. She had been going to spend the 40 cents at the canteen, but decided to donate it instead. It made all the rainy days hanging around Hobart feel worthwhile.

The library was a significant comfort to me in Hobart. The times I didn't have speaking appointments, I settled in with a pile of non-fiction books to skim through or a novel to lose myself in. At closing time, I'd check out as many books as I could carry back to my tent for the evening.

I tried to gain some useful information in my reading. I spent a few hours on a self-help manual about how to deal with solitude and got some tips from a book on Genghis Khan about how I should be getting the most out of my mount. I warned Bike that when we hit the road again, he should be ready to tenderise raw meat under his saddle as we rode, and that I might be nicking his jugular to drink some of his blood while riding, to save time on snack breaks. I also got some inspiration from a book on Zen to add some haiku to my Latrobe notebook.

Throughout the past week, I had also been receiving regular updates from my family in Adelaide on the health of my grandmother. When I left, she was (as she had been for the past few years) quite deaf, sometimes confused, but otherwise physically in good shape. I'd received a typed letter from her every few weeks as I rode the mainland and she kept a close eye on my travels on the maps my parents brought over for her with regular print-outs of my blog. When I arrived home, she was proud of my ride, but anxiously asked every time I visited if I was home for good now.

Last weekend Grandma became sick rapidly and had an emergency procedure performed on Sunday afternoon. I knew the doctor who carried out the procedure, and was able to speak to him afterwards, as well as to my parents. He assured me that it had all gone well, they had a good idea of what was making my grandmother sick, and she should recover.

I am not a big worrier, and the news was reassuring. Nevertheless, when not distracting myself with library books, I spent a large part of my time feeling bad that I wasn't in Adelaide with my grandmother and the rest of the family. Cycle of Learning was no longer a big, exciting, outdoor adventure. It was a job that was my responsibility to carry out. I needed to make it through the roads and speaking engagements of the next ten days, and then I could go home, where I belonged.

Wednesday 5 April
Oatlands to Kempton (to Hobart), Tasmania
37 kilometres – 2 hours 39 minutes

My departure from Hobart on Tuesday was delayed when I realised I had inadvertently packed a library book into Trailer. I think my subconscious was in action, as the book was not only by one of my favourite authors,

Kazuo Ishiguro, but also had made an excellent pillow. After a detour to the library, I headed out of town. The bridge over the Derwent River was one of my trip's worst, with no shoulder and plenty of cars and trucks to compete with for space. I sang my way over: singing flicked the switch in my brain to make me ride steadier and feel calmer in stressful riding conditions.

Although there was some rain in the morning, the sun made a brief but welcome appearance in the early afternoon. This cheered me up no end, reminding me of how uplifting it was to be out on the road in the middle of life at its simplest. By 4 pm, however, the rain and clouds were back with a vengeance, as were the hills. I plodded on and on, finally arriving in Oatlands completely drenched. I bought a tin of spaghetti and a chocolate bar, then found an undercover barbeque area in a quiet part of town by a lake and set up for the night. What else could you want of an evening when you have mint triple-decker chocolate, shelter from the rain, a barbeque to heat up your spaghetti, and warm dry clothes to change into? Nothing. Maybe just a pillow-sized book, but besides that, not much else.

I woke up the next morning to freezing gale-force winds that had destroyed my makeshift clothesline under the barbeque shelter. Between thwarting my laundry efforts, the wind had also dried my tent out, so I didn't complain too much. Once I packed up, I headed into town where it was just as windy and cold as my spot by the lake had been. It was much more bearable, though, because chocolate bars were on special in the supermarket and there was a cafe to sit in to sip a hot drink. However, I made the mistake of choosing the wrong brochure from the windowsill as reading material for the morning. It was disguised as a magazine called "Heat" and profiled the company's huge range of home heating systems. Feeling colder and colder as I read on, I decided I'd like to install embedded floor heating, radiant ceiling heating, and reverse cycle air-conditioning in my tent, and maybe an electric blanket onto Bike.

Luckily, my next stop at Oatlands District School was not only very friendly and hospitable, but it also had an extremely well heated staff room for me to wait in and be plied with hot coffee.

I had a while to wait because I'd arrived ridiculously early, but I spent my time constructively by clearing up an identity crisis. Apparently, a few people at the school had been expecting me to be "the hand cyclist". The main problem with this assumption was that I was not Andreas. In addition, if I were indeed him, I would have just finished my circumnavigation of the country yesterday in Brisbane. I explained to the staff who I was, and that I had just a normal bike, and wouldn't be beating any world records that day, and went on to speak to the student cohort. To begin, I shared the story of Malar with the group.

Malar

My name is Malar. I am 13 years old and in Year 6 at school. I have one younger brother and one younger sister. Until recently, nobody in my village studied.

There are caste problems in my village. Recently some Dalit people, including my mother, went to get water from the village well. The so-called higher-caste people attacked them for using the water. The Dalit people of my village suffer.

I want to study to get a good job when I am older, like being a government official.

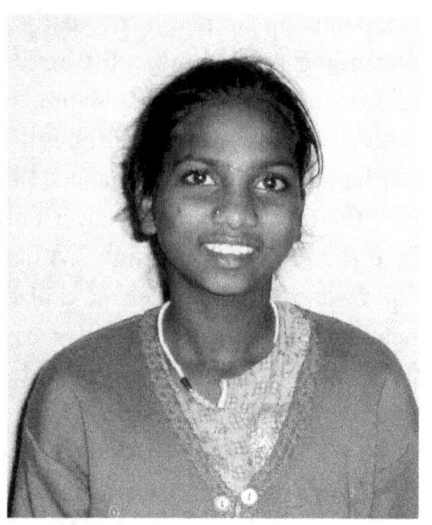

Malar, aged 13 in 2004.

*

When the talk was over, I was reluctant to leave the school, not just because the students were so pleasant or the heating of such high quality, but because an almighty storm had picked up in the past hour. Waiting for me outside were driving winds, icy rain and air so cold that my breath turned to vapour. I waterproofed up and brought out my secret weapons: Matt's wetsuit booties.

I pedalled off and spent the first few kilometres feeling very impressed by how, even though the booties let water in, the wind didn't get through at all. The novelty soon wore off as my body temperature dropped and I slowed down. I inched my way through the rain and the wind, feeling progressively sorrier for myself as all feeling drained out of my hands.

I did my best to muster some motivation by reminding myself of the content of some motivational emails I had received throughout my journey. Harley, the bike shop attendant who had helped me find Bike and vegetarianism in the months before I started my ride, had been in touch throughout my journey. He had done a lot of long-distance cycling himself and was a dynamo of motivation. His latest email had been to "forge myself on the road", which felt like a slightly more heroic perspective to take than being miserable and soggy and cold. To keep my thoughts in check I also kept reminding myself of the tattoo Harley has on one of his wrists – PMAR, which stands for Positive Mental Attitude Regardless. This didn't do much for my speed or my temperature, but did succeed in making me refuse a lift from a friendly passing motorist with an empty trailer.

The extreme cold drained me of my energy quickly, and when I stopped on the roadside, the sultanas I carried in my handlebar bag tasted exquisite. With clumsy, shaking, numb hands, I pushed fistfuls of them into my mouth, and felt their sugar surge through my body almost instantaneously.

The unpleasant weather continued and I rode on, not because my body felt like it could do so, but because there were no other options. I kept telling myself that either the rain would stop or I would get to a town at some stage. However, part of me was sure I had entered some sort of hell through which I would have to keep cycling for the rest of eternity.

The rain finally did stop and, as I reached the top of a huge hill, the sun made an appearance as well. I had an awe-inspiring view of the hills, fields and mountains all around. I stood at the peak, retrieved my phone from its triple plastic-bagged protection, and saw I'd missed a phone call from my mother. I felt a calm certainty that it would be about my grandmother, but paused and watched the rays of sun coming through the clouds for a few moments more before calling her back. When I did, I listened to her tell me that although the doctors didn't seem worried, she could tell that my grandmother didn't have long. I had to go home.

I had two schools, one Rotary club and the entire west coast still expecting me to visit in Tasmania. I'd been planning to turn off for the west just five kilometres from where I stood, but instead I rode right past the turnoff, and got to Kempton. I went through the motions: apologetic phone calls to cancel visits, text messages to friends who were expecting me, booking bus tickets, changing out of my cold, soggy clothes, and eating half my body weight in muesli.

I had a few hours to wait for the bus that would take me into Hobart, and during that time I put an end to my life on the road. I stripped Bike of all his touring accessories and threw out the water bottles, insulating socks, ockie straps, bent water-bottle cages, plastic tubing, and bits and pieces that had been part of my journey for thousands of kilometres. In different circumstances I might have felt some nostalgic grief over this process, but instead I felt detached and ruthless, ready to ditch my life on the road without hesitation.

I felt jolted between worlds. In the moment I got the call from my mum I suddenly went from embarking on a week of battling the elements and being the public face of Cycle of Learning to being alone on the highway hundreds of kilometres from where I needed to be. It had been easy to forget that life – and illness and death – keeps marching on while you are off on adventures.

Finally, the Hobart-bound bus arrived. I loaded Bike, Trailer and myself on board, and soon found myself back in town. I tracked down the closest backpackers' hostel and curled up in a bunk.

Conclusion

Hobart – Adelaide

Total: $50,000

June 2006
Adelaide, South Australia

From Hobart I boarded a flight to Adelaide. On arrival I went straight to the hospital with my mother and sister to see my grandmother. When she woke up, the joy of seeing her daughter and granddaughters was evident through her exhaustion. She slipped into a coma on Saturday and died soon after.

I wasn't sure how I should feel about not completing the ride. I felt bad about the three speaking engagements I missed, but I reminded myself that the rest of the state donated generously. There was still $8000 to go to reach the $50,000 target but then I received a call from the Australian Lutheran World Service. They told me that they had decided to contribute the final amount from their general funds, so we could wrap up the project by the end of the financial year. I suddenly felt a huge, $8000 burden fall off my shoulders – and off the shoulders of all the family and friends who were propping me up, emotionally, financially and logistically. I almost heard the universe heave a sigh of relief too. "We did it", it muttered. "We got you around Australia safely. We kept you out of the way of the road trains. We found people for you to speak to. We found you $50,000. We gave you the fly net you wanted. We put good people in your path. Please do something easier next time and give us a break."

We did it. Not in the easy, professional, high profile, overflowing-with-donations way that I had imagined two years ago, but it was done.

Epilogue

December 2007
Kodaikanal, India

I returned to the Kodai hills taking the scenic route via a couple of years, a few different jobs and several countries. Children I knew in my last visits were now young men and young women. The young women from the Grihini program that I met in 2001 were now wives and mothers, looking wiser, a bit more gaunt, and a lot more worn out. I can't be sure, but I'm guessing that getting married, having children, running a home, and all the work that goes along with those things, takes a large toll in this place where women do the lion's share of the work, and usually end up with the least food, rest and freedom. I must have been looking a bit older too: instead of calling me "Ackaa" (big sister) the children switched to "Mami" (auntie) this time.

I felt different, too. Instead of coming to Kodaikanal with just my backpack, I came bearing the well wishes, thoughts, prayers and friendship for the students of Kodaikanal from so many Australians.

My first evening in the hills was spent at the senior boys' hostel. Even though their exams started the next day, they put on a short program for my arrival. There was dancing, singing, a drama, and speeches on the theme of helping others and appreciation for the opportunities that the Cycle of Learning funds would provide. There at the boys' hostel I passed on the message that I went on to deliver at the two junior hostels and the senior girls' hostel later in the week.

I told them that every time I visited Kodaikanal, I am really impressed. I am impressed by the students' dedication to their study, and what they want to do with their education. Going to school comes at a cost to them: they have to live away from their parents and villages. They aren't able to be working and earning money for their family. These determined students are studying hard away from home because of the dreams they have for the future – to finish high school, to go to university, to become teachers, doctors, nurses or government officials. Beyond these professional goals, they have dreams to improve the position of their families and to change their villages and our world for the better: to make it more just, healthier and more equitable.

When I had shared the stories of these young people with students in Australia they were just as impressed as I was, but also curious. What are their schools like? What do they eat? What are the dots on their foreheads? What games do they play? Why can't they go to school in their own villages? Why do they all have black hair?

The Kodai students had their own questions about Australia. What animals are there? How many palaces are there in Australia? Are children healthy? Do we have drains? How do Australians get water?

What I was most eager to tell the Kodai children, though, was what they had done for their peers in Australia. While Australian students had raised money that would help students in Kodai to study and have the skills to change their communities, the young people of Kodaikanal had inspired and challenged their Australian peers. Reflecting on the importance that education plays for Kodai children helped to reveal the importance that education has for them as Australians – they reflected that education was not just to get a good job and earn a nice pile of money, but also to help their communities and make changes to society. They also learned that our world is shared by Aussie kids, with good drains but no palaces, and Kodaikanal boys and girls, who have lots of songs and dances but a more difficult path to access their basic human rights.

With Chandramathi (left) and Kamileshwari (front), 2013.

Chandramathi is the one person I've been able to catch up with on every one of my six visits to Kodai. The first time I was there she was working as an Ackaa (big sister) in the children's home. Since then she has changed roles to work as a receptionist at Sacred Heart College, married a local stonemason, and had a gorgeous daughter, Kamileshwari.

2013
Kodaikanal, India

After my ride, I spent some years teaching, both in Japan and in some different schools around Australia. I have ended up, after some more study, in a job I love, working for the Australian Lutheran World Service as a Program Officer. In my leave I have returned to Kodai for the fifth time since my first visit. The staff of PEAK have changed over the years, but I have been back often enough and in contact through email and Skype to remain in touch and familiar with the team, their work and the progress of the trust fund and the educational scholarships it provides.

PEAK has reached the target it requires for the interest from the trust fund to be able to support over 100 secondary and college students. The approximately 30 students in college are studying courses such as teaching,

Rakkammal for many years was the Auntie at the senior boys hostel. She would cook for them, and did whatever she could to make the hostel feel like a home for the boys who were away from their families.

Rakkammal, 2004

nursing and engineering. The demand for these scholarships is steadily increasing, as is the capacity and determination of families to contribute what they can to their children's education. In this latest visit, I managed to meet with a number of the young people I interviewed originally in 2004 when they were in high school. I heard their reflections about the impact of their time in PEAK hostels (for many of them for the twelve years of primary and secondary school) and the college educations they have received with PEAK support.

PEAK continues its work with, and for, the Dalit and Adhivasi communities of the Kodai hills. The team see some small improvements in the material aspects of people's lives. A government initiative to guarantee 100 days of paid work to all adults has seen average incomes increase slightly. Likewise, there is state support for improved housing and a new government scheme that gives poor people the opportunity to access and own their own land. In communities, families are increasingly recognising political, economic and caste injustice, and finding ways of challenging it when it occurs. This has come about through a number of contributing

With Rakkammal, 2013

factors – greater access to media; more travel outside villages which gives exposure to alternative views and situations; Grihini's work with local young women; PEAK's work to raise awareness within villages and within the children in their hostels.

Along with this search for justice and equality, families are seeking out opportunities for their children's education. In the past PEAK had to work hard in the villages to motivate families to send their children to school. Now families come to PEAK, having already set aside their own money for their children's education, eager to access extra support from PEAK to make this education a reality.

In 2010 Grihini responded to the increasing levels of education in the Kodai Hills by becoming a certified community college. Most young women in the area were now completing at least up to Year 10, so there was little need for the non-formal education course that used to cater for girls who had not been able to access formal primary or secondary schooling. Instead, Grihini now offers vocational diplomas to young women who cannot access higher education elsewhere. Students conclude the ten-month live-in course with an internship that generally leads to long-term employment. Even though Grihini offers a higher level of education now, the focus still remains on social awareness for the students and their families.

Eswaran, who is from the village that takes two bus trips and a three-hour climb to reach, is now 22 and on the verge of completing a Bachelor of Engineering through PEAK's support. He will be the first Adhivasi engineer in this district. The remote nature of his village has meant that there have only been a few improvements there – ten houses have been built, electricity for streetlights is connected and a pump for water installed. His people earn below average wages still – 100 rupees a day for agricultural work for men, and 80 for women. Eswaran feels proud that he is in a position to show the rest of society

Eswaran, aged 22 in 2013.

what Tribal people can achieve and to be an ambassador for his culture. He appreciates how in his village everyone is treated with equal respect and that discrimination is not tolerated. This is something that he feels that wider society could learn from his culture.

Pandimeena finished her work as a nurse for Grihini in 2006. She is now married with three children and works in the school in her home village. She looks after the logistics and accounts of its nutrition program. The women that she grew up with work in the fields and tell their daughters to look to Pandimeena for inspiration in their study, because she is respected by everyone in the village. Pandimeena sees some big changes in her village. In the past, Dalit families were cheated out of their land, by being convinced to exchange it for food or for less than its value. However, now the Dalit community is aware this was unjust and are claiming their rights and trying to get their land back. This awareness has come through PEAK holding community meetings about human rights and social issues. It has also come through the education of the young people. Parents listen to what their children share with them about social justice.

Kalaivani is now 24 years old and has achieved the goals she shared in 2004. She finished high school, then completed a teaching course with PEAK's support and returned to her village as a teacher. She was proud that although she is from the Dalit community, which used to experience high levels of discrimination, she was well respected at the school, and parents were happy to send their children to be taught by her. The standard of the local school has improved considerably compared to when she was younger. Social changes have also happened in her village. Dalits are no longer treated as badly – they are not expected to beat drums at death ceremonies, people are not insulted by being called their caste name and at the tea shop there are no longer two sets of cups for Dalits and non-Dalits. Recently she came to work as a staff member at one of PEAK's primary hostels. She supports the students with their studies and shares the story of her life with them to motivate them. Kalaivani's hope for the future is that all issues that divide people – caste, poverty, gender – will be resolved and that people will "become more human".

Karuppusamy, who comes from a village with just 28 families, is 21 now. After completing a Bachelor of Arts with PEAK's support, he spent some time working in the same boys' hostel he attended as a teenager. Since then he has been working as a radio announcer on local Kodaikanal radio. Although he enjoys this, he realises that he felt most fulfilled when working with students, particularly helping the weaker ones improve and grow. He has decided to return to study to become a teacher, and teach in poor communities. He noted, sadly, that the trend now is for young people to leave his village, to work as far away as north India. The culture and way of life he knew as a boy are being lost. Even so, positive changes have come through the improvements in levels of education. In the past, when so-called higher-caste people came to his village and demanded that his people come to work in their fields, or prepare land for burials, his people would go, without question. Now, they have realised that they can voice their opinion and refuse if they don't want to do this work. They have also been speaking out to local politicians and lobbying for increased services. They are starting to be noticed by politicians who have long ignored them.

Karuppusamy, aged 21 in 2013.

Murugulakshmi completed high school, has worked in the accounts department of a mill, and also in one of PEAK's primary hostels. She currently is living in her home village with her husband and two children and does daily agricultural labour for income. These days wages are 100 rupees a day for women and 120 for men. Dalits no longer need to beg for leftover food as they have enough income to buy and cook their own. Murugulakshmi looks back on her 12 years as a student in PEAK hostels and reflects that she developed a strong social awareness through her time there. She sees clearly the discrimination that still occurs in her community, but has been among those who increasingly challenge it. Her education has given her a boldness to stand up to those who discriminate against Dalits, and an ability to speak freely and without hesitation about issues that are important to her. Her analysis of the situation in her community is that the problem for Dalits there is that they have no land, and so depend on the so-called higher-caste people for work. With this dependency come exploitation, domination and discrimination. As Dalit people become educated, they have more opportunities to get other work and their dependency on the caste people disappears along with the accompanying domination and discrimination. Education also gives people the social awareness to know it is their right to challenge unfair situations.

Karnan remained in PEAK's hostel until he completed Year 10. He didn't go any further as he needed to go home to help earn income for his family. He is married now and has a nine-month-old daughter. He works as a day labourer, earning 200 rupees a day, which is an improvement to the 70 rupees a day that men earned ten years ago.

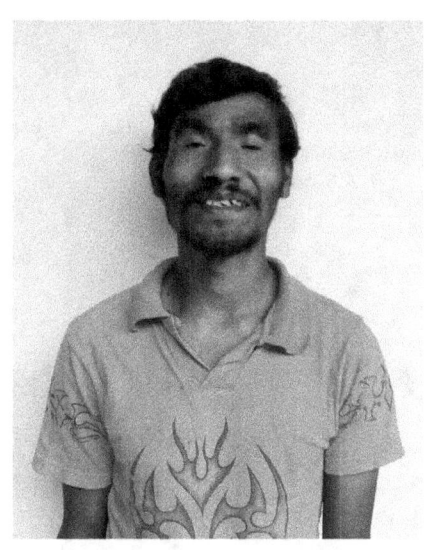

Karnan, aged 23 in 2013.

The material changes in his village are that there are better roads, better water supply, people have been able to use tiles for the roofs of their homes instead of thatch, and electricity comes to all homes in the village. While the older generation still do retain discriminatory customs such as not letting Dalits enter non-Dalit homes, the younger generation is abandoning these practices. This has come through education, and also because the younger people mix more outside of the village and continue to be friendly with each other, no matter their caste status, inside the village as well. Karnan feels that his time in the PEAK hostels taught him confidence that he can look after himself and his family and that he does not need to be subservient to anyone. When he was studying, his dream was to become a doctor. Now he wishes that for his daughter. He has already started saving for her education. Karnan thinks that since he has witnessed so much change in his lifetime already, surely there will be true equality by the time his daughter is grown.

Malar always had a strong desire to be educated. Once she finished high school her parents wanted her to come home and be married. She eventually convinced them to let her attend college. After the first semester when she achieved high marks, her parents put their full support behind her and no longer put pressure on her to get married. She is studying a Bachelor of History and hopes to follow this degree by studying law. As a lawyer she wishes to help the poor and fight injustice by providing access

Malar, aged 22 in 2013.

to legal representation. She has seen her own father have to give up his legal claim for land that was unjustly taken from him after he couldn't afford the legal fees. Malar feels that it was her education in PEAK hostels that opened her eyes to social issues. While she sees that much of the open discrimination towards Dalits has disappeared now, she feels that there is still some way to go. The key is education. When Dalits are educated, they gain respect from all of the community, and also do not have to depend on the so-called higher-caste community for work. She is glad that most of the young people from the Dalit community are finishing at least Year 10 or Year 12, through the support of PEAK. She sees a time when this support will no longer be needed in her village, and families will be able to educate their children from their own income. For herself, Malar feels that it was only through PEAK's help that she was able to study, improve her life and have a vision for her and her community's future.

Visit the Cycle of Learning website:

http://cycleoflearning.wordpress.com/

www.ingramcontent.com/pod-product-compliance
Lightning Source LLC
Chambersburg PA
CBHW050349230426
43663CB00010B/2050